The Power of Eloquence

The
Power of Eloquence

A TREASURY OF BRITISH SPEECH
Selected and edited by
ANDREW SCOTLAND

CASSELL · LONDON

CASSELL & COMPANY LTD
35 Red Lion Square · London WC1
and at
MELBOURNE · SYDNEY · TORONTO
CAPE TOWN · AUCKLAND

———

© in this anthology under the
title *The Power of Eloquence*
Cassell & Co. Ltd. 1961

First published 1961

Printed in Great Britain
by Ebenezer Baylis & Son, Limited
The Trinity Press, Worcester, and London
F.1260

PREFACE

At all periods in history, ability in public speaking has been the lever which has raised people to influence and authority over their fellows. There is power in the spoken word; and in the case of great speeches their power can be felt over the centuries. In this collection the attempt has been made to choose speeches which are great because of their literary qualities and their abiding interest. The choice has been deliberately restricted to Britain. Many of the speeches inevitably deal with politics. Speech is the expression of politics and it would be strange if political speeches did not occupy a prominent place. Political topics, however, invariably have a short life. The great talking points of one House of Commons are so often forgotten by another. When one reform has been accomplished another takes its place. The greatness of a political speech arises not from the topic which touches off the speech but from the principles underlying it and the language in which it is expressed.

Sometimes speeches make history; always they are the footnotes of history. The history of Britain is told in the speeches which follow. Crisis has always produced the speech and the speaker. Elizabeth's speech is evoked by the threat of the Armada. Wentworth faces death, and, all unknowingly, speaks a prologue to the Civil War and to the death of King Charles himself. The Revolt of the American Colonies and the struggle with Napoleon are made more memorable by the speeches of men like Burke, the Pitts, Cobden, Fox and Erskine. The optimism of the Victorian age is surely reflected in the speeches of Macaulay. Cobden and Bright introduce new ideas and new accents into government. The emergence of modern political parties is not only the cause of, but the result of, the speeches of Disraeli and Gladstone. In the twentieth century the speeches of Asquith and Lloyd George are a part of the history of the First World War. In the Second World War, the speeches of Winston Churchill were as much deeds as words.

But men have souls to save as well as votes to give. The seventeenth-century poet and preacher Donne and the more modern Cardinal

Newman exercised great influence in their own time and their message is ever new.

It is also interesting to note how many of the great speeches have liberty as their theme. Liberty has two sides. It has to be extended and it has to be preserved. The theme of liberty moves great minds to great expression. To that extent speeches are biographical. The spoken words reflect the personality and the beliefs of the speakers. So long as there are men and women who are prepared to defend liberty there will always be great speeches when liberty is threatened. The theme of liberty runs through this book like a golden thread.

The modern inventions of radio and television have increased the power of the spoken word and have brought about new techniques. Elizabeth's speech was heard by the merest handful of those around her. In the seventeenth and eighteenth centuries, the great speeches were heard by those who were in the chambers when the speeches were delivered. In his Midlothian campaign Gladstone extended the range of his audience by the frequency of his speeches, and in the twentieth century Lloyd George realized that the popular Press was a useful ally to the spoken word. It was, however, in the Second World War that the power of the radio speech became gloriously manifest in the speeches of Winston Churchill. Where Elizabeth had inspired a handful, Churchill inspired millions.

This book is intended for students of history and of literature. It is also intended for those whose career depends on their ability to speak in public. Those contemplating careers in politics, at the Bar and in the Church must attain proficiency in public speaking and the great models of the past and present must be studied. Lord Birkett in his own great address on Advocacy reminds us that in the modern world the ability to speak in public is in increasing demand. Moreover, radio and television have provided new platforms for the public speaker; and examples of good radio speeches have been introduced to remind people—if such a reminder is necessary—that in the future the way to men's hearts and minds might lie through the transistor and the cathode ray tube.

A.S.

CONTENTS

CONTENTS

ACKNOWLEDGMENTS

THE publishers acknowledge with thanks the permission of the under-mentioned to reprint the speeches indicated:

The Rt. Hon. Lord Birkett for 'Advocacy'; the Baroness Eliot of Harewood and Messrs. Constable & Co., Ltd., for 'Anniversary, 3rd September, 1942', by the late Walter Elliot, which appeared in *Long Distance*; Messrs. Dent & Sons, Ltd., for 'Holiday Memory' by Dylan Thomas from *Quite Early One Morning*; Messrs. Hodder & Stoughton, Ltd., for 'Courage' by Sir James Barrie; the Hutchinson Group for 'A Call to Arms' by Lord Oxford and Asquith; and *The Times* and Messrs. Dent & Sons, Ltd., for 'The Freedom of the Press' by Lord Rosebery (*Historical and Political Orations*—Everyman's Library).

QUEEN ELIZABETH I

1534–1603

Speech at Tilbury

In the summer of 1588 the threat of invasion lay over England. The Spanish Armada had set sail from Spain, and on 19th July, 1588, it was reported to be off The Lizard. At the same time a Spanish army, with transports, under the command of the Duke of Parma, was in the Netherlands. The Spanish plan was for the Armada to destroy the English fleet and thereafter to cover the crossing of the army of Parma.

On 21st July battle was joined between the Armada and the English fleet. A running fight took place down the Channel. The Spanish Armada was driven into the North Sea, and all hope of making contact with Parma was lost.

Nevertheless, the fear remained that Parma would attempt an invasion on his own.

In August Queen Elizabeth visited her army at Tilbury. On 8th August, 'full of princely resolution and more than feminine courage she passed like some Amazonian empress through all her army'. The soldiers fell on their knees as she passed through the ranks. 'Lord bless you all!' she cried.

The following day, mounted on a horse and with a staff in her hands, she reviewed her army and delivered this speech to them.

MY loving people, we have been persuaded by some that are careful of our safety, to take heed how we commit ourselves to armed multitudes, for fear of treachery. But I assure you, I do not desire to live to distrust my faithful and loving people. Let tyrants fear. I have always so behaved myself that, under God, I have placed my chiefest strength and safeguard in the loyal hearts and goodwill of my subjects; and therefore I am

1

come amongst you, as you see, at this time, not for my recreation and disport, but being resolved, in the midst and heat of the battle, to live or die amongst you all, to lay down for my God, and for my Kingdom, and for my people, my honour and my blood, even in the dust. I know I have the body of a weak and feeble woman, but I have the heart and stomach of a King, and of a King of England, too, and think foul scorn that Parma or Spain, or any prince of Europe should dare to invade the borders of my realm; to which, rather than any dishonour shall grow by me, I myself will take up arms, I myself will be your general, judge, and rewarder of every one of your virtues in the field. I know, already for your forwardness you have deserved rewards and crowns; and we do assure you, in the word of a prince, they shall be duly paid you.

JOHN DONNE

1572–1631

In the Shadow of Thy Wings

John Donne is remembered as a poet and as a preacher. As a poet he has had a great influence on modern poetry. His ideas and his great command of words are strangely in tune with modern thought. He was a master of the unexpected phrase.

> *'I long to talk with some old lover's ghost*
> *Who died before the god of love was born.'*

He became Dean of St. Paul's and his fame as a preacher was considerable. In his sermons one finds many of the characteristics of his poetry. There is the same concern for mankind. 'Any man's death diminishes me because I am involved in mankind: therefore never send to know for whom the bell tolls: it tolls for thee.'

The sermon which follows shows his power as a preacher. The text is thoroughly examined and, in language suited to the theme, he develops its meaning. Notice the majesty and beauty of the last paragraph where his words soar, as it were, up to Heaven.

In the shadow of Thy wings will I rejoice.

FIRST then, lest any man in his dejection of spirit, or of fortune, should stray into a jealousy or suspicion of God's power to deliver him, as God has spangled the firmament with stars, so has He His Scriptures with names, and metaphors, and denotations of power. Sometimes He shines

3

out in the name of a Sword, and of a Target, and of a Wall, and of a Tower, and of a Rock, and of a Hill; and sometimes in that glorious and manifold constellation of all together, *Dominus exercituum*, The Lord of Hosts. God, as God, is never represented to us, with defensive arms; He needs them not. When the poets present their great heroes, and their worthies, they always insist upon their arms, they spend much of their invention upon the description of their arms; both because the greatest valour and strength need arms (Goliath himself was armed), and because to expose oneself to danger unarmed, is not valour, but rashness.

But God is invulnerable in Himself, and is never represented armed; you find no shirts of mail, no helmets, no cuirasses in God's Armoury. In that one place of essay, where it may seem to be otherwise, where God is said to have put on righteousness as a breastplate, and a helmet of salvation upon His head; in that prophecy God is Christ, and is therefore in that place, called the Redeemer. Christ needed defensive arms, God does not. God's word does; His Scriptures do; and therefore St. Jerome hath armed them, and set before every book his *Prologum galeatum*, that prologue that arms and defends every book from calumny. But though God need not, nor receive defensive arms for Himself, yet God is to us as a helmet, a breastplate, a strong tower, a rock, everything that may give us assurance and defence; and as often as He will, He can refresh that proclamation, *Nolite tangere Christos meas*, our enemies shall not so much as touch us.

But here, by occasion of his metaphor in this text, (*Sub umbra alarum*, In the Shadow of Thy Wings), we do not so much consider an absolute immunity, that we shall not be touched, as a refreshing and consolation, when we are touched, though we be pinched and wounded. The Names of God, which are most frequent in the Scriptures, are these three, Elohim, and Adonai, and Jehovah; and to assure us of His Power to deliver us, two of these three are Names of Power. Elohim is *Deus fortis*, the mighty, the powerful God: and (which deserves a particular consideration), Elohim is a plural Name. It is not *Deus fortis*, but *Dei fortes*, powerful Gods. God is all kind of Gods; all kinds, which either idolators and Gentiles can imagine, (as riches, or injustice, or wisdom, or valour, or such) and all kinds which God Himself has called gods, (as princes, and magistrates, and prelates, and all that assist and help one another). God is Elohim, all these Gods, and all these in their height and best of

4

their power; for Elohim is *Dei fortes*, Gods in the plural, and those plural gods in their exaltation.

The second name of God, is a name of power too, Adonai. For Adonai is Dominus, the Lord, such a Lord, as is Lord and Proprietary of all His creatures, and all creatures are His creatures. And then, *Dominium est potestas tum utendi, tum abutendi*, says the law; to be absolute Lord of anything, gives that Lord a power to do what He will with that thing. God, as He is Adonai, the Lord, may give and take, quicken and kill, build and throw down, where and whom He will. So then two of God's three Names are names of absolute power, to imprint, and re-imprint an assurance in us, that He can absolutely deliver us, and full revenge us, if He will.

Then, His third Name, and that Name which He chooses for Himself, and in the signification of which Name, He employs Moses, for the relief of His people under Pharaoh, that Name Jehovah, is not a Name of Power, but only of Essence, of Being, of Subsistence, and yet in the virtue of that Name, God relieved His people. And if, in my afflictions, God vouchsafe to visit me in that Name, to preserve me in my being, in my subsistence in Him, that I be not shaked out of Him, disinherited in Him, excommunicate from Him, devested of Him, annihilated towards Him, let him, at His good pleasure, reserve His Elohim, and His Adonai, the exercises and declarations of His mighty power, to those great public causes, that more concern His Glory, than anything that can befall me . . . But if He imparts his Jehovah, enlarge Himself, so far towards me, as that I may live, and move, and have my being in Him, though I be not instantly delivered, nor mine enemies absolutely destroyed, yet this is as much as I should promise myself, this is as much as the Holy Ghost intends in this metaphor, *sub umbra alarum*, under the shadow of Thy wings, that is a Refreshing, a Respiration, a Conservation, a Consolation in all afflictions that are inflicted upon me.

Yet is not this metaphor of Wings without a denotation of Power. As no Act of God's, though it seems to imply but spiritual comfort, is without a denotation of power, (for it is the power of God that comforts me; to overcome that sadness of soul, and that dejection of spirit, which the Adversary by temporal afflictions would induce upon me, is an act of His Power), so this metaphor, the shadow of His wings, (which in this place expresses no more, than consolation and refreshing in misery, and not a powerful deliverance out of it) is so often in the Scriptures made a denotation of Power too, as that we can doubt of no act of power, if we have the shadow of His wings.

For, in this metaphor of Wings, doth the Holy Ghost express the Maritime power, the power of some Nations at Sea, in navies, (Woe to the land shadowing with wings;) that is, that hovers over the world, and intimidates it with her sails and ships. In this metaphor does God remember His people, of His powerful deliverance of them, (You have seen what I did unto the Egyptians; and how I bare you on eagle's wings, and brought you to Myself.) In this metaphor does God threaten His and their enemies, what He can do, (The noise of the wings of His Cherubins, are as the voice of great waters, and of an army.) So also, what He will do, (He shall spread His wings over Bozrah, and at that day shall the hearts of the mighty men of Edom be as the heart of a woman in her pangs.)

So that, if I have the shadow of His wings, I have the earnest of the power of them too. If I have refreshing, and respiration from them, I am able to say, (as those three Confessors did to Nebuchadnezzar) My God is able to deliver me, I am sure He has power. And my God will deliver me, when it conduces to His glory, I know He will. But, if He do not, be it known unto thee, O King, we will not serve thy gods. Be it known unto thee, O Satan, how long soever God defer my Deliverance, I will not seek false comforts, the miserable comforts of this world. I will not, for I need not, for I can subsist under this shadow of these wings, though I have no more.

The Mercy-seat itself was covered with the Cherubim's wings. And who would have more than Mercy? And a Mercy-seat; that is, established, resident Mercy, permanent and perpetual Mercy; present and familiar Mercy; a Mercy-seat. Our Saviour Christ intends as much as would have served their turn, if they had laid hold upon it, when He says, that He would have gathered Jerusalem, as a hen gathers her chickens under her wings. And though the other Prophets (as ye have heard) mingle the signification of Power, and actual deliverance, in this metaphor of Wings, yet our Prophet, whom we have now in especial consideration, David, never does so; but in every place where he uses this metaphor of Wings, (which are in five or six several Psalms), still he rests and determines in that sense, which is his meaning here; that, though God do not actually deliver us, nor actually destroy our enemies, yet if He refresh us in the shadow of His wings, if He maintain our subsistence (which is a religious constancy) in Him, this should not only establish our patience, (for that is but half the work), but it should also produce a joy, and rise to an exultation, which is our last circumstance, therefore in the shadow of Thy wings, I will rejoice.

I would always raise your hearts, and dilate your hearts, to a holy joy, to a joy in the Holy Ghost. There may be a just fear, that men do not grieve enough for their sins; but there may be a just jealousy, and suspicion too, that they may fall into inordinate grief, and diffidence of God's mercy. And God has reserved us to such times, as being the later times, given us even the dregs and lees of misery to drink. For, God has not only let loose into the world a new spiritual disease; which is, an equality, and an indifferency, which religion our children, or our servants, or our companions profess; (I would not keep company with a man that thought me a knave, or a traitor; with him that thought I loved not my Prince, or were a faithless man, not to be believed, I would not associate myself; and yet I will make him my bosom companion, that thinks I do not love God, that thinks I cannot be saved) but God has accompanied, and complicated almost all our bodily diseases of these times, with an extraordinary sadness, a predominant melancholy, a faintness of heart, a cheerlessness, a joylessness of spirit, and therefore I return often to this endeavour of raising your hearts, dilating your hearts with a holy joy, joy in the Holy Ghost, for under the shadow of His wings, you may, you should rejoice.

TWO HEMISPHERES

If you look upon this world in a map, you find two hemispheres, two half-worlds. If you crush heaven into a map, you may find two hemispheres too, two half heavens; and the glory of heaven, is all heaven often represented unto us. And as of those two hemispheres of the world, the first has been known long before, but the other (that of America, which is the richer in treasure) God reserved for later discoveries; so, though He reserve that hemisphere of heaven, which is the Glory thereof, to the Resurrection, yet the other hemisphere, the Joy of heaven, God opens to our discovery, and delivers for our habitation even whilst we dwell in this world.

As God has cast upon the unrepentant sinner two deaths, a temporal, and a spiritual death, so has He breathed into us two lives; for so, as the word for death is doubled, *Morte morieris*, Thou shalt die the death, so is the word of life expressed in the plural, *chaiim, vitarum*, God breathed into his nostrils the breath of lives, of divers lives. Though our natural life were no life, but rather a continual dying, yet we have two lives besides that, an eternal life reserved for heaven, but yet a heavenly life too, a spiritual life, even in this world. And, as God does thus inflict two deaths, and infuse two lives, so does He also pass two judgments upon man, or rather repeats the same judgment twice. For, that which Christ shall say to thy conscience now, Enter into thy Master's joy. He says to thy conscience now, Enter into thy Master's joy. The everlastingness of the joy is the blessedness of the next life, but the entering, the inchoation is afforded here.

For that which Christ shall say then to us, *Venite benedicti*, Come ye blessed, are words intended to persons that are coming, that are upon the way, though not at home. Here in this world He bids us Come, there in the next, he shall bid us Welcome. The Angels of heaven have joy in thy conversion, and canst thou be without that joy in thyself? If thou desire revenge upon thy enemies, as they are God's enemies that God would be pleased to remove, and root out all such as oppose Him, that affectation appertains to Glory. Let that alone till thou come to the hemisphere of Glory; there join with those Martyrs under the Altar, *Usquequo Domine*, How long, O Lord, dost Thou defer judgment? and thou shalt have thine answer there for that. Whilst thou art here, here join with David, and the other Saints of God, in that holy increpation of a dangerous sadness, Why art thou cast down, O my soul? why art thou disquieted in me? That soul that is dissected and anatomized to God, in a sincere confession, washed in the tears of true contrition, embalmed in the blood of reconciliation, the blood of Christ Jesus, can assign no reason, can give no just answer to that interrogatory, Why art thou cast down, O my soul? why art thou disquieted in me? No man is so little, as that he can be lost under these wings, no man is so great, as that they cannot reach him; *Semper ille major est, quantumcumque creverimus*.

To what temporal, to what spiritual greatness soever we grow, still pray we Him to shadow us under His wings; for the poor need those wings against oppression, and the rich against envy. The Holy Ghost, who is a Dove, shadowed in the whole world under His wings. *Incubabat aquis*, He hovered over the waters, He sat upon the waters, and He hatched all that was produced, and all that was produced so, was good. Be thou a Mother where the Holy Ghost would be a Father; conceive by Him; and be content that He produce joy in thy heart here. First think, that as a man must have some land, or else he cannot be in wardship, so a man must have some of the love of God, or else he could not fall under God's correction; God would not give him His physic, God would not study his cure, if He cared not for him.

And then, think also, that if God afford thee the shadow of His wings, that is, consolation, respiration, refreshing, though not as present and plenary deliverance, in thy afflictions, not to thank God, is a murmuring, and not to rejoice in God's ways, is an unthankfulness. Howling is the noise of hell, singing the voice of heaven; sadness the damp of hell, rejoicing the serenity of heaven. And he that has not this joy here, lacks one of the best pieces of his evidence for the joys of heaven; and has neglected or refused that earnest, by which God uses to bind His bargain, that true joy in this world shall flow into the joy of heaven, as a river flows into the sea.

This joy shall not be put out in death, and a new joy kindled in me in heaven; but as my soul, as soon as it is out of my body, is in heaven, and does not stay for the possession of heaven, nor for the fruition of the fight of God, till it be ascended through air, and fire, and moon, and sun, and planets, and firmament, to that place which we conceive to be heaven, but without the thousandth part of a minute's stop, as soon as it issues, is in a glorious light, which is heaven, (for all the way to heaven is heaven; and as those Angels which came from heaven hither, bring heaven with them, and are in heaven here, so that soul that goes to heaven meets heaven here; and as those Angels do not devest heaven by coming, so these souls invest heaven, in their going). As my soul shall not go towards heaven, but go by heaven to heaven, to the heaven of Heavens. So the true joy of a good soul in this world is the very joy of heaven; and we go thither, not that being without joy, we might have joy infused into us, but that as Christ says, Our joy might be full, perfected, sealed with an everlastingness; for, as He promises that no man shall take our joy from us, so neither shall Death itself take it away, nor so much as interrupt it, or discontinue it. But as in the face of Death, when he lays hold upon me, and in the face of the Devil, when he attempts me, I shall see the face of God, (for everything shall be glass, to reflect God upon me) so in the agonies of Death, in the anguish of that dissolution, in the sorrows of that valediction, in the irreversibleness of that transmigration, I shall have a joy, which shall no more evaporate, than my soul shall valediction, in the irreversibleness of that transmigration, I shall have a joy, which shall no more evaporate, than my soul shall evaporate, a joy, that shall pass up, and put on a more glorious garment above, and be joy superinvested in glory. Amen.

THOMAS WENTWORTH, EARL OF STRAFFORD

1593–1641

Defence Against Impeachment

One of the most famous trials in history is the trial of Thomas Wentworth, Earl of Strafford, who was impeached by the Long Parliament of 1640 on a charge of High Treason.

In the great struggle between Crown and Parliament in the seventeenth century, Strafford was the faithful servant and adviser of King Charles I. His proving ground as an administrator was Ireland, where he was virtual dictator from 1632 until 1639. Under him the country flourished, but his methods were harsh and arbitrary. Liberty was precarious and freedom depended upon his judgment and not upon the rule of law.

Although resident in Ireland he kept a close watch on events in England. His chief friend and ally was Archbishop Laud. Between them they carried out the policy of 'Thorough'. Charles's personal rule was beginning to break down and Strafford was recalled to England. The Civil War had really begun with the revolt by the Scots in 1638. Strafford advised Charles to summon Parliament. This was done early in 1640, but the Commons refused to discuss Charles's needs until he redressed their grievances. This Parliament, the Short Parliament, was accordingly dismissed.

Again Strafford advised the King to summon Parliament. This was done and the Parliament, the Long Parliament, lasted until 1653 when the Rump was ignominiously dismissed by Cromwell. The Scots rebels were already in the North of England. Charles was in a position of extreme danger. The Parliament was led by Pym, a man of great determination. He demanded the dismissal and punishment of both Strafford and Laud.

Strafford was found guilty and sentenced to death in 1641. Charles signed the death warrant of his great servant. On the way to execution, Strafford passed the cell in which Laud was lying a prisoner. Laud put his hands out to bless Strafford. Strafford murmured: 'Put not your trust in princes.'

But Charles had signed more than the death warrant of Strafford. This act was to lead to his own death in 1649.

Strafford's speech in defence is rightly regarded as one of the great speeches in British history. It is reasoned yet charged with emotion; it is dignified yet impassioned. He was ill and in mortal danger—as he well knew—but his courage and his hope never faltered.

MY Lords,—This day I stand before you, charged with high treason. The burden of the charge is heavy, yet far the more so because it hath borrowed the authority of the House of Commons. If they were not interested, I might expect a no less easy, than I do a safe issue. But let neither my weakness plead my innocence, nor their power my guilt. If your Lordships will conceive of my defences as they are in themselves, without reference to either party—and I shall endeavour so to present them—I hope to go hence as clearly justified by you, as I now am in the testimony of a good conscience by myself.

My Lords, I have all along during this charge, watched to see that poisoned arrow of treason, which some men would fain have feathered in my heart; but, in truth, it hath not been in my quickness to discover any such evil yet within my breast, though now, perhaps, by sinister information, sticking to my clothes.

They tell me of a two-fold treason—one against the Statute, another by the common law; this direct, that consecutive; this individual, that accumulative; this in itself, that by way of construction.

As to this charge of treason, I must and do acknowledge that if I had the least suspicion of my own guilt, I would save your Lordships the pains. I would cast the first stone. I would pass the first sentence of condemnation against myself. And whether it be so or not, I now refer to your Lordships' judgment and deliberation. You, and you only, under the care and protection of my gracious master, are my judges. I shall ever celebrate the providence and wisdom of your noble ancestors, who have put the keys of life and death, so far as concerns you and your posterity, into your own hands. None but your own selves, my Lords, know the rate of your noble blood; none but yourselves must hold the balance in disposing of the same. . . .

If that one article had been proved against me, it contained more weighty matter than all the charges besides. It would not only have been treason, but villainy, to have betrayed the trust of his Majesty's army. But, as the managers have been sparing, by reason of the times, as to insisting on that article, I have resolved to keep the same method, and not utter the least expression which might disturb the happy agreement intended between the two kingdoms. I only admire how I, being an incendiary against the Scots in the twenty-third article, am become a confederate with them in the twenty-eighth article! How could I be charged for betraying Newcastle, and also for fighting with the Scots at Newburne, since fighting against them was no possible means of betraying the town into their hands, but rather to hinder their passage thither! I never advised war any further than, in my poor judgment, it concerned the very life of the King's authority, and the safety and honour of his kingdom. Nor did I ever see that any advantage could be made by a war in Scotland, where nothing could be gained but hard blows. For my part, I honour that nation, but I wish they may ever be under their own climate. I have no desire that they should be too well acquainted with the better soil of England.

My Lords, you see what has been alleged for this constructive, or rather destructive treason. For my part, I have not the judgment to conceive that such treason is agreeable to the fundamental grounds either of reason or of law. Not of reason, for how can that be treason in the lump or mass, which is not so in any of its parts? or how can that make a thing treasonable which is not so in itself? Not of law, since neither statute, common law nor practice hath, from the beginning of the government, ever mentioned such a thing.

It is hard, my Lords, to be questioned upon a law which cannot be shown! Where hath this fire lain hid for so many hundred years, without smoke to discover it, till it thus bursts forth to consume me and my children? My Lords, do we not live under laws? And must we be punished by laws before they are made? For better were it to live by no laws at all, but to be governed by those characters of virtue and discretion which Nature hath stamped upon us, than to put this necessity of divination upon a man, and to accuse him of a breach of law before it is a law at all! If a waterman upon the Thames split his boat by grating upon an anchor, and the same have no buoy appended to it, the owner of the anchor is to pay the loss; but if a buoy be set there, every man passeth upon his own peril. Now, where is the mark, where is the token set upon the crime to declare it to be high treason?

My Lords, be pleased to give that regard to the peerage of England as never to expose yourselves to such moot points, such constructive interpretations of law. If there must be a trial of wits, let the subject matter be something else than the lives and honour of peers! It will be wisdom for yourselves and your posterity to cast into the fire those bloody and mysterious volumes of constructive and arbitrary treason, as the primitive Christians did their books of curious arts, and betake yourselves to the plain letter of the law and statute, which telleth what is, and what is not, treason, without being ambitious to be more learned in the art of killing than our forefathers. These gentlemen tell us that they speak in defence of the Commonwealth against my arbitrary laws. Give me leave to say I speak in defence of the Commonwealth against their arbitrary treason!

It is now full two hundred and forty years since any man was touched for this alleged crime to this height before myself. Let us not awaken those sleeping lions to our destruction, by taking up a few musty records that have lain by the walls for so many ages, forgotten or neglected.

My Lords, what is my present misfortune may be for ever yours! It is not the smallest part of my grief that not the crime of treason, but my other sins, which are exceeding many, have brought me to this bar; and, except your Lordships' wisdom provide against it, the shedding of my blood may make way for the tracing out of yours. You, your estates, your posterity, lie at the stake!

For my poor self, if it were not for your Lordships' interest, and the interest of a saint in heaven, who hath left me here two pledges on earth, I should never take the pains to keep up this ruinous cottage of mine. It is loaded with such infirmities that, in truth, I have no great pleasure to carry it about with me any longer. Nor could I ever leave it at a fitter time than this, when I hope that the better part of the world would perhaps think that by my misfortunes I have given a testimony of my integrity to my God, my King, and my country. I thank God I count not the afflictions of the present life to be compared to that glory which is to be revealed in the time to come!

My Lords! my Lords! my Lords! something more I have intended to say, but my voice and my spirit fail me. Only I do, in all humility and submission, cast myself down at your Lordships' feet, and desire that I may be a beacon to keep you from shipwreck. Do not put such rocks in your own way, which no prudence, no circumspection, can eschew or satisfy, but by your utter ruin!

And so, my Lords, even so, with all tranquillity of mind, I submit myself to your decision. And whether your judgment in my case—I wish it were not the case of you all—be for life or for death, it shall be righteous in my eyes, and shall be received with a *Te Deum laudamus*, we give God the praise.

WILLIAM PITT, EARL OF CHATHAM

1708-1778

An Army of Impotence

William Pitt was the architect of victory in the Seven Years War. It was from him that the inspiration stemmed to win a war which extended from India to America. His task was no easy one. He had to deal with a hostile House of Commons and hostile kings (George II and George III); he was racked with ill-health; but he was inflexible in his purpose and untiring in effort.

He, more than any other man, evolved the strategy which was necessary for an island people to succeed in war. He made no attempts to raise large British armies to fight on the continent of Europe. He subsidized the King of Prussia; the armies of Frederick the Great bore the burden of the war in Europe. He realized the importance of sea power. When the command of the seas has been won an enemy can be defeated on its outposts and flanks. The successes of Wolfe in Canada and Clive in India were consolidated by the victories obtained by the British fleets. The French were unable to reinforce their troops in America and India.

Not only did Pitt have a correct conception of strategy but he had the ability to choose the right leaders. Men like Wolfe, Conway, Howe, Keppel and Rodney were his personal choice. His oratory matched his deeds. He had the power to inspire his hearers. He was well in advance of his time because he realized that a victory in the House of Commons was not enough for the successful prosecution of the war. He had to unite the people to his own purpose. This he did with consummate success. To the masses Pitt was the 'Great Commoner'; his speeches united the country. It is interesting to reflect that the Highlanders who stormed the Heights of Quebec in 1759 were the brothers of men who had been killed at Culloden in 1746—thirteen years before. The Stuart cause was forgotten—except by a few.

AN ARMY OF IMPOTENCE

At the end of the Seven Years War Britain was at the pinnacle of her power and renown; but the new king—George III—who succeeded in 1760 disliked Pitt. He was excluded from office and when the quarrel broke out between Britain and the American Colonies, Pitt, who was of the same opinion as Burke, sat in Parliament 'unconnected and unconsulted'. He urged that there should be conciliation, but the King and the 'King's Friends' would have none of it.

In the speech which follows, delivered in 1775, Pitt pleads for conciliation. This is one of his great speeches. It shows his eloquence and his power, the balance of his sentences and his command of the memorable phrase. Like all great orators, Pitt had the ability to weld together the particular with the general. Speeches like this infuriated the King. It is strange, looking back on these years, to record that George III called Chatham, the man who had done so much for his country, the 'Trumpet of Sedition'. Also he opposed the plan to erect a monument, saying it would be an 'offensive measure'. But the City of London defied the King and Burke's inscription is well and nobly said: 'The means by which Providence raises a nation to greatness are the virtues infused into great men.'

As I have not the honour of access to His Majesty, I will endeavour to transmit to him, through the constitutional channel of his House, my ideas of America, to rescue him from the misadvice of his present ministers. I congratulate your Lordships that the business is at last entered upon by the noble Lords laying the papers before you. As I suppose your Lordships too well apprized of their contents, I hope I am not premature in submitting to you my present motion—

'That an humble address be presented to his Majesty humbly to desire and beseech His Majesty that, in order to open the way towards a happy settlement of the dangerous troubles in America, by beginning to allay ferments and soften animosities there; and, above all, for preventing in the meantime any sudden and fatal catastrophe at Boston, now suffering under the daily irritation of an army before their eyes posted in their town: it may graciously please His Majesty that immediate orders be despatched to General Gage for removing His Majesty's forces from the town of Boston as soon as the rigour of the season, and other circumstances indispensable to the safety and accommodation of the said troops, may render the same practicable.'

I wish, my Lords, not to lose a day in this urgent, pressing crisis; an hour now lost in allaying ferments in America may produce years of calamity. For my own part, I will not desert for a moment the conduct of this weighty business from the first to the last, unless nailed to my bed by the extremity of sickness. I will give it unremitted attention; I will knock at the door of this sleeping and confounded ministry; and will rouse them to a sense of their important danger.

When I state the importance of the Colonies to this country, and the magnitude of danger hanging over this country from the present plan of misadministration practised against them, I desire not to be understood to argue for a reciprocity of indulgence between England and America. I contend not for indulgence, but justice to America; and I shall ever contend that the Americans justly owe obedience to us in a limited degree—they owe obedience to our ordinance of trade and navigation; but let the line be skilfully drawn between the objects of those ordinances and their private, internal property; let the sacredness of their property remain inviolate; let it be taxable only by their own consent, given in their provincial assemblies, else it will cease to be property. As to the metaphysical refinements, attempting to show that the Americans are equally free from obedience and commercial restraints as from taxation for revenue, as being unrepresented here, I pronounce them as futile, frivolous, and groundless.

When I urge this measure of recalling the troops from Boston, I urge it on this pressing principle—that it is necessarily preparatory to the restoration of your peace and the establishment of your prosperity. It will then appear that you are disposed to treat amicably and equitably; and to consider, revise, and repeal, if it should be found necessary, as I affirm it will, those violent acts and declarations which have disseminated confusion throughout your Empire.

Resistance to your acts was necessary, as it was just; and your vain declarations of the omnipotence of Parliament, and your imperious doctrines of the necessity of submission, will be found equally impotent to convince, or to enslave, your fellow-subjects in America, who feel that that tyranny, whether ambitioned by an individual part of the legislature, or the bodies who comprise it, is equally intolerable to British subjects.

The means of enforcing this thraldom are found to be as ridiculous and weak in practice as they are unjust in principle. Indeed, I cannot but feel the most anxious sensibility for the situation of General Gage and the troops under his command; thinking him, as I do, a man of humanity and understanding, and entertaining, as I ever will, the highest respect, the warmest love, for the British troops. Their situation is truly unworthy; penned up—pining in inglorious inactivity. They are an army of impotence. You may call them an army of safety and guard, but they are in truth an army of impotence and contempt; and, to make the folly equal to the disgrace, they are an army of irritation and vexation. But I find a report creeping abroad, that ministers censure General Gage's inactivity; let them censure him—it becomes them—it becomes their justice and their honour. I mean not to censure his inactivity; it is a prudent and necessary inaction; but it is a miserable condition, where disgrace is prudence, and where it is necessary to be contemptible. This tameness, however contemptible, cannot be censured; for the first drop of blood shed in civil and unnatural war might be *immedicabile pulnus*.

I therefore urge and conjure your Lordships immediately to adopt this conciliating measure. I will pledge myself for its immediately producing conciliatory effects by its being thus well timed; but if you delay till your vain hope shall be accomplished of triumphantly dictating reconciliation, you delay for ever. But admitting that this hope, which in truth is desperate, should be accomplished, what do you gain by the imposition of your victorious amnity? You will be untrusted and unthanked. Adopt, then, the grace while you have the opportunity of reconcilement, or at least prepare the way. Allay the ferment prevailing in America, by removing the obnoxious hostile cause—obnoxious and unserviceable, for their merit can be only inaction.

THEIR WOODS AND THEIR LIBERTY

But His Majesty is advised that the union in America cannot last. Ministers have more eyes than I, and should have more ears; but with all the information I have been able to procure, I can pronounce it a union, solid, permanent, and effectual. Ministers may satisfy themselves and delude the public with the report of what they call commercial bodies in America. They are not commercial; they are your packers and factors; they live upon nothing—for I call commission nothing. I mean the ministerial authority for this American intelligence;

the runners of government, who are paid for their intelligence. But these are not the men, nor this the influence, to be considered in America when we estimate the firmness of their union. Even to extend the question, and to take in the really mercantile circle, will be totally inadequate to the consideration. Trade indeed increases the wealth and glory of a country; but its real strength and stamina are to be looked for amongst the cultivators of the land; in their simplicity of life is found the simpleness of virtue—the integrity and courage of freedom. These true, genuine sons of the earth are invincible; and they surround and hem in the mercantile bodies; even if these bodies, which supposition I totally disclaim, could be supposed disaffected to the cause of liberty. Of this general spirit existing in the British nation (for so I wish to distinguish the real and genuine Americans from the pseudo-traders I have described), of this spirit of independence animating the nation of America, I have the most authentic information. It is not new among them; it is, and has ever been, their established principle, their confirmed persuasion; it is their nature and their doctrine.

I remember some years ago, when the repeal of the Stamp Act was in agitation, conversing in a friendly confidence with a person[1] of undoubted respect and authenticity on that subject; and he assured me with a certainty which his judgment and opportunity gave him, that these were the prevalent and steady principles of America—that you might destroy their towns, and cut them off from the superfluities, perhaps the conveniences of life; but that they were prepared to despise your power, and would not lament their loss, whilst they have—what, my Lords?—their woods and their liberty. The name of my authority, if I am called upon, will authenticate the opinion irrefragably.

If illegal violences have been, as it is said, committed in America, prepare the way, open the door of possibility, for acknowledgment and satisfaction; but proceed not to such coercion, such prescription; cease your indiscriminate inflictions; amerce not thirty thousand; oppress not three millions, for the fault of forty or fifty individuals. Such severity of injustice must for ever render incurable the wounds you have already given your colonies; you irritate them to unappeasable rancour. What though you march from town to town, and from province to province; though you should be able to secure the obedience of the country you leave behind you in your progress, to grasp the dominion of eighteen

[1] Dr Benjamin Franklin.

hundred miles of continent, populous in numbers possessing valour, liberty and resistance?

To such united force, what force shall be opposed? What, my Lords? A few regiments in America, and seventeen or eighteen thousand men at home! The idea is too ridiculous to take up a moment of your Lordships' time. Nor can such a rational and principled union be resisted by the tricks of office or ministerial manœuvre. Laying of papers on your table, or counting numbers on a division, will not avert or postpone the hour of danger; it must arrive, my Lords, unless these fatal Acts are done away; it must arrive in all its horrors, and then these boastful ministers, spite of all their confidence, and all their manœuvres, shall be forced to hide their heads. They shall be forced to a disgraceful abandonment of their present measures and principles, which they avow but cannot defend—measures which they presume to attempt, but cannot hope to effectuate. They cannot, my Lords, they cannot stir a step; they have not a move left; they are checkmated.

The Kingdom is Undone

But it is not repealing this Act of Parliament, it is not repealing a piece of parchment, that can restore America to our bosom; you must repeal her fears and her resentments; and you may then hope for her love and gratitude. But now, insulted with an armed force posted at Boston, irritated with an hostile array before her eyes, her concessions, if you could force them, would be suspicious and insecure; they will be *irato animo*; they will not be the sound, honourable passions of freemen, they will be dictates of fear, and extortions of force. But it is more than evident that you cannot force them, united as they are, to your unworthy terms of submission—it is impossible; and when I hear General Gage censured for inactivity, I must retort with indignation on those whose intemperate measures and improvident councils have betrayed him into his present situation. His situation reminds me, my Lords, of the answer of a French general in the civil wars of France—Monsieur Condé opposed to Monsieur Turenne. He was asked how it happened that he did not take his adversary prisoner, as he was often very near him: 'J'ai peur,' replied Condé very honestly, 'J'ai peur qu'il ne me prenne.'[1]

When your Lordships look at the papers transmitted us from America,

[1] I'm afraid he'll take me.

when you consider their decency, firmness, and wisdom, you cannot but respect their cause, and wish to make it your own. For myself, I must declare and avow that in all my reading and observation—and it has been my favourite study: I have read Thucydides, and have studied and admired the master-states of the world—that for solidity of reasoning, force of sagacity, and wisdom of conclusion, under such a complication of difficult circumstances, no nation or body of men can stand in preference to the General Congress at Philadelphia. I trust it is obvious to your Lordships, that all attempts to impose servitude upon such men, to establish despotism over such a mighty continental nation, must be vain, must be fatal. We shall be forced ultimately to retract; let us restrain while we can, not when we must. I say we must necessarily undo these violent oppressive Acts; they must be repealed—you will repeal them; I pledge myself for it, that you will in the end repeal them; I stake my reputation on it:—I will consent to be taken for an idiot, if they are not finally repealed. Avoid, then, this humiliating, disgraceful necessity. With a dignity becoming your exalted situation, make the first advances to concord, to peace, and happiness; for that is your true dignity, to act with prudence and justice. That you should first concede is obvious, from sound and rational policy. Concession comes with better grace and more salutary effect from superior power with the feelings of men, and establishes solid confidence on the foundations of affection and gratitude.

Every motive, therefore, of justice and of policy, of dignity and prudence, urges you to allay the ferment in America—by a removal of your troops from Boston, by a repeal of your Acts of Parliament, and by demonstration of amicable dispositions towards your Colonies. On the other hand, every danger and every hazard impend to deter you from perseverance in your present ruinous measures—foreign war hanging over your heads by a slight and brittle thread; France and Spain watching your conduct, and waiting for the maturity of your errors; with a vigilant eye to America, and the temper of your Colonies, more than to their own concerns, be they what they may.

To conclude, my Lords, if the ministers thus persevere in misadvising and misleading the King, I will not say that they can alienate the affections of his subjects from his crown; but I will affirm that they will make the crown not worth his wearing. I will not say that the King is betrayed; but I will pronounce that the kingdom is undone.

JOHN WILKES

1727-1797

The Commons and its Rights

In 1763 a newspaper called the North Briton *attacked the government. It was accused of being nothing but a reflection of the unpopular Lord Bute. King George III was so angry that he issued a general warrant commanding that those connected with No. 45 of the* North Briton *should be arrested.*

Among them was John Wilkes, who was a Member of Parliament. He was in some ways a worthless figure, but overnight he found himself the centre of a political storm. He was sent to the Tower. He protested, that because he was a Member of Parliament he could claim Parliamentary privilege. He further claimed that general warrants, which named no offender, were illegal.

Wilkes was charged with seditious libel, and he was outlawed. He returned to fight his constituency—Middlesex—and in 1768 he was elected. In the following February he was expelled from the House of Commons, and once again there was a by-election. Once again he was elected, and this election, too, was declared void. In the end Wilkes was released from gaol in 1770, and all London turned out to greet him. Later he was elected Lord Mayor, and again a Member of Parliament.

He was on the whole a disreputable figure, but the cause for which he fought commanded much support and sympathy. As a speaker, Wilkes was not without power, and even charm, as the following speech, made in 1776, shows. It is worth noting that although he was the centre of violent scenes his speeches could be reasonable and thoughtful. Indeed, he forecast many reforms, which had to wait until the nineteenth century, when the great Reform Bills were passed. It is curious that a single incident should have given Wilkes a secure place in history.

C

ALL wise governments and well-regulated states have been particularly careful to mark and correct the various abuses which a considerable length of time almost necessarily creates. Among these, one of the most striking and important in our country is the present unfair and inadequate state of the representation of the people of England in Parliament. It is now become so partial and unequal, from the lapse of time, that I believe almost every gentleman in the House will agree with me in the necessity of its being taken into our most serious consideration, and of our endeavouring to find a remedy for this great and growing evil.

I wish, sir, my slender abilities were equal to a thorough investigation of this momentous business; very diligent and well-meant endeavours have not been wanting to trace it from the first origin. The most natural and perfect idea of a free government is, in my mind, that of the people themselves assembling to determine by what laws they choose to be governed, and to establish the regulations they think necessary for the protection of their property and liberty against all violence and fraud. Every member of such a community would submit with alacrity to the observance of whatever had been enacted by himself, and assist with spirit in giving efficacy and vigour to laws and ordinances which derived all their authority from his own approbation and concurrence. In small inconsiderable states, this mode of legislation has been happily followed, both in ancient and modern times. The extent and populousness of a great empire seems scarcely to admit it without confusion or tumult, and therefore, our ancestors, more wise in this than the ancient Romans, adopted the representation of the many by a few, as answering more fully the true ends of government. Rome was enslaved from inattention to this very circumstance, and by one other fatal act, which ought to be a strong warning to the people, even against their own representatives here—the leaving power too long in the hands of the same persons by which the armies of the republic became the armies of Sylla, Pompey, and Caesar. When all the burghers of Italy obtained the freedom of Rome, and voted in public assemblies, their multitudes rendered the distinction of the citizen of Rome, and the alien, impossible. Their assemblies and deliberations became disorderly and tumultuous. Unprincipled and ambitious men found out the secret of turning them to the ruin of the Roman liberty and the commonwealth. Among us this evil is avoided by representation, and yet the justice of this principle is preserved. Every Englishman is supposed to be present in Parliament, either in person or by deputy chosen by himself; and therefore the resolution of Parliament is taken to be the resolution of every individual, and to give to the public the consent and approbation of every free agent of the community.

According to the first formation of this excellent constitution, so long and so justly our greatest boast and best inheritance, we find that the people thus took care no laws should be enacted, no taxes levied, but by their consent, expressed by their representatives in the great council of the nation. The mode of representation in ancient times being tolerably adequate and proportionate, the sense of the people was known by that of Parliament; their share of power in the legislature was preserved, and founded in equal justice; at present it is become insufficient, partial, and unjust. From so pleasing a view as that of the equal power which our ancestors had, with great wisdom and care, modelled for the commons of this realm, the present scene gives us not very venerable ruins of that majestic and beautiful fabric, the English constitution.

It will be objected, I foresee, that a time of perfect calm and peace throughout this vast empire is the most proper to propose internal regulations of this importance; and that while intestine discord rages in the whole northern continent of America, our attention ought to be fixed upon the most alarming object, and all our efforts employed to extinguish the devouring flame of a civil war. In my opinion, sir, the American war is, in this truly critical area, one of the strongest arguments for the regulations of our representation which I now submit to the House. During the rest of our lives, likewise, I may venture to prophesy, America will be the leading feature of this age. In our late disputes with the Americans, we have always taken it for granted that the people of England justified all the iniquitous, cruel, arbitrary, and mad proceedings of administration, because they had the approbation of the majority of this House. The absurdity of such an argument is apparent; for the majority of this House, we know, speak only the sense of 5,723 persons, even supposing, according to the constitutional custom of our ancestors, the constituent had been consulted on this great national point as he ought to have been. We have seen in what manner the acquiescence of a majority here is obtained. The people in the southern part of this island amount to upwards of five millions, the sense, therefore, of five millions cannot be ascertained by the opinion of not six thousand, even supposing it had been collected. The Americans with great reason insist that the present war is carried on contrary to the sense of the nation, by a ministerial junto, and an arbitrary faction, equally hostile to the rights of Englishmen and the claims of Americans. The various addresses to the throne from the most numerous bodies, praying that the sword may be returned to the scabbard, and all hostilities cease, confirm this assertion. The capital of our country has repeatedly declared by various public acts, its abhorrence of the present unnatural civil war, begun on principles subversive of our constitution.

Our history furnishes frequent instances of the sense of Parliament running directly counter to the sense of the nation. It was notoriously of late the case in the business of the Middlesex election. I believe the fact to be equally certain in the grand American dispute, at least as to the actual hostilities now carrying on against our brethren and fellow-subjects. The proposal before us will bring the case to an issue, and from a fair and equal representation of the people, America may at length distinguish the real sentiments of freemen and Englishmen. I do not mean, sir, at this time, to go into a tedious detail of all the various proposals which have been made for redressing this irregularity in the representation of the people. I will not intrude on the indulgence of the House, which I have always found so favourable to me. When the bill is brought in, and sent to a committee, it will be the proper time to examine all the minutiae of this great plan, and to determine on the propriety of what ought now to be done, as well as of what formerly was actually accomplished.

The journals of Cromwell's Parliaments prove that a more equal representation was settled, and carried by him into execution. That wonderful, comprehensive mind embraced the whole of this powerful empire. Ireland was put on a par with Scotland, and each kingdom sent thirty members to Parliament, which consisted likewise of 400 from England and Wales, and was to be triennial. Our colonies were then a speck on the face of the globe; now they cover half the New World. I will at this time, sir, only throw out general ideas, that every free agent in this kingdom should, in my wish, be represented in Parliament; that the metropolis, which contains in itself a ninth part of the people, and the counties of Middlesex, York, and others, which so greatly abound with inhabitants, should receive an increase in their representation; that the mean and insignificant boroughs, so emphatically styled the rotten part of our constitution, should be lopped off, and the electors in them thrown into the counties; and the rich, populous, trading towns, Birmingham, Manchester, Sheffield, Leeds, and others, be permitted to send deputies to the great council of the nation. The disfranchising of the mean, venal, and dependent boroughs, would be laying the axe to the root of corruption and treasury influence, as well as aristocratical tyranny. We ought equally to guard against those who sell themselves, or whose lords sell them. Burgage tenures, and private property in a share of the legislature, are monstrous absurdities in a free state, as well as an insult to common sense. I wish, sir, an English Parliament to speak the free, unbiassed sense of the body of the English people, and of every man among us, of each individual who may be justly supposed to be comprehended in a fair majority.

A DELUSIVE NAME

The meanest mechanic, the poorest peasant and day-labourer, has important rights respecting his personal liberty, that of his wife and children, his property, however inconsiderable, his wages, his earnings, the very price and value of each day's hard labour, which are in many trades and manufactures regulated by the power of Parliament. Every law relative to marriage, to the protection of a wife, sister, or daughter, against violence and brutal lust, to every contract or agreement with a rapacious or unjust master, interest the manufacturer, the cottager, the servant, as well as the rich subjects of the state. Some share, therefore, in the power of making those laws which deeply interest them, and to which they are expected to pay obedience, should be referred even to this inferior, but most useful set of men in the community; and we ought always to remember this important truth, acknowledged by every free state—that all government is instituted for the good of the mass of the people to be governed; that they are the original fountain of power, and even of revenue, and in all events, the last resource. The various instances of partial injustice throughout this kingdom will likewise become the proper subjects of inquiry in the course of the bill before the committee, such as the many freeholds in the city of London, which are not represented in this House. These freeholds being within the particular jurisdiction of the city, are excluded from giving a vote in the county of Middlesex, and by Act of Parliament only liverymen can vote for Members of Parliament in London. These, and other particulars, I leave. I mention them now to show the necessity of a new regulation of the representation of this kingdom.

My inquiries, sir, are confined to the southern part of the island. Scotland I leave to the care of its own careful and prudent sons. I hope they will spare a few moments from the management of the arduous affairs of England and America, which at present so much engross their time, to attend to the state of representation among their own people, if they have not all emigrated to this warmer and more fruitful climate. I am almost afraid that the forty-five Scottish gentlemen among us represent themselves. Perhaps in my plan for the improvement of the representation of England, almost all the natives of Scotland may be included. I shall only remark, that the proportion of representations between the two countries cannot be changed. In the twenty-second article of the Treaty of Union, the number of forty-five is to be the representative body of the Parliament of Great Britain for the northern part of this island. To increase the members for England and Wales beyond the number of which the English Parliament consisted at the period of that treaty, in 1706, would be a breach of public faith, and a violation of a solemn treaty between two independent states.

My proposition has for its basis the preservation of that compact, the proportional share of each kingdom in the legislative body remaining exactly according to its establishment. The monstrous injustice and glaring partiality of the present representation of the commons of England has been fully stated, and is, I believe, almost universally acknowledged, as well as the necessity of our recurring to the great leading principle of our free constitution, which declares this House of Parliament to be only a delegated power from the people at large. Policy, no less than justice, calls our attention to this momentous point; and reason, not custom, ought to be our guide in a business of this consequence, where the rights of a free people are materially interested. Without a true representation of the commons our constitution is essentially defective, our Parliament is a delusive name, a mere phantom, and all other remedies to recover the pristine purity of the form of government established by our ancestors, would be ineffectual; even the shortening the period of Parliaments, and a place and pension bill, both which I highly approve, and think absolutely necessary. I therefore flatter myself, sir, that I have the concurrence of the House with the motion which I have now the honour of making, 'That leave be given to bring in a bill for a just and equal representation of the people of England in Parliament.'

EDMUND BURKE
1729–1797

Speech on American Taxation

In 1763, at the end of the Seven Years War, the reputation of Britain throughout the world was high. The country was admired and respected not only because of her achievements in that war but because she was recognized as the champion of liberty. But in the next twenty years, between 1763 and 1783, her reputation at home and abroad sank to a low level. It was only restored after 1783 when William Pitt the Younger, son of William Pitt the Elder (Lord Chatham) who had inspired the British effort in the Seven Years War, formed a government.

The main reason for the decline in Britain's fortunes and reputation during the years 1763–83 lay in the impossible position of the King. George III was expected both to reign and rule, while individual Members of Parliament contested with each other for the great Offices of State.

Modern historians do not now hold the view that George III was an ambitious schemer determined to dominate the political scene. There was no well-defined system of parties. Because of the limited franchise, Parliament was not completely representative of the country. It represented interests rather than the people as a whole. George III was compelled to play an active political rôle, otherwise he would have been completely dominated by his ministers. He destroyed the great Whig empire of power, but it would be a mistake to suppose that he always acted unconstitutionally. Indeed, he revived some of the constitutional practices which his predecessors, George I and George II, had allowed to lapse.

In his long reign from 1760 to 1820 there were many changes and events which would have taxed the resources of the wisest of men. George III could not be regarded as the personification of wisdom. But he was no fool—at any rate not in the early part of his reign—and he was not a tyrant. At this period, he tried to achieve his ambitions by playing one interest against another and by skilful use of the government party—the King's Friends. There was much corruption, but the King was no more corrupt than many of his ministers.

The King's attitude towards the American Colonies did not meet with the approval of the Irishman, Edmund Burke. He is, without doubt, the outstanding philosopher-politician writing in English. It is ironical that he never held high office; his greatest work was done in opposition. He disagreed with the popular conception of the time regarding politicians not in office, and he tried to gather round him a small group of men who would advocate a consistent programme of opposition.

Burke was totally opposed to the King's policy towards the American colonies. In two great speeches he set out his ideas in language at once elevated and sustained. As Hazlitt said of him: 'Chatham's eloquence was calculated to make men act; Burke's was calculated to make them think.' His speeches are read and studied today, not only because of the events which gave rise to them but because of the sentiments which he expressed and the manner in which he expressed them. In a striking phrase Matthew Arnold said of his speeches: 'He saturates politics with thought.' Never before or since has the relationship of a mother-country to colonies been better expressed than in his speeches on America.

Burke could not tolerate tyranny in anything, great or small. His speech to the Bristol electors is a classic, defining once and for all what should be the relationship between a Member of Parliament and his constituents.

Inevitably Indian affairs attracted his attention as well as American affairs. The excesses of the East India Company filled him with horror. Warren Hastings, one of the Governors, was impeached by Burke. He was unsuccessful in bringing Hastings to book but the effect of Burke's action has never been forgotten.

It is worth noting that although Burke was one of the greatest orators which this country has ever known he was singularly ineffective in the House of Commons. His speech was indistinct: he had a strong Irish accent; and very few members stayed in the House of Commons to listen to what he had to say. This neglect is in itself a commentary on the House of Commons of the day. But when his speeches were published they were immediately read and studied, not only in this country, but abroad. They were rightly regarded as being among the great expositions made by mankind on the subject of government. They had an immediate effect on the educated opinion of Europe. Burke was a member of that literary group which acknowledged

Dr Johnson as its leader. His friend, Goldsmith, speaking of his style, said that he 'winds into his subject like a serpent'. That is an acute observation.

Anyone who essays speaking in the grand style must study the speeches of Burke. He has no facile tricks of expression. He was a learned man and a thoughtful man. He brought great powers of intellect and imagination to the matter on hand; and he had a feeling for the use of the English language. His speeches are constructed as majestically as noble buildings. They are built up on the three stages of thought, image, and sentiment.

The beginning of the first speech which follows shows this pattern.

'In this eventful history of the revolutions of America the characters of men are of much importance.' (Thought.)

'Great men are the guide-posts and land-marks in the state.' (Image.)

'The credit of such men at court or in the nation is the sole cause of all the public measures.' (Sentiment.)

At the present time when the relationship of colonies to mother countries throughout the world is the concern of the world, the speeches of Burke are being studied by politicians in their assemblies and by scholars in their studies. These speeches are not only great literature but a body of principles capable of universal application.

The first speech which follows was delivered by Burke in the House of Commons on 19th April, 1774, on a motion to repeal the tea duty.

IN this eventful history of the revolutions of America, the characters of men are of much importance. Great men are the guide-posts and land-marks in the state. The credit of such men at court, or in the nation, is the sole cause of all the public measures. It would be an invidious thing (most foreign, I trust, to what you think my disposition) to remark the errors into which the authority of great names has brought the nation, without doing justice at the same time to the great qualities whence that authority arose. The subject is instructive to those who wish to form themselves on whatever of excellence has gone before them. There are many young members in the House (such of late has been the rapid succession of public men) who never saw that prodigy, Charles Townshend, nor of course know what a ferment he was able to excite in everything by the violent ebullition of his mixed virtues and failings. For failings he had undoubtedly—many of us remember them; we are this day considering the effect of them. But he had no failings which were not owing to a noble cause, to an ardent, generous, perhaps an immoderate, passion for fame—a passion which is the instinct of all great souls. He worshipped that goddess wheresoever she appeared; but he paid his particular devotions to her in her favourite habitation in her chosen temple, the House of Commons.

Besides the characters of the individuals that compose our body, it is impossible, Mr Speaker, not to observe that this House has a collective character of its own. That character too, however imperfect, is not unamiable. Like all great public collections of men, you possess a marked love of virtue and an abhorrence of vice. But among vices, there is none which the House abhors in the same degree with obstinacy. Obstinacy, Sir, is certainly a great vice; and in the changeful state of political affairs it is frequently the cause of great mischief. It happens, however, very unfortunately, that almost the whole line of the great and masculine virtues, constancy, gravity, magnanimity, fortitude, fidelity, and firmness, are closely allied to this disagreeable quality, of which you have so just an abhorrence, and, in their excess, all these virtues very easily fall into it. He who paid such a punctilious attention to all your feelings certainly took care not to shock them by that vice which is the most disgustful to you.

That fear of displeasing those who ought most to be pleased betrayed him sometimes into the other extreme. He had voted, and, in the year 1765, had been an advocate, for the Stamp Act. Things and the disposition of men's minds were changed. In short, the Stamp Act began to be no favourite in this House. He therefore attended at the private meeting, in which the resolutions moved by a right honourable gentleman were settled, resolutions leading to the repeal. The next day he voted for that repeal, and he would have spoken for it too if an illness (not, as was then given out, a political, but to my knowledge a very real illness) had not prevented it.

The very next session, as the fashion of this world passeth away, the repeal began to be in as bad an odour in this House as the Stamp Act had been in the session before. To conform to the temper which began to prevail, and to prevail mostly amongst those most in power, he declared very early in the winter that a revenue must be had out of America. Instantly he was tied down to his engagements by some who had no objection to such experiments when made at the cost of persons for whom they had no particular regard. The whole body of courtiers

33

drove him onward. They always talked as if the King stood in a sort of humiliated state until something of the kind should be done.

Here this extraordinary man, then Chancellor of the Exchequer, found himself in great straits. To please universally was the object of his life, but to tax and to please, no more than to love and to be wise, is not given to men. However, he attempted it. To render the tax palatable to the partisans of American revenue, he had a preamble stating the necessity of such a revenue. To close with the American distinction, this revenue was external or port duty; but again, to soften it to the other party, it was a duty of supply. To gratify the colonists, it was laid on British manufactures; to satisfy the merchants of Britain, the duty was trivial, and (except that on tea, which touched only the devoted East India Company) on none of the grand objects of commerce. To counterwork the American contraband, the duty on tea was reduced from a shilling to threepence. But to secure the favour of those who would tax America, the scene of collection was changed, and, with the rest, it was levied in the colonies. What need I say more? This fine-spun scheme had the usual fate of all exquisite policy. But the original plan of the duties and the mode of executing that plan both arose singly and solely from a love of our applause. He was truly the child of the House. He never thought, did, or said anything, but with a view to you. He every day adapted himself to your disposition, and adjusted himself before it as at a looking-glass.

He had observed (indeed it could not escape him) that several persons, infinitely his inferiors in all respects, had formerly rendered themselves considerable in this House by one method alone. They were a race of men (I hope in God the species is extinct) who, when they rose in their place, no man living could divine, from any known adherence to parties, to opinions, or to principles, from any order or system in their politics, or from any sequel or connection in their ideas, what part they were going to take in any debate. It is astonishing how much this uncertainty, especially at critical times, called the attention of all parties on such men. All eyes were fixed on them, all ears open to hear them; each party gaped, and looked alternately for their vote, almost to the end of their speeches. While the House hung in this uncertainty, now the *hear hims* rose from this side—now they rebelled from the other; and that party to whom they fell at length from their tremulous and dancing balance always received them in a tempest of applause. The fortune of such men was a temptation too great to be resisted by one to whom a single whiff of incense withheld gave much greater pain than he received delight in the clouds of it which daily rose about him from the prodigal superstition of innumerable admirers. He was a candidate for contradictory honours, and his great aim was to make those agree in admiration of him who never agreed in anything else.

THE ANGEL OF PEACE

Hence arose this unfortunate Act, the subject of this day's debate; from a disposition which, after making an American revenue to please one, repealed it to please others, and again revived it in hopes of pleasing a third, and of catching something in the ideas of all.

This Revenue Act of 1767 formed the fourth period of American policy. How we have fared since then—what woeful variety of schemes have been adopted; what enforcing and what repealing; what bullying and what submitting; what doing and undoing; what straining and what relaxing; what assemblies dissolved for not obeying and called again without obedience; what troops sent out to quell resistance and, on meeting that resistance, re-called; what shiftings and changes and jumblings of all kinds of men at home, which left no possibility of order, consistency, vigour, or even so much as a decent unity of colour in any one public measure—it is a tedious, irksome task. My duty may call me to open it out some other time; on a former occasion I tried your temper on a part of it, for the present I shall forbear.

After all these changes and agitations, your immediate situation upon the question on your paper is at length brought to this. You have an Act of Parliament, stating that 'it is expedient to raise a revenue in America'. By a partial repeal you annihilated the greatest part of that revenue which this preamble declares to be so expedient. You have substituted no other in the place of it. A Secretary of State has disclaimed, in the King's name, all thoughts of such a substitution in future. The principle of this disclaimer goes to what has been left as well as what has been repealed. The tax which lingers after its companions (under a preamble declaring an American revenue expedient, and for the sole purpose of supporting the theory of that preamble) militates with the assurance authentically conveyed to the colonies, and is an exhaustless source of jealousy and animosity. On this state, which

I take to be a fair one, not being able to discern any grounds of honour, advantage, peace, or power, for adhering either to the Act or to the preamble, I shall vote for the question which leads to the repeal of both.

If you do not fall in with this motion, then secure something to fight for consistent in theory and valuable in practice. If you must employ your strength, employ it to uphold you in some honourable right or some profitable wrong. If you are apprehensive that the concession recommended to you, though proper, should be a means of drawing on you further, but unreasonable claims, why then employ your force in supporting that reasonable concession against those unreasonable demands. You will employ it with more grace, with better effect, and with great probable concurrence of all the quiet and rational people in the provinces, who are now united with, and hurried away by, the violent—having indeed different dispositions, but a common interest. If you apprehend that on a concession you shall be pushed by meta-physical process to the extreme lines and argued out of your whole authority, my advice is this: when you have recovered your old, your strong, your tenable position, then face about—stop short—do nothing more—reason not at all—oppose the ancient policy and practice of the empire as a rampart against the speculations of innovators on both sides of the question, and you will stand on great, manly, and sure ground. On this solid basis fix your machines, and they will draw worlds towards you.

Your ministers, in their own and His Majesty's name, have already adopted the American distinction of internal and external duties. It is a distinction, whatever merit it may have, that was originally moved by the Americans themselves, and I think they will acquiesce in it, if they are not pushed with too much logic and too little sense, in all the conse-quences. That is, if external taxation be understood, as they and you understand it, when you please, to be not a distinction of geography, but of policy; that it is a power for regulating trade, and not for supporting establishments. The distinction, which is as nothing with regard to right, is of most weighty consideration in practice. Recover your old ground and your old tranquillity—try it—I am persuaded the Americans will compromise with you. When confidence is once restored, the odious and suspicious *summum jus* will perish of course. The spirit of practicability, of moderation, and mutual convenience will never call in geometrical exactness as the arbitrator of amicable settlement. Consult and follow your experience. Let not the long story with which I have exercised your patience prove fruitless to your interests.

For my part, I should choose (if I could have my wish) that the proposition of the honourable gentleman for the repeal could go to America without the attendance of the penal bills. Alone I could almost answer for its success. I cannot be certain of its reception in the bad company it may keep. In such heterogeneous assortments, the most innocent person will lose the effect of his innocency. Though you should send out this angel of peace, yet you are sending out a destroying angel too; and what would be the effect of the conflict of these two adverse spirits, or which would predominate in the end, is what I dare not say: whether the lenient measures would cause American passion to subside, or the severe would increase its fury—all this is in the hand of Providence. Yet now, even now, I should confide in the prevailing virtue and efficacious operation of lenity, though working in darkness and in chaos, in the midst of all this unnatural and turbid combination, I should hope it might produce order and beauty in the end.

OUR CHILDREN

Let us, Sir, embrace some system or other before we end this session. Do you mean to tax America and to draw a productive revenue from thence? If you do, speak out; name, fix, ascertain this revenue; settle its quantity; define its objects; provide for its collection; and then fight when you have something to fight for. If you murder, rob; if you kill, take possession: and do not appear in the character of madmen as well as assassins, violent, vindictive, bloody, and tyrannical, without an object. But may better counsels guide you!

Again and again revert to your own principles—seek peace and ensue it—leave America, if she has taxable matter in her, to tax herself. I am not here going into the distinctions of rights, not attempting to mark their boundaries. I do not enter into these metaphysical distinctions; I hate the very sound of them. Leave the Americans as they anciently stood, and these distinctions, born of our unhappy contest, will die along with it. They and we, and their and our ancestors, have been happy under that system. Let the memory of all actions in contradiction to that good old mode, on both sides, be extinguished for ever. Be content to bind America by laws of trade; you have always done it. Let this be your reason for binding their trade. Do not burthen them by taxes; you were not used to do so from the beginning. Let this be your reason for not taxing. These are the arguments of states and kingdoms. Leave the rest to the schools for there only they may be discussed with safety. But if, intemperately, unwisely, fatally, you sophisticate and poison the very source of government, by urging subtle deductions and consequences odious to those you govern, from the unlimited and illimitable nature of supreme sovereignty, you will teach them by these means to call that sovereignty itself in question. When you drive him hard, the boar will surely turn upon the hunters. If that sovereignty and their freedom cannot be reconciled, which will they take? They will cast your sovereignty in your face. Nobody will be argued into slavery. Sir, let the gentlemen on the other side call forth all their ability, let the best of them get up and tell me, what one character of liberty the Americans have, and what one brand of slavery they are free from, if they are bound in their property and industry by all the restraints you can imagine on commerce, and at the same time are made pack-horses of every tax you choose to impose, without the least share in granting them. When they bear the burthens of unlimited monopoly, will you bring them to bear the burthens of unlimited revenue too? The Englishman in America will feel that this is slavery—that it is legal slavery will be no compensation either to his feelings or his understanding.

A noble lord[1], who spoke some time ago, is full of the fire of ingenuous youth; and when he has modelled the ideas of a lively imagination by further experience he will be an ornament to his country in either House. He has said that the Americans are our children, and how can they revolt against their parent? He says that if they are not free in their present state, England is not free, because Manchester and other considerable places are not represented. So then, because some towns in England are not represented, America is to have no representative at all. They are 'our children'; but when children ask for bread we are not to give a stone. Is it because the natural resistance of things and the various mutations of time hinder our Government, or any scheme of government, from being any more than a sort of approximation to the right, is it therefore that the colonies are to recede from it infinitely? When this child of ours wishes to assimilate to its parent and to reflect with a true filial resemblance the beauteous countenance of British liberty, are

---

[1] Lord Carmarthen.

we to turn to them the shameful parts of our constitution? are we to give them our weakness for their strength? our opprobrium for their glory? and the slough of slavery, which we are not able to work off, to serve them for their freedom?

If this be the case, ask yourselves this question, Will they be content in such a state of slavery? If not, look to the consequences. Reflect how you are to govern a people who think they ought to be free and think they are not. Your scheme yields no revenue, it yields nothing but discontent, disorder, disobedience; and such is the state of America, that after wading up to your eyes in blood, you could only end just where you began; that is, to tax where no revenue is to be found, to—my voice fails me; my inclination indeed carries me no farther—all is confusion beyond it.

THE IMPERIAL CHARACTER OF BRITAIN

Well, Sir, I have recovered a little, and before I sit down I must say something to another point with which gentlemen urge us. What is to become of the Declaratory Act asserting the entireness of British legislative authority if we abandon the practice of taxation?

For my part I look upon the rights stated in that Act exactly in the manner in which I viewed them on its very first proposition, and which I have often taken the liberty, with great humility, to lay before you. I look, I say, on the imperial rights of Great Britain and the privileges which the colonists ought to enjoy under these rights to be just the most reconcilable things in the world. The Parliament of Great Britain sits at the head of her extensive empire in two capacities: one as the local legislature of this island, providing for all things at home, immediately, and by no other instrument than the executive power; the other, and I think her nobler capacity, is what I call her imperial character, in which as from the throne of heaven, she superintends all the several inferior legislatures, and guides and controls them all, without annihilating any. As all these provincial legislatures are only co-ordinate to each other, they ought all to be subordinate to her; else they can neither preserve mutual peace, nor hope for mutual justice, nor effectually afford mutual assistance. It is necessary to coerce the negligent, to restrain the violent, and to aid the weak and deficient by the overruling plenitude of her power. She is never to intrude into the place of the others, whilst they are equal to the common ends of their institution. But in order to enable Parliament to answer all these ends of provident and beneficent superintendence, her powers must be boundless. The gentlemen who think the powers of Parliament limited, may please themselves to talk of requisitions. But suppose the requisitions are not obeyed? What! Shall there be no reserved power in the empire, to supply a deficiency which may weaken, divide, and dissipate the whole? We are engaged in war—the Secretary of State calls upon the colonies to contribute—some would do it, I think most would cheerfully furnish whatever is demanded—one or two, suppose, hang back, and, easing themselves, let the stress of the draft lie on the others—surely it is proper, that some authority might legally say—'Tax yourselves for the common supply, or Parliament will do it for you.' This backwardness was, as I am told, actually the case of Pennsylvania for some short time towards the beginning of the last war, owing to some internal dissensions in the colony. But whether the fact were so, or otherwise, the case is equally to be provided for by a competent sovereign power. But then this ought to be no ordinary power, nor ever used in the first instance. This is what I meant, when I have said at various times that I consider the power of taxing in Parliament as an instrument of empire and not as a means of supply.

Such, Sir, is my idea of the constitution of the British empire, as distinguished from the constitution of Britain; and on these grounds I think subordination and liberty may be sufficiently reconciled through the whole, whether to serve a refining speculatist or a facetious demagogue, I know not, but enough surely for the ease and happiness of man.

Sir, whilst we held this happy course, we drew more from the colonies than all the impotent violence of despotism ever could extort from them. We did this abundantly in the last war. It has never been once denied—and what reason have we to imagine that the colonies would not have proceeded in supplying government as liberally, if you had not stepped in and hindered them from contributing, by interrupting the channel in which their liberality flowed with so strong a course, by attempting to take, instead of being satisfied to receive? Sir William Temple says that Holland has loaded itself with ten times the impositions which it revolted from Spain rather than submit to. He says true. Tyranny is a poor provider. It knows neither how to accumulate nor how to extract.

I charge therefore to this new and unfortunate system the loss not only of peace, of union, and of commerce, but even of revenue, which its friends are contending for. It is morally certain that we have lost at least a million of free grants since the peace. I think we have lost a great deal more, and that those who look for a revenue from the provinces never could have pursued, even in that light, a course more directly repugnant to their purposes.

Now, Sir, I trust I have shown, first on that narrow ground which the honourable gentleman measured, that you are likely to lose nothing by complying with the motion, except what you have lost already. I have shown afterwards, that in time of peace you flourished in commerce, and, when war required it, had sufficient aid from the colonies while you pursued your ancient policy; that you threw everything into confusion when you made the Stamp Act; and that you restored everything to peace and order when you repealed it. I have shown that the revival of the system of taxation has produced the very worst effects, and that the partial repeal has produced, not partial good, but universal evil. Let these considerations, founded on facts not one of which can be denied, bring us back to our reason by the road of our experience.

I cannot, as I have said, answer for mixed measures; but surely this mixture of lenity would give the whole a better chance of success. When you once regain confidence, the way will be clear before you. Then you may enforce the Act of Navigation when it ought to be enforced. You will yourselves open it where it ought still further to be opened. Proceed in what you do, whatever you do, from policy and not from rancour. Let us act like men, let us act like statesmen. Let us hold some sort of consistent conduct.—It is agreed that a revenue is not to be had in America. If we lose the profit, let us get rid of the odium.

On this business of America I confess I am serious even to sadness. I have had but one opinion concerning it since I sat, and before I sat, in Parliament. The noble lord[1] will, as usual, probably attribute the part taken by me and my friends in this business to a desire of getting his places. Let him enjoy this happy and original idea. If I deprived him of it, I should take away most of his wit and all his argument. But I had rather bear the brunt of all his wit, and indeed blows much heavier, than stand answerable to God for embracing a system that tends to the destruction of some of the very best and fairest of his works. But I know

[1] Lord North.

the map of England as well as the noble lord, or as any other person, and I know that the way I take is not the road to preferment. My excellent and honourable friend[1] under me on the floor has trod that road with great toil for upwards of twenty years together. He is not yet arrived at the noble lord's destination. However, the tracks of my worthy friend are those I have ever wished to follow, because I know they lead to honour. Long may we tread the same road together, whoever may accompany us, or whoever may laugh at us on our journey! I honestly and solemnly declare, I have in all seasons adhered to the system of 1766, for no other reason than that I think it laid deep in your truest interest—and that, by limiting the exercise, it fixes on the firmest foundations a real, consistent, well-grounded authority in Parliament. Until you come back to that system there will be no peace for England.

Speech to the Electors of Bristol

This speech was made by Burke on being elected to Parliament for that City in November, 1774. His colleague, a Bristol merchant named Cruger, had promised to vote according to the wishes of the constituents. In this speech Burke sets out what he considers should be the relationship between a Member of Parliament and his constituents.

GENTLEMEN—I cannot avoid sympathizing strongly with the feelings of the gentleman who has received the same honour that you have conferred on me. If he, who was bred and passed his whole life amongst you; if he, who through the easy gradations of acquaintance, friendship, and esteem, has obtained the honour, which seems of itself, naturally and almost insensibly, to meet with those, who, by the even tenor of pleasing manners and social virtues, slide into the love and confidence of their fellow-citizens;—if he cannot speak but with great emotion on this subject, surrounded as he is on all sides with his old friends; you

[1] Mr Dowdeswell.

will have the goodness to excuse me, if my real, unaffected embarrassment prevents me from expressing my gratitude to you as I ought.

I was brought hither under the disadvantage of being unknown, even by sight, to any of you. No previous canvass was made for me. I was put in nomination after the poll was opened. I did not appear until it was far advanced. If, under all these accumulated disadvantages, your good opinion has carried me to this happy point of success; you will pardon me, if I can only say to you collectively, as I said to you individually, simply, and plainly, I thank you—I am obliged to you—I am not insensible of your kindness.

This is all that I am able to say for the inestimable favour you have conferred upon me. But I cannot be satisfied, without saying a little more in defence of the right you have to confer such a favour. The person that appeared here as counsel for the candidate, who so long and so earnestly solicited your votes, thinks proper to deny, that a very great part of you have any votes to give. He fixes a standard period of time in his own imagination, not what the law defines, but merely what the convenience of his client suggests, by which he would cut off, at one stroke, all those freedoms which are the dearest privileges of your corporation; which the common law authorizes; which your magistrates are compelled to grant; which come duly authenticated into this court; and are saved in the clearest words, and with the most religious care and tenderness, in that very act of Parliament, which was made to regulate the elections by freemen, and to prevent all possible abuses in making them.

I do not intend to argue the matter here. My learned counsel has supported your cause with his usual ability; the worthy sheriffs have acted with their usual equity, and I have no doubt, that the same equity, which dictates the return, will guide the final determination. I had the honour, in conjunction with many far wiser men, to contribute a very small assistance, but, however, some assistance, to the forming the judicature which is to try such questions. It would be unnatural in me to doubt the justice of that court, in the trial of my own cause, to which I have been so active to give jurisdiction over every other.

I assure the worthy freemen, and this corporation, that, if the gentleman perseveres in the intentions which his present warmth dictates to him, I will attend their cause with diligence, and I hope with effect.

For, if I know anything of myself, it is not my own interest in it, but my full conviction, that induces me to tell you—I think there is not a shadow of doubt in the case.

I do not imagine that you find me rash in declaring myself, or very forward in troubling you. From the beginning to the end of the election, I have kept silence in all matters of discussion. I have never asked a question of a voter on the other side, or supported a doubtful vote on my own. I respected the abilities of my managers; I relied on the candour of the court. I think the worthy sheriffs will bear me witness, that I have never once made an attempt to impose upon their reason, to surprise their justice, or to ruffle their temper. I stood on the hustings (except when I gave my thanks to those who favoured me with their votes) less like a candidate, than an unconcerned spectator of a public proceeding. But here the face of things is altered. Here is an attempt for a general massacre of suffrages; an attempt, by a promiscuous carnage of friends and foes, to exterminate above two thousand votes, including seven hundred polled for the gentleman himself, who now complains, and who would destroy the friends whom he has obtained, only because he cannot obtain as many of them as he wishes.

How he will be permitted, in another place, to stultify and disable himself, and to plead against his own acts, is another question. The law will decide it. I shall only speak of it as it concerns the propriety of public conduct in this city. I do not pretend to lay down rules of decorum for other gentlemen. They are best judges of the mode of proceeding that will recommend them to the favour of their fellow-citizens. But I confess I should look rather awkward, if I had been the very first to produce the new copies of freedom, if I had persisted in producing them to the last; if I had ransacked, with the most unremitting industry and the most penetrating research, the remotest corners of the kingdom to discover them; if I were then, all at once, to turn short, and declare, that I had been sporting all this while with the right of election; and that I had been drawing out a poll, upon no sort of rational grounds, which disturbed the peace of my fellow-citizens for a month together—I really, for my part, should appear awkward under such circumstances.

It would be still more awkward in me, if I were gravely to look the sheriffs in the face, and to tell them, they were not to determine my cause on my own principles; not to make the return upon those votes upon which I had rested my election. Such would be my appearance to the court and magistrates.

But how should I appear to the voters themselves? If I had gone round to the citizens entitled to freedom, and squeezed them by the hand—'Sir, I humbly beg your vote—I shall be eternally thankful—may I hope for the honour of your support?—Well!—come—we shall see you at the council-house.'—If I were then to deliver them to my managers, pack them into tallies, vote them off in court, and when I heard from the bar—'Such a one only! and such a one for ever!—he's my man!'—'Thank you, good sir—Hah! my worthy friend! thank you kindly—that's an honest fellow—how is your good family?'—Whilst these words were hardly out of my mouth, if I should have wheeled round at once, and told them—'Get you gone, you pack of worthless fellows! you have no votes—you are usurpers! you are intruders on the rights of real freemen! I will have nothing to do with you! you ought never to have been produced at this election, and the sheriff ought not to have admitted you to poll.'

Gentlemen, I should make a strange figure if my conduct had been of this sort. I am not so old an acquaintance of yours as the worthy gentleman. Indeed I could not have ventured on such kind of freedoms with you. But I am bound, and I will endeavour, to have justice done to the rights of freemen; even though I should, at the same time, be obliged to vindicate the former part of my antagonist's conduct against his own present inclinations.

I owe myself, in all things, to all the freemen of this city. My particular friends have a demand on me that I should not deceive their expectations. Never was cause or man supported with more constancy, more activity, more spirit. I have been supported with a zeal indeed and heartiness in my friends, which (if their object had been at all proportioned to their endeavours) could never be sufficiently commended. They supported me upon the most liberal principles. They wished that the members for Bristol should be chosen for the city, and for their country at large, and not for themselves.

So far they are not disappointed. If I possess nothing else, I am sure I possess the temper that is fit for your service. I know nothing of Bristol, but by the favours I have received, and the virtues I have seen exerted in it.

I shall ever retain, what I now feel, the most perfect and grateful attachment to my friends—and I have no enmities; no resentment. I never can consider fidelity to engagements, and constancy in friendships, but with the highest approbation; even when those noble qualities are employed against my own pretensions. The gentleman, who is not so fortunate as I have been in this contest, enjoys, in this respect, a consolation full of honour both to himself and to his friends. They have certainly left nothing undone for his service.

As for the trifling petulance, which the rage of party stirs up in little minds, though it should show itself even in this court, it has not made the slightest impression on me. The highest flight of such clamorous birds is winged in an inferior reign of the air. We hear them, and we look upon them, just as you, gentlemen, when you enjoy the serene air on your lofty rocks, look down upon the gulls that skim the mud of your river, when it is exhausted of its tide.

I am sorry I cannot conclude without saying a word on a topic touched upon by my worthy colleague. I wish that topic had been passed by at a time when I have so little leisure to discuss it. But since he has thought proper to throw it out, I owe you a clear explanation of my poor sentiments on that subject.

He tells you that 'the topic of instructions has occasioned much altercation and uneasiness in this city'; and he expresses himself (if I understand him rightly) in favour of the coercive authority of such instructions.

NOT MEMBER OF BRISTOL BUT MEMBER OF PARLIAMENT

Certainly, gentlemen, it ought to be the happiness and glory of a representative to live in the strictest union, the closest correspondence, and the most unreserved communication with his constituents. Their wishes ought to have great weight with him; their opinion, high respect; their business, unremitted attention. It is his duty to sacrifice his repose, his pleasures, his satisfactions, to theirs; and above all, ever, and in all cases, to prefer their interest to his own. But his unbiassed opinion, his mature judgment, his enlightened conscience, he ought not to sacrifice to you, to any man, or to any set of men living. These he does not derive from your pleasure; no, nor from the law and the constitution. They are a trust from Providence, for the abuse of which he is deeply answerable. Your representative owes you, not his industry only, but his judgment;

and he betrays, instead of serving you, if he sacrifices it to your opinion.

My worthy colleague says, his will ought to be subservient to yours. If that be all, the thing is innocent. If government were a matter of will upon any side, yours, without question, ought to be superior. But government and legislation are matters of reason and judgment, and not of inclination; and what sort of reason is that, in which the determination precedes the discussion; in which one set of men deliberate, and another decide; and where those who form the conclusion are perhaps three hundred miles distant from those who hear the arguments?

To deliver an opinion, is the right of all men; that of constituents is a weighty and respectable opinion, which a representative ought always to rejoice to hear; and which he ought always most seriously to consider. But authoritative instructions; mandates issued, which the member is bound blindly and implicitly to obey, to vote, and to argue for, though contrary to the clearest conviction of his judgment and conscience—these are things utterly unknown to the laws of this land, and which arise from a fundamental mistake of the whole order and tenor of our constitution.

Parliament is not a congress of ambassadors from different and hostile interests; which interests each must maintain, as an agent and advocate, against other agents and advocates; but parliament is a deliberate assembly of one nation, with one interest, that of the whole; where, not local purposes, not local prejudices, ought to guide, but the general good, resulting from the general reason of the whole. You choose a member indeed, but when you have chosen him, he is not member of Bristol, but he is a Member of Parliament. If the local constituent should have an interest, or should form an hasty opinion, evidently opposite to the real good of the rest of the community, the member for that place ought to be as far, as any other, from any endeavour to give it effect. I beg pardon for saying so much on this subject. I have been unwillingly drawn into it; but I shall ever use a respectful frankness of communication with you. Your faithful friend, your devoted servant, I shall be to the end of my life: a flatterer you do not wish for. On this point of instructions, however, I think it scarcely possible we ever can have any sort of difference. Perhaps I may give you too much, rather than too little, trouble.

From the first hour I was encouraged to court your favour, to this happy day of obtaining it, I have never promised you anything but humble and persevering endeavours to do my duty. The weight of that duty, I confess, makes me tremble; and whoever well considers what it is, of all things in the world, will fly from what has the least likeness to a positive and precipitate engagement. To be a good Member of Parliament is, let me tell you, no easy task; especially at this time, when there is so strong a disposition to run into the perilous extremes of servile compliance or wild popularity. To unite circumspection with vigour, is absolutely necessary; but it is extremely difficult. We are now members for a rich commercial city; this city, however, is but a part of a rich commercial nation, the interests of which are various, multiform, and intricate. We are members for that great nation, which however is itself but part of a great empire, extended by our virtue and our fortune to the farthest limits of the east and of the west. All these wide-spread interests must be considered; must be compared; must be reconciled, if possible. We are members for a free country; and surely we all know, that the machine of a free constitution is no simple thing; but as intricate and as delicate as it is valuable. We are members in a great and ancient monarchy; and we must preserve religiously the true legal rights of the sovereign, which form the key-stone that binds together the noble and well-constructed arch of our empire and our constitution. A constitution made up of balanced powers must ever be a critical thing. As such I mean to touch that part of it which comes within my reach. I know my inability, and I wish for support from every quarter. In particular I shall aim at the friendship, and shall cultivate the best correspondence, of the worthy colleague you have given me.

I trouble you no further than once more to thank you all; you, gentlemen, for your favours; the candidates, for their temperate and polite behaviour; and the sheriffs, for a conduct which may give a model for all who are in public stations.

On Conciliation with the Colonies

This speech was made by Burke in the House of Commons on 22nd March, 1775. This was the last of several efforts made by those who opposed the government, and who sought to bring about a reconciliation. In fact hostilities began at Lexington on 19th April, less than a month after this speech was delivered.

To restore order and repose to an empire so great and so distracted as ours is, merely in the attempt, an undertaking that would ennoble the flights of the highest genius and obtain pardon for the efforts of the meanest understanding. Struggling a good while with these thoughts, by degrees I felt myself more firm. I derived at length some confidence from what in other circumstances usually produces timidity. I grew less anxious, even from the idea of my own insignificance. For, judging of what you are by what you ought to be, I persuaded myself that you would not reject a reasonable proposition because it had nothing but its reason to recommend it. On the other hand, being totally destitute of all shadow of influence, natural or adventitious, I was very sure that, if my proposition were futile or dangerous, if it were weakly conceived or improperly timed, there was nothing exterior to it of power to awe, dazzle, or delude you. You will see it just as it is; and you will treat it just as it deserves.

The proposition is peace. Not peace through the medium of war; not peace to be hunted through the labyrinth of intricate and endless negotiations; not peace to arise out of universal discord fomented from principle in all parts of the empire; not peace to depend on the juridical determination of perplexing questions or the precise marking the shadowy boundaries of a complex government. It is simple peace, sought in its natural course, and in its ordinary haunts—it is peace sought in the spirit of peace, and laid in principles purely pacific. I propose, by removing the ground of the difference, and by restoring the former unsuspecting confidence of the colonies in the mother-country, to give permanent satisfaction to your people; and (far from a scheme of ruling by discord) to reconcile them to each other in the same act, and by the bond of the very same interest which reconciles them to British government.

My idea is nothing more. Refined policy ever has been the parent of confusion, and ever will be so as long as the world endures. Plain good intention, which is as easily discovered at the first view as fraud is surely detected at last, is, let me say, of no mean force in the government of mankind. Genuine simplicity of heart is an healing and cementing principle. My plan, therefore, being formed upon the most simple grounds imaginable, may disappoint some people when they hear it. It has nothing to recommend to it the pruriency of curious ears. There is nothing at all new and captivating in it. It has nothing of the splendour of the project which has been lately laid upon your table by the noble lord in the blue riband. It does not propose to fill your lobby with squabbling colony agents, who will require the interposition of your mace at every instant to keep the peace amongst them. It does not institute a magnificent auction of finance, where captivated provinces come to general ransom by bidding against each other, until you knock down the hammer and determine a proportion of payments beyond all the powers of algebra to equalize and settle.

THE SPIRIT OF LIBERTY

I pass therefore to the colonies in another point of view, their agriculture. This they have prosecuted with such a spirit that, besides feeding plentifully their own growing multitude, their annual export of grain, comprehending rice, has some years ago exceeded a million in value. Of their last harvest, I am persuaded they will export much more. At the beginning of the century some of these colonies imported corn from the mother-country. For some time past, the Old World has been fed from the New. The scarcity which you have felt would have been a desolating famine if this child of your old age, with a true filial piety, with a Roman charity, had not put the full breast of its youthful exuberance to the mouth of its exhausted parent.

As to the wealth which the colonies have drawn from the sea by their fisheries, you had all that matter fully opened at your bar. You surely thought these acquisitions of value, for they seemed even to excite your envy; and yet the spirit by which that enterprising employment has been exercised ought rather, in my opinion, to have raised your esteem and admiration. And pray, Sir, what in the world is equal to it? Pass by the other parts, and look at the manner in which the people of New England have of late carried on the whale fishery. Whilst we follow them among the tumbling mountains of ice, and behold them penetrating into the deepest frozen recesses of Hudson's Bay and Davis's Straits, whilst we are looking for them beneath the Arctic

Circle, we hear that they have pierced into the opposite region of Polar cold, that they are at the Antipodes, and engaged under the frozen serpent of the south. Falkland Island, which seemed too remote and romantic an object for the grasp of national ambition, is but a stage and resting-place in the progress of their victorious industry. Nor is the equinoctial heat more discouraging to them than the accumulated winter of both the poles. We know that whilst some of them draw the line and strike the harpoon on the coast of Africa, others run the longitude and pursue their gigantic game along the coast of Brazil. No sea but what is vexed by their fisheries. No climate that is not witness to their toils. Neither the perseverance of Holland, nor the activity of France, nor the dexterous and firm sagacity of English enterprise ever carried this most perilous mode of hard industry to the extent to which it has been pushed by this recent people—a people who are still, as it were, but in the gristle, and not yet hardened into the bone of manhood. When I contemplate these things, when I know that the colonies in general owe little or nothing to any care of ours, and that they are not squeezed into this happy form by the constraints of watchful and suspicious government, but that, through a wise and salutary neglect, a generous nature has been suffered to take her own way to perfection; when I reflect upon these effects, when I see how profitable they have been to us, I feel all the pride of power sink, and all presumption in the wisdom of human contrivances melt and die away within me. My rigour relents. I pardon something to the spirit of liberty.

I am sensible, Sir, that all which I have asserted in my detail, is admitted in the gross, but that quite a different conclusion is drawn from it. America, gentlemen say, is a noble object. It is an object well worth fighting for. Certainly it is, if fighting a people be the best way of gaining them. Gentlemen in this respect will be led to their choice of means by their complexions and their habits. Those who understand the military art will of course have some predilection for it. Those who wield the thunder of the state may have more confidence in the efficacy of arms. But I confess, possibly for want of this knowledge, my opinion is much more in favour of prudent management than of force, considering force not as an odious, but a feeble instrument for preserving a people so numerous, so active, so growing, so spirited as this in a profitable and subordinate connection with us.

First, Sir, permit me to observe that the use of force alone is but temporary. It may subdue for a moment, but it does not remove the necessity of subduing again; and a nation is not governed which is perpetually to be conquered.

My next objection is its uncertainty. Terror is not always the effect of force, and an armament is not a victory. If you do not succeed, you are without resource; for, conciliation failing, force remains, but, force failing, no further hope of reconciliation is left. Power and authority are sometimes bought by kindness, but they can never be begged as alms by an impoverished and defeated violence.

A further objection to force is, that you impair the object by your very endeavours to preserve it. The thing you fought for is not the thing which you recover, but depreciated, sunk, wasted, and consumed in the contest. Nothing less will content me than whole America. I do not choose to consume its strength along with our own, because in all parts it is the British strength that I consume. I do not choose to be caught by a foreign enemy at the end of this exhausting conflict; and still less in the midst of it. I may escape, but I can make no assurance against such an event. Let me add, that I do not choose wholly to break the American spirit, because it is the spirit that has made the country.

Lastly, we have no sort of experience in favour of force as an instrument in the rule of our colonies. Their growth and their utility has been owing to methods altogether different. Our ancient indulgence has been said to be pursued to a fault. It may be so. But we know, if feeling is evidence, that our fault was more tolerable than our attempt to mend it, and our sin far more salutary than our penitence.

These, sir, are my reasons for not entertaining that high opinion of untried force by which many gentlemen, for whose sentiments in other particulars I have great respect, seem to be so greatly captivated. But there is still behind a third consideration concerning this object, which serves to determine my opinion on the sort of policy which ought to be pursued in the management of America, even more than its population and its commerce—I mean its temper and character.

THE SIX CAPITAL SOURCES

In this character of the Americans, a love of freedom is the predominating feature which marks and distinguishes the whole; and as an ardent is always a jealous affection, your colonies become suspicious, restive, and untractable whenever they see the least attempt to wrest from them by force or shuffle from them by chicane what they think the only advantage worth living for. This fierce spirit of liberty is stronger in the English colonies probably than in any other people of the earth; and this from a great variety of powerful causes, which, to understand the true temper of their minds and the direction which this spirit takes, it will not be amiss to lay open somewhat more largely.

First, the people of the colonies are descendants of Englishmen. England, Sir, is a nation which still I hope respects, and formerly adored, her freedom. The colonists emigrated from you when this part of your character was most predominant, and they took this bias and direction the moment they parted from your hands. They are therefore not only devoted to liberty, but to liberty according to English ideas and on English principles. Abstract liberty, like other mere abstractions, is not to be found. Liberty inheres in some sensible object; and every nation has formed to itself some favourite point, which by way of eminence becomes the criterion of their happiness. It happened you know, Sir, that the great contests for freedom in this country were from the earliest times chiefly upon the question of taxing. Most of the contests in the ancient commonwealths turned primarily on the right of election of magistrates, or on the balance among the several orders of the state. The question of money was not with them so immediate. But in England it was otherwise. On this point of taxes the ablest pens and most eloquent tongues have been exercised; the greatest spirits have acted and suffered. In order to give the fullest satisfaction concerning the importance of this point, it was not only necessary for those who in argument defended the excellence of the English constitution to insist on this privilege of granting money as a dry point of fact, and to prove that the right had been acknowledged in ancient parchments and blind usages to reside in a certain body called a House of Commons. They went much further; they attempted to prove, and they succeeded, that in theory it ought to be so, from the particular nature of a House of Commons, as an immediate representative of the people, whether the old records had delivered this oracle or not. They took infinite pains to inculcate, as a fundamental principle, that in all monarchies the people must in effect themselves, mediately or immediately, possess the power of granting their own money, or no shadow of liberty could subsist. The colonies draw from you, as with their life-blood, these ideas and principles. Their love of liberty, as with you, fixed and attached on this specific point of taxing. Liberty might be safe or might be endangered in twenty other particulars, without their being much pleased or alarmed. Here they felt its pulse, and as they found that beat they thought themselves sick or sound. I do not say whether they were right or wrong in applying your general arguments to their own case. It is not easy indeed to make a monopoly of theorems and corollaries. The fact is, that they did thus apply those general arguments; and your mode of governing them, whether through lenity or indolence, through wisdom or mistake, confirmed them in the imagination that they, as well as you, had an interest in these common principles.

They were further confirmed in this pleasing error by the form of their provincial legislative assemblies. Their governments are popular in a high degree, some are merely popular, in all the popular representative is the most weighty, and this share of the people in their ordinary government never fails to inspire them with lofty sentiments and with a strong aversion from whatever tends to deprive them of their chief importance.

If anything were wanting to this necessary operation of the form of government, religion would have given it a complete effect. Religion, always a principle of energy, in this new people is no way worn out or impaired, and their mode of professing it is also one main cause of this free spirit. The people are Protestants, and of that kind which is the most adverse to all implicit submission of mind and opinion. This is a persuasion not only favourable to liberty, but built upon it. I do not think, Sir, that the reason of this averseness in the dissenting churches, from all that looks like absolute government, is so much to be sought in their religious tenets as in their history. Every one knows that the Roman Catholic religion is at least coeval with most of the governments where it prevails, that it has generally gone hand in hand with them, and received great favour and every kind of support from authority. The Church of England, too, was formed from her cradle under the nursing care of regular government. But the dissenting interests have sprung up in direct opposition to all the ordinary powers of the world, and could justify that opposition only on a strong claim to natural liberty. Their very existence depended on the powerful and unremitted assertion of that claim. All Protestantism, even the most cold and passive, is a sort of dissent. But the religion most prevalent in our northern colonies is a refinement on the principle of resistance; it is the dissidence of dissent and the Protestantism of the Protestant religion. This religion, under a variety of denominations agreeing in nothing but in the communion of the spirit of liberty, is predominant in most of the northern provinces, where the Church of England, notwithstanding its legal rights, is in reality no more than a sort of private sect, not composing most probably the tenth of the people. The colonists left England when this spirit was high, and in the emigrants was the highest of all; and even that stream of foreigners, which has been constantly flowing into these colonies, has, for the greatest part, been composed of dissenters from the establishments of their several countries, who have brought with them a temper and character far from alien to that of the people with whom they mixed.

Sir, I can perceive by their manner that some gentlemen object to the latitude of this description; because in the southern colonies the Church of England forms a large body and has a regular establishment. It is certainly true. There is, however, a circumstance attending these colonies which, in my opinion, fully counterbalances this difference, and makes the spirit of liberty still more high and haughty than in those to the northward. It is, that in Virginia and the Carolinas they have a vast multitude of slaves. Where this is the case in any part of the world, those who are free are by far the most proud and jealous of their freedom. Freedom is to them not only an enjoyment, but a kind of rank and privilege. Not seeing there that freedom, as in countries where it is a common blessing and as broad and general as the air, may be united with much abject toil, with great misery, with all the exterior of servitude, liberty looks amongst them like something that is more noble and liberal. I do not mean, Sir, to commend the superior morality of this sentiment, which has at least as much pride as virtue in it; but I cannot alter the nature of man. The fact is so; and these people of the southern colonies are much more strongly, and with a higher and more stubborn spirit, attached to liberty than those to the northward. Such were all the ancient commonwealths, such were our Gothic ancestors, such in our days were the Poles, and such will be all masters of slaves who are not slaves themselves. In such a people, the haughtiness of domination combines with the spirit of freedom, fortifies it, and renders it invincible.

Permit me, Sir, to add another circumstance in our colonies, which contributes no mean part towards the growth and effect of this untractable spirit. I mean their education. In no country perhaps in the world is the law so general a study. The profession itself is numerous and powerful, and in most provinces it takes the lead. The greater number of the deputies sent to the congress were lawyers. But all who read, and most do read, endeavour to obtain some smattering in that science. I have been told by an eminent bookseller that in no branch of his business, after tracts of popular devotion, were so many books as those on the law exported to the plantations. The colonists have now fallen into the way of printing them for their own use. I hear that they have sold nearly as many of Blackstone's Commentaries in America as in England. General Gage marks out this disposition very particularly in a letter on your table. He states that all the people in his government are lawyers, or smatterers in law, and that in Boston they have been enabled, by successful chicane, wholly to evade many parts of one of your capital penal constitutions. The smartness of debate will say, that this knowledge ought to teach them more clearly the rights of legislature, their obligations to obedience, and the penalties of rebellion. All this is mighty well. But my honourable and learned friend on the floor, who condescends to mark what I say for animadversion, will disdain that ground. He has heard, as well as I, that when great honours and great emoluments do not win over this knowledge to the service of the state, it is a formidable adversary to government. If the spirit be not tamed and broken by these happy methods, it is stubborn and litigious. This study renders men acute, inquisitive, dexterous, prompt in attack, ready in defence, full of resources. In other countries, the people, more simple and of a less mercurial cast, judge of an ill principle in government only by an actual grievance; here they anticipate the evil and judge of the pressure of the grievance by the badness of the principle. They augur misgovernment at a distance, and snuff the approach of tyranny in every tainted breeze.

The last cause of this disobedient spirit in the colonies is hardly less powerful than the rest, as it is not merely moral, but laid deep in the natural constitution of things. Three thousand miles of ocean lie between you and them. No contrivance can prevent the effect of this distance in weakening government. Seas roll, and months pass, between the order and the execution, and the want of a speedy explanation of a single point is enough to defeat a whole system. You have, indeed, winged ministers of vengeance, who carry your bolts in their pounces to the remotest verge of the sea. But there a power steps in that limits the arrogance of raging passions and furious elements, and says, 'So far shalt thou go, and no farther.' Who are you, that should fret and rage and bite the chains of nature? Nothing worse happens to you than does to all nations who have extensive empire; and it happens in all the forms into which empire can be thrown. In large bodies, the circulation of power must be less vigorous at the extremities. Nature has said it. The Turk cannot govern Egypt, and Arabia, and Curdistan, as he governs Thrace; nor has he the same dominion in Crimea and Algiers which he has at Brusa and Smyrna. Despotism itself is obliged to truck and huckster. The Sultan gets such obedience as he can. He governs with a loose rein that he may govern at all; and the whole of the force and vigour of his authority in his centre is derived from a prudent relaxation in all his borders. Spain, in her provinces, is, perhaps, not so well obeyed as you are in yours. She complies too, she submits, she watches times. This is the immutable condition, the eternal law, of extensive and detached empire.

Then, Sir, from these six capital sources: of descent, of form of government, of religion in the northern provinces, of manners in the southern, of education, of the remoteness of situation from the first mover of government—from all these causes a fierce spirit of liberty has grown up. It has grown with the growth of the people in your colonies and increased with the increase of their wealth; a spirit that unhappily meeting with an exercise of power in England which, however lawful, is not reconcilable to any ideas of liberty, much less with theirs, has kindled this flame that is ready to consume us.

I do not mean to commend either the spirit in this excess or the moral causes which produce it. Perhaps a more smooth and accommodating spirit of freedom in them would be more acceptable to us. Perhaps ideas of liberty might be desired more reconcilable with an arbitrary and boundless authority. Perhaps we might wish the colonists to be persuaded that their liberty is more secure when held in trust for them by us (as their guardians during a perpetual minority) than with any part of it in their own hands. The question is, not whether their spirit deserves praise or blame, but—what, in the name of God, shall we do with it? You have before you the object, such as it is, with all its glories, with all its imperfections on its head. You see the magnitude, the importance, the temper, the habits, the disorders. By all these considerations we are strongly urged to determine something concerning it. We are called upon to fix some rule and line for our future conduct which may give a little stability to our politics and prevent the return of such unhappy deliberations as the present. Every such return will bring the matter before us in a still more untractable form. For, what astonishing and incredible things have we not seen already! What monsters have not been generated from this unnatural contention!

JUSTICE IS THE SAME

Perhaps, Sir, I am mistaken in my idea of an empire as distinguished from a single state or kingdom. But my idea of it is this: that an empire is the aggregate of many states under one common head, whether this head be a monarch or a presiding republic. It does, in such constitutions, frequently happen (and nothing but the dismal, cold, dead uniformity of servitude can prevent its happening) that the subordinate parts have many local privileges and immunities. Between these privileges and the supreme common authority the line may be extremely nice. Of course disputes, often, too, very bitter disputes, and much ill blood, will arise. But though every privilege is an exemption (in the case) from the ordinary exercise of the supreme authority, it is no denial of it. The claim of a privilege seems rather to imply a superior power. For to talk of the privileges of a state, or of a person, who has no superior, is hardly any better than speaking nonsense. Now, in such unfortunate quarrels among the component parts of a great political union of communities, I can scarcely conceive anything more completely impudent than for the head of the empire to insist that, if any privilege is pleaded against his will or his acts, his whole authority is denied—instantly to proclaim rebellion, to beat to arms, and to put the offending provinces under the ban. Will not this, Sir, very soon teach the provinces to make no distinctions on their part? Will it not teach them that the government, against which a claim of liberty is tantamount to high treason, is a government to which submission is equivalent to slavery? It may not always be quite convenient to impress dependent communities with such an idea.

We are, indeed, in all disputes with the colonies, by the necessity of things, the judge. It is true, Sir. But I confess that the character of judge in my own cause is a thing that frightens me. Instead of filling me with pride, I am exceedingly humbled by it. I cannot proceed with a stern, assured, judicial confidence, until I find myself in something more like a judicial character. I must have these hesitations as long as I am compelled to recollect that, in my little reading upon such contests as these, the sense of mankind has, at least, as often decided against the superior as the subordinate power. Sir, let me add too, that the opinion of my having some abstract right in my favour would not put me much at my ease in passing sentence, unless I could be sure that there were no rights which, in their exercise under certain circumstances, were not the most odious of all wrongs and the most vexatious of all injustice. Sir, these considerations have great weight with me, when I find things so circumstanced that I see the same party at once a civil litigant against me in point of right and a culprit before me; while I sit as a criminal judge on acts of his whose moral quality is to be decided upon the merits of that very litigation. Men are every now and then put, by the complexity of human affairs, into strange situations; but justice is the same, let the judge be in what situation he will. There is, Sir, also a circumstance which convinces me that this mode of criminal proceeding is not (at least in the present stage of our contest) altogether expedient; which is nothing less than the conduct of those very persons who have seemed to adopt that mode by lately declaring a rebellion in Massachusetts Bay, as they had formerly addressed to have traitors brought hither, under an Act of Henry VIII, for trial. For though rebellion is declared, it is not proceeded against as such, nor have any steps been taken towards the apprehension or conviction of any individual offender, either on our late or our former address; but modes of public coercion have been adopted, and such as have much more resemblance to a sort of qualified hostility towards an independent power than the punishment of rebellious subjects. All this seems rather inconsistent, but it shows how difficult it is to apply the juridical ideas to our present case.

In this situation, let us seriously and coolly ponder. What is it we have got by all our menaces, which have been many and ferocious? What advantage have we derived from the penal laws we have passed, and which for the time have been severe and numerous? What advances have we made towards our object by the sending of a force which, by land and sea, is no contemptible strength? Has the disorder abated?

Nothing less. When I see things in this situation, after such confident hopes, bold promises, and active exertions, I cannot, for my life, avoid a suspicion that the plan itself is not correctly right.

If then the removal of the causes of this spirit of American liberty be, for the greater part, or rather entirely, impracticable; if the ideas of criminal process be inapplicable, or, if applicable, are in the highest degree inexpedient—what way yet remains? No way is open, but the third and last—to comply with the American spirit as necessary, or, if you please, to submit to it as a necessary evil.

Compromise and Barter

I do not know that the colonies have, in any general way, or in any cool hour, gone much beyond the demand of immunity in relation to taxes. It is not fair to judge of the temper or dispositions of any man or any set of men, when they are composed and at rest from their conduct, or their expressions in a state of disturbance and irritation. It is besides a very great mistake to imagine that mankind follow up practically any speculative principle, either of government or of freedom, as far as it will go in argument and logical illation. We Englishmen stop very short of the principles upon which we support any given part of our constitution, or even the whole of it together. I could easily, if I had not already tired you, give you very striking and convincing instances of it. This is nothing but what is natural and proper. All government, indeed every human benefit and enjoyment, every virtue and every prudent act, is founded on compromise and barter. We balance inconveniences, we give and take, we remit some rights that we may enjoy others, and we choose rather to be happy citizens than subtle disputants. As we must give away some natural liberty to enjoy civil advantages, so we must sacrifice some civil liberties for the advantages to be derived from the communion and fellowship of a great empire. But in all fair dealings the thing bought must bear some proportion to the purchase paid. None will barter away the immediate jewel of his soul. Though a great house is apt to make slaves haughty, yet it is purchasing a part of the artificial importance of a great empire too dear to pay for it all essential rights and all the intrinsic dignity of human nature. None of us who would not risk his life rather than fall under a government purely arbitrary. But although there are some amongst us who think our constitution wants many improvements to make it a complete system of liberty, perhaps none who are of that opinion would think it right to aim at such improvement by disturbing his country and risking everything that is dear to him. In every arduous enterprise we consider what we are to lose as well as what we are to gain, and the more and better stake of liberty every people possess the less they will hazard in a vain attempt to make it more. These are the cords of man. Man acts from adequate motives relative to his interest, and not on metaphysical speculations. Aristotle, the great master of reasoning, cautions us, and with great weight and propriety, against this species of delusive geometrical accuracy in moral arguments as the most fallacious of all sophistry.

The Americans will have no interest contrary to the grandeur and glory of England, when they are not oppressed by the weight of it; and they will rather be inclined to respect the acts of a superintending legislature, when they see them the acts of that power which is itself the security, not the rival, of their secondary importance. In this assurance my mind most perfectly acquiesces; and I confess I feel not the least alarm from the discontents which are to arise from putting people at their ease, nor do I apprehend the destruction of this empire from giving, by an act of free grace and indulgence, to two millions of my fellow-citizens some share of those rights upon which I have always been taught to value myself.

THE SANCTUARY OF LIBERTY

My hold of the colonies is in the close affection which grows from common names, from kindred blood, from similar privileges, and equal protection. These are ties which, though light as air, are as strong as links of iron. Let the colonies always keep the idea of their civil rights associated with your government; they will cling and grapple to you, and no force under heaven will be of power to tear them from their allegiance. But let it be once understood that your government may be one thing and their privileges another, that these two things may exist without any mutual relation; the cement is gone, the cohesion is loosened, and everything hastens to decay and dissolution. As long as you have the wisdom to keep the sovereign authority of this country as the sanctuary of liberty, the sacred temple consecrated to our common faith, wherever the chosen race and sons of England worship freedom, they will turn their faces towards you. The more they multiply, the more friends you will have; the more ardently they love liberty, the more perfect will be their obedience. Slavery they can have anywhere. It is a weed that grows in every soil. They may have it from Spain, they may have it from Prussia. But until you become lost to all feeling of your true interest and your natural dignity, freedom they can have from none but you. This is the commodity of price of which you have the monopoly. This is the true act of navigation which binds to you the commerce of the colonies, and through them secures to you the wealth of the world. Deny them this participation of freedom and you break that sole bond which originally made and must still preserve the unity of the empire. Do not entertain so weak an imagination as that your registers and your bonds, your affidavits and your sufferances, your cockets and your clearances are what form the great securities of your commerce. Do not dream that your letters of office, and your instructions, and your suspending clauses are the things that hold together the great contexture of the mysterious whole. These things do not make your government. Dead instruments, passive tools as they are, it is the spirit of the English communion that gives all their life and efficacy to them. It is the spirit of the English constitution which, infused through the mighty mass, pervades, feeds, unites, invigorates, vivifies every part of the empire, even down to the minutest member.

Is it not the same virtue which does everything for us here in England? Do you imagine then that it is the Land Tax Act which raises your revenue, that it is the annual vote in the committee of supply which gives you your army? or that it is the Mutiny Bill which inspires it with bravery and discipline? No! surely no! It is the love of the people, it is their attachment to their government, from the sense of the deep stake they have in such a glorious institution, which gives you your army and your navy, and infuses into both that liberal obedience, without which your army would be a base rabble, and your navy nothing but rotten timber.

All this, I know well enough, will sound wild and chimerical to the profane herd of those vulgar and mechanical politicians, who have no place among us; a sort of people who think that nothing exists but what is gross and material; and who, therefore, far from being qualified to be directors of the great movement of empire, are not fit to turn a wheel in the machine. But to men truly initiated and rightly taught, these ruling and master principles which, in the opinion of such men as I have mentioned, have no substantial existence, are in truth everything and all in all. Magnanimity in politics is not seldom the truest wisdom; and a great empire and little minds go ill together. If we are conscious of our situation, and glow with zeal to fill our place as becomes our station and ourselves, we ought to auspicate all our public proceedings on America with the old warning of the Church, '*Sursum corda*'.[1] We ought to elevate our minds to the greatness of that trust to which the order of Providence has called us. By adverting to the dignity of this high calling, our ancestors have turned a savage wilderness into a glorious empire, and have made the most extensive, and the only honourable conquests, not by destroying, but by promoting the wealth, the number, the happiness of the human race.

The Devastation of the Carnatic

In 1780, Hyder Ali, the Maharajah of Mysore, descended upon the Carnatic and ravaged the district. Here is Burke's description of what took place. It shows how India gripped his imagination and stirred his feelings.

This is one of the greatest pieces of descriptive prose in the English language. It shows Burke's gifts at their best—his ability to project himself into the subject matter, his imagination, his feeling and his superlative mastery of English.

WHEN at length Hyder Ali found that he had to do with men who either would sign no convention, or whom no treaty and no signature could bind, and who were the determined enemies of human intercourse itself, he decreed to make the country possessed by these incorrigible and predestinated criminals a memorable example to mankind. He resolved, in the gloomy recesses of a mind capacious of such things, to leave the whole Carnatic an everlasting monument of vengeance, and to put perpetual desolation as a barrier between him and

[1] Lift up your hearts.

those against whom the faith which holds the moral elements of the world together was no protection. He became at length so confident of his force, so collected in his might, that he made no secret whatsoever of his dreadful resolution. Having terminated his disputes with every enemy, and every rival, who buried their mutual animosities in their common detestation against the creditors of the nabob of Arcot, he drew from every quarter whatever a savage ferocity could add to his new rudiments in the arts of destruction; and compounding all the materials of fury, havoc, and desolation into one black cloud, he hung for a while on the declivities of the mountains. Whilst the authors of all these evils were idly and stupidly gazing on this menacing meteor, which blackened all their horizon, it suddenly burst, and poured down the whole of its contents upon the plains of the Carnatic. Then ensued a scene of woe, the like of which no eye had seen, no heart conceived, and which no tongue can adequately tell. All the horrors of the war before known or heard of, were mercy to that new havoc. A storm of universal fire blasted every field, consumed every house, destroyed every temple. The miserable inhabitants flying from their flaming villages, in part were slaughtered; others, without regard to sex, to age, to the respect of rank, or sacredness of function, fathers torn from children, husbands from wives, enveloped in a whirlwind of cavalry and amidst the goading spears of drivers, and the trampling of pursuing horses, were swept into captivity in an unknown and hostile land. Those who were able to evade this tempest fled to the walled cities. But escaping from fire, sword and exile, they fell into the jaws of famine.

The alms of the settlement, in this dreadful exigency, were certainly liberal; and all was done by charity that private charity could do; but it was a people in beggary; it was a nation which stretched out its hands for food. For months together these creatures of sufferance, whose very excess and luxury in their most plenteous days had fallen short of the allowance of our austerest fasts, silent, patient, resigned, without sedition or disturbance, almost without complaint, perished by a hundred a day in the streets of Madras; every day seventy at least laid their bodies in the streets, or on the glacis of Tanjore, and expired of famine in the granary of India. I was going to awake your justice towards this unhappy part of our fellow-citizens by bringing before you some of the circumstances of this plague of hunger. Of all the calamities which beset and waylay the life of man, this comes the nearest to our heart, and is that wherein the proudest of us all feels himself to be nothing more than he is. But I find myself unable to manage it with decorum. These details are a species of horror so nauseous and disgusting; they are so degrading to the sufferers and to the hearers; they are so humiliating to human nature itself that, on better thoughts, I find it more advisable to throw a pall over this hideous object, and to leave it to your general conceptions.

For eighteen months, without intermission, this destruction raged from the gates of Madras to the gates of Tanjore; and so completely did these masters in their art, Hyder Ali, and his more ferocious son, absolve themselves of their impious vow, that when the British armies traversed, as they did, the Carnatic for hundreds of miles in all directions, through the whole line of their march they did not see one man, not one woman, not one child, not one four-footed beast of any description whatever. One dead, uniform silence reigned over the whole region, with the inconsiderable exceptions of the narrow vicinage of some few forts. I wish to be understood as speaking literally; I mean to produce to you more than three witnesses, above all exception, who will support this assertion in its full extent. That hurricane of war passed through every part of the central provinces of the Carnatic. Six or seven districts to the north and to the south (and these not wholly untouched) escaped the general ravage.

The Carnatic is a country not much inferior in extent to England. Figure to yourself, Mr Speaker, the land in whose representative chair you sit; figure to yourself the form and fashion of your sweet and cheerful country from Thames to Trent, north and south, and from the Irish to the German sea, east and west, emptied and embowelled (may God avert the omen of our crimes!) by so accomplished a desolation. Extend your imagination a little farther, and then suppose your ministers taking a survey of this scene of waste and desolation; what would be your thoughts if you should be informed, that they were computing how much had been the amount of the excises, how much the customs, how much the land and malt tax, in order that they should charge (take it in the most favourable light) for public service, upon the relics of the satiated vengeance of relentless enemies, the whole of what England had yielded in the most exuberant seasons of peace and abundance? What would you call it? To call it tyranny sublimed into madness, would be too faint an image; yet this very madness is the principle upon which the ministers at your right hand have proceeded in their estimate of the revenues of the Carnatic, when they were providing, not supply for the establishment of its protection, but rewards for the authors of its ruin.

The Carnatic is not by the bounty of nature a fertile soil. The general size of its cattle is proof enough that it is much otherwise. It is some days since I moved that a curious and interesting map, kept in the India House, should be laid before you. The India House is not yet in readiness to send it; I have therefore brought down my own copy, and there it lies for the use of any gentleman who may think such a matter worthy of his attention. It is indeed a noble map, and of noble things; but it is decisive against the golden dreams and sanguine speculations of avarice run mad. In addition to what you know must be the case in every part of the world (the necessity of a previous provision of habitation, seed, stock, capital), that map will show you that the uses of the influences of Heaven itself are in that country a work of art. The Carnatic is refreshed by few or no living brooks or running streams, and it has rain only at one season. This is the National Bank of the Carnatic on whom it must have perpetual credit, or it perishes irretrievably. For that reason, in the happier times of India, a number, almost incredible, of reservoirs have been made in chosen places throughout the whole country; they are formed for the greater part of mounds of earth and stones, with sluices of solid masonry; the whole constructed with admirable skill and labour, and maintained at a mighty charge. In the territory contained in that map alone, I have been at the trouble of reckoning the reservoirs, and they amount to upwards of eleven hundred, from the extent of two or three acres to five miles in circuit. From these reservoirs currents are occasionally drawn over the fields, and these watercourses again call for a considerable expense to keep them properly scoured and duly levelled. Taking the district in that map as a measure, there cannot be in the Carnatic and Tanjore fewer than ten thousand of these reservoirs of the larger and middling dimensions, to say nothing of those for domestic services and the uses of religious purification. These are not the enterprises of your power, nor in a style of magnificence suited to the taste of your minister. These are the monuments of real kings, who were the fathers of their people; testators to a posterity which they embraced as their own. These are the grand sepulchres built by ambition; but by the ambition of an insatiable benevolence, which, not contented with reigning in the dispensation of happiness during the contracted term of human life, had strained, with all the reachings and graspings of a vivacious mind, to extend the dominion of their bounty beyond the limits of nature, and to perpetuate themselves through generations of generations, the guardians, the protectors, the nourishers of mankind.

The Impeachment of Warren Hastings

The conduct of the East India Company shocked Burke. Officers of the Company who had held high office lived vulgar, ostentatious lives when they returned to England on the fortunes which they had amassed in India.

Warren Hastings had been a Governor of Bengal, and after his return a Parliamentary inquiry into his conduct was set on foot. On 13th February, 1788, the trial of Warren Hastings was opened in Westminster Hall. It lasted for seven years. In the end Hastings was acquitted.

Although Burke might have seemed to have failed, he gained acceptance for the view that India should be administered 'by those laws which are to be found in Europe, Africa and Asia that are found common to all mankind —these principles of equity and humanity implanted in our hearts'.

These two extracts show the power of Burke in presenting his case.

THERE is a sacred veil to be drawn over the beginnings of all governments. Ours, in India, had an origin like those which time has sanctified by obscurity. Time, in the origin of most governments, has thrown this mysterious veil over them; prudence and discretion make it necessary to throw something of the same drapery over more recent foundations, in which otherwise the fortune, the genius, the talents, and military virtue of this nation never shone more conspicuously. But, whatever necessity might hide or excuse or palliate in the acquisition of power, a wise nation, when it has once made a revolution upon its own principles and for its own ends, rests there. The first step to empire is revolution, by which power is conferred; the next is good laws, good orders, good institutions, to give that power stability . . .

He[1] have arbitrary power! My Lords, the East India Company have not arbitrary power to give him; the King has no arbitrary power to give him; your Lordships have not; nor the Commons; nor the whole legislature. We have no arbitrary power to give, because arbitrary power is a thing which neither any man can hold nor any man can give. No man can lawfully govern himself according to his own will, much less can one person be governed by the will of another. We are all born in subjection, all born equally, high and low, governors and governed, in subjection to one great, immutable, pre-existent law, prior to all our devices, and prior to all our contrivances, paramount to all our ideas and all our sensations, antecedent to our very existence, by which we are knit and connected in the eternal frame of the universe, out of which we cannot stir.

This great law does not arise from our conventions or compacts; on the contrary, it gives to our conventions and compacts all the force and sanction they can have;—it does not arise from our vain institutions. Every good gift is of God; all power is of God;—and He, who has given the power, and from whom alone it originates, will never suffer the exercise of it to be practised upon any less solid foundation than the power itself. If then all dominion of man over man is the effect of the Divine disposition, it is bound by the eternal laws of Him that gave it, with which no human authority can dispense; neither he that exercises it, nor even those who are subject to it: and, if they were mad enough to make an express compact that should release their magistrate from his duty, and should declare their lives, liberties, and properties dependent upon, not rules and laws, but his mere capricious will, that covenant would be void. The acceptor of it has not his authority increased, but he has his crime doubled. Therefore can it be imagined, if this be true, that He will suffer this great gift of government, the greatest, the best that was ever given by God to mankind, to be the plaything and the sport of the feeble will of a man who, by a blasphemous, absurd, and petulant usurpation, would place his own feeble, contemptible, ridiculous will in the place of the Divine wisdom and justice?

[1] i.e., Warren Hastings.

THE IMPEACHMENT OF WARREN HASTINGS

The Charges Against Hastings

My Lords, I do not mean now to go farther than just to remind your Lordships of this—that Mr Hastings's government was one whole system of oppression, of robbery of individuals, of spoilation of the public, and of supersession of the whole system of the English government, in order to vest in the worst of the natives all the power that could possibly exist in any government; in order to defeat the ends which all governments ought, in common, to have in view. In the name of the Commons of England, I charge all this villainy upon Warren Hastings, in this last moment of my application to you.

My Lords, what is it that we want here, to a great act of national justice? Do we want a cause, my Lords? You have the cause of oppressed princes, of undone women of the first rank, of desolated provinces and of wasted kingdoms.

Do you want a criminal, my Lords? When was there so much iniquity ever laid to the charge of any one? No, my Lords, you must not look to punish any other such delinquent from India. Warren Hastings has not left substance enough in India to nourish such another delinquent.

My Lords, is it a prosecutor you want? You have before you the Commons of Great Britain as prosecutors; and I believe, my Lords, that the sun, in his beneficent progress round the world, does not behold a more glorious sight than that of men, separated from a remote people by the material bounds and barriers of nature, united by the bond of a social and moral community—all the Commons of England resenting, as their own, the indignities and cruelties that we offered to all the people of India.

Do we want a tribunal? My Lords, no example of antiquity, nothing in the modern world, nothing in the range of human imagination, can supply us with a tribunal like this. We commit safely the interests of India and humanity into your hands. Therefore, it is with confidence that, ordered by the Commons:

I impeach Warren Hastings, Esquire, of high crimes and misdemeanours.

I impeach him in the name of the Commons of Great Britain in Parliament assembled, whose parliamentary trust he has betrayed.

I impeach him in the name of all the Commons of Great Britain, whose national character he has dishonoured.

I impeach him in the name of the people of India, whose laws, rights, and liberties he has subverted; whose properties he has destroyed; whose country he has laid waste and desolate.

I impeach him in the name and by virtue of those eternal laws of justice which he has violated.

I impeach him in the name of human nature itself, which he has cruelly outraged, injured, and oppressed, in both sexes, in every age, rank, situation, and condition of life.

My Lords, at this awful close, in the name of the Commons and surrounded by them, I attest the retiring, I attest the advancing generations, between which, as a link in the great chain of eternal order, we stand. We call this nation, we call the world to witness, that the Commons have shrunk from no labour; that we have been guilty of no prevarication; that we have made no compromise with crime; that we have not feared any odium whatsoever, in the long warfare which we have carried on with the crimes, with the vices, with the exorbitant wealth, with the enormous and overpowering influence of Eastern corruption.

My Lords, it has pleased Providence to place us in such a state that we appear every moment to be upon the verge of some great mutations. There is one thing, and one thing only, which defies all mutation: that which existed before the world, and will survive the fabric of the world itself—I mean justice; that justice which, emanating from the Divinity, has a place in the breast of every one of us, given us for our guide with regard to ourselves and with regard to others, and which will stand, after this globe is burned to ashes, our advocate or our accuser, before the great Judge, when He comes to call upon us for the tenor of a well-spent life.

My Lords, the Commons will share in every fate with your Lordships; there is nothing sinister which can happen to you, in which we shall not all be involved; and, if it should so happen that we shall be subjected to some of those frightful changes which we have seen— if it should happen that your Lordships, stripped of all the decorous distinctions of human society, should, by hands at once base and cruel, be led to those scaffolds and machines of murder upon which great kings and glorious queens have shed their blood, amidst the prelates,

amidst the nobles, amidst the magistrates, who supported their thrones
—may you in those moments feel that consolation which I am persuaded
they felt in the critical moments of their dreadful agony!

My Lords, if you must fall, may you so fall! But, if you stand—and
stand I trust you will—together with the fortune of this ancient monarchy, together with the ancient laws and liberties of this great and
illustrious kingdom, may you stand as unimpeached in honour as in
power; may you stand, not as a substitute for virtue, but as an ornament
of virtue, as a security for virtue; may you stand long, and long stand
the terror of tyrants; may you stand the refuge of afflicted nations; may
you stand a sacred temple, for the perpetual residence of an inviolable
justice!

RICHARD BRINSLEY SHERIDAN

1751–1816

The Impeachment of Warren Hastings

At the height of his career Richard Brinsley Sheridan was one of the brightest stars in the firmament of eighteenth century London society. He was married to a lovely wife. He was the author of The Rivals *and* The School for Scandal, *two of the outstanding plays of the period. He was Member of Parliament for Stafford and renowned for his speeches in the House of Commons. He moved at ease in the company of men like his fellow-Irishman Burke, Pitt, Fox, Garrick and Dr Johnson. He was famous for his wit and his humour. He had a large income most of which was derived from the revenues of the famous Drury Lane Theatre.*

His last years, however, were spent in abject misery. The crowning blow came when Drury Lane Theatre was destroyed by fire in 1809. Yet even in the face of this disaster his wit did not desert him. It is said that he was found seated at one of the coffee houses near Covent Garden 'swilling port by the tumblerful' and watching the flames consume the theatre. One of his friends suggested that he might leave. His answer was: 'Surely a man may be allowed to take a glass of wine by his own fireside.'

His renown as an orator rests upon the speeches which he made against Warren Hastings. He and Burke were the chief advocates for the prosecution. Macaulay has painted the scene in some of his most picturesque pages. The Great Hall of Westminster was packed to capacity: the peers and judges in their robes; the walls hung with scarlet; and all London society in the audience. The speeches of both Burke and Sheridan were so overwhelming that it seemed there was no hope for Hastings. People were carried out fainting. Others were struck dumb with admiration and astonishment.

The following extract is taken from the closing stages of Sheridan's speech. Although it gives the impression of careless ease the speech was carefully prepared. It was delivered by a man who knew that a court is not unlike a theatre, and that effects can be created by the spoken word. He was a master of the incisive phrase and the set picture. After he uttered the words: 'My Lords, I have done', he sank back, exhausted, into the arms of Burke. Even this was a theatrical gesture.

Sheridan's speeches show that for maximum effect a speech has not only to be good in itself, but it has to be carefully delivered. It is clear from contemporary records that in this respect he excelled his great contemporary Burke.

INSINUATIONS have been thrown out that my honourable colleagues and myself are actuated by motives of malignity against the unfortunate prisoner at the bar. An imputation of so serious a nature cannot be permitted to pass altogether without comment; though it comes in so loose a shape, in such whispers and oblique hints as to prove to a certainty that it was made in the consciousness, and, therefore, with the circumspection of falsehood.

I can, my Lords, most confidently aver, that a prosecution more disinterested in all its motives and ends; more free from personal malice or personal interest; more perfectly public, and more purely animated by the simple and unmixed spirit of justice, never was brought in any country, at any time, by any body of men, against any individual. What possible resentment can we entertain against the unfortunate prisoner? What possible interest can we have in his conviction? What possible object of a personal nature can we accomplish by his ruin? For myself, my Lords, I make this solemn asseveration, that I discharge my breast of all malice, hatred, and ill-will against the prisoner, if at any time indignation at his crimes has planted in it these passions; and I believe, my Lords, that I may with equal truth answer for every one of my colleagues.

We are, my Lords, anxious, in stating the crimes with which he is charged, to keep out of recollection the person of the unfortunate prisoner. In prosecuting him to conviction, we are impelled only by a sincere abhorrence of his guilt, and a sanguine hope of remedying future delinquency. We can have no private incentive to the part we have taken. We are actuated singly by the zeal we feel for the public welfare, and by an honest solicitude for the honour of our country, and the happiness of those who are under its dominion and protection.

With such views, we really, my Lords, lose sight of Mr Hastings, who, however great in some other respects, is too insignificant to be blended with these important circumstances. The unfortunate prisoner is, at best, to my mind, no mighty object. Amid the series of mischiefs and enormities to my sense seeming to surround him, what is he but a petty nucleus, involved in its laminae, scarcely seen or heard of?

This prosecution, my Lords, was not, as is alleged, 'begot in prejudice, and nursed in error'. It originated in the clearest conviction of the wrongs which the natives of Hindostan have endured by the maladministration of those in whose hands this country had placed extensive powers; which ought to have been exercised for the benefit of the governed, but which was used by the prisoner for the shameful purpose of oppression. I repeat with emphasis, my Lords, that nothing personal or malicious has induced us to institute this prosecution. It is absurd to suppose it.

You see, my Lords, that the British government, which ought to have been a blessing to the powers in India connected with it, has proved a scourge to the natives, and the cause of desolation to their most flourishing provinces.

Behold, my Lords, this frightful picture of the consequences of a government of violence and oppression! Surely the condition of wretchedness to which this once happy and independent prince is reduced by our cruelty, and the ruin which in some way has been brought upon his country, call loudly upon your Lordships to interpose, and to rescue the national honour and reputation from the infamy to which both will be exposed if no investigation be made into the causes of their calamities, and no punishment inflicted on the authors of them. By policy as well as justice you are vehemently urged to vindicate the English character in the East; for, my Lords, it is manifest that the native powers have so little reliance on our faith, that the preservation of our possessions in that division of the world can only be effected by convincing the princes that a religious adherence to its engagements with them shall hereafter distinguish our India government.

It will not, I trust, be concluded that because Mr Hastings has not marked every passing shade of guilt, and because he has only given the bold outline of cruelty, he is therefore to be acquitted. It is laid down by the law of England, that law which is the perfection of reason, that a person ordering an act to be done by his agent is answerable for that act with all its consequences. *Quod facit per alium, facit per se.* Middleton was appointed, in 1777, the confidential agent, the second self, of Mr Hastings. The Governor-General ordered the measure. Even if he never saw nor heard afterwards of its consequences, he was therefore answerable for every pang that was inflicted, and for all the blood that was shed. But he did hear, and that instantly, of the whole. He wrote to accuse Middleton of forbearance and of neglect! He commanded him to work upon the hopes and fears of the princesses, and to leave no means untried, until, to speak his own language, which was better suited to the banditti of a cavern, 'he obtained possession of the secret hoards of the old ladies.' He would not allow even of a delay of two days to smooth the compelled approaches of a son to his mother, on this occasion! His orders were peremptory. After this, my Lords, can it be said that the prisoner was ignorant of the acts, or not culpable for their consequences? It is true he did not direct the guards, the famine, and the bludgeons; he did not weigh the fetters, nor number the lashes to be inflicted on his victims; but yet he is just as guilty as if he had borne an active and personal share in each transaction. It is as if he had commanded that the heart should be torn from the bosom, and enjoined that no blood should follow. He is in the same degree accountable to the law, to his country, to his conscience, and to his God!

THE NATURE OF JUSTICE

The prisoner has endeavoured also to get rid of a part of his guilt by observing that he was but one of the supreme council, and that all the rest had sanctioned those transactions with their approbation. Even if it were true that others did participate in the guilt, it cannot tend to diminish his criminality. But the fact is, that the council erred in nothing so much as in a reprehensible credulity given to the declarations of the Governor-General. They know not a word of those transactions until they were finally concluded. It was not until the January following that they saw the mass of falsehood which had been published under the title of 'Mr Hastings' Narrative'. They were, then, unaccountably duped to permit a letter to pass, dated the twenty-ninth of November, intended to seduce the directors into a belief that they had received intelligence at that time, which was not the fact. These observations, my Lords, are not meant to cast any obloquy on the council; they undoubtedly were deceived; and the deceit practised on them is a decided proof of his consciousness of guilt. When tired of corporeal infliction Mr Hastings was gratified by insulting the understanding. The coolness and reflection with which this act was managed and concerted raises its enormity and blackens its turpitude. It proves the prisoner to be that monster in nature, a deliberate and reasoning tyrant! Other tyrants of whom we read, such as a Nero, or a Caligula, were urged to their crimes by the impetuosity of passion. High rank disqualified them from advice, and perhaps equally prevented reflection. But in the prisoner we have a man born in a state of mediocrity; bred to mercantile life; used to system; and accustomed to regularity; who was accountable to his masters, and therefore was compelled to think and to deliberate on every part of his conduct. It is this cool deliberation, I say, which renders his crimes more horrible, and his character more atrocious.

When, my Lords, the Board of Directors received the advices which Mr Hastings thought proper to transmit, though unfurnished with any other materials to form their judgment, they expressed very strongly their doubts, and properly ordered an inquiry into the circumstances of the alleged disaffection of the begums, declaring it, at the same time, to be a debt which was due to the honour and justice of the British nation. This inquiry, however, Mr Hastings thought it absolutely necessary to elude. He stated to the council, in answer, 'that it would revive those animosities that subsisted between the begums and the nabob (Asoph Dowlah), which had then subsided. If the former were inclined to appeal to a foreign jurisdiction, they were the best judges of their own feeling, and should be left to make their own complaint.' All this, however, my Lords, is nothing to the magnificent paragraph which concludes this communication. 'Besides,' says he, 'I hope it will not be a departure from official language to say that the majesty of justice ought not to be approached without solicitation. She ought not to descend to inflame or provoke, but to withold her judgment until she is called on to determine.' What is still more astonishing is that Sir John Macpherson, who, though a man of sense and honour, is rather Oriental in his imagination, and not learned in the sublime and beautiful from the immortal leader of this prosecution,[1] was caught by this bold, bombastic quibble, and joined in the same words, 'That the majesty of

[1]Edmund Burke.

justice ought not to be approached without solicitation.' But, my Lords, do you, the judges of this land, and the expounders of its rightful laws— do you approve of this mockery and call it the character of justice, which takes the form of right to excite wrong? No, my Lords, justice is not this halt and miserable object; it is not the ineffective bauble of an Indian pagod; it is not the portentous phantom of despair; it is not like any fabled monster, formed in the eclipse of reason, and found in some unhallowed grove of superstitious darkness and political dismay! No, my Lords. In the happy reverse of all this, I turn from the disgusting caricature to the real image! Justice I have now before me august and pure! The abstract idea of all that would be perfect in the spirits and the aspirings of men!—where the mind rises; where the heart expands; where the countenance is ever placid and benign; where her favourite attitude is to stoop to the unfortunate; to hear their cry and to help them; to rescue and relieve, to succour and save; majestic, from its mercy; venerable, from its utility; uplifted, without pride; firm, without obduracy; beneficent in each preference; lovely, though in her frown!

On that justice I rely—deliberate and sure, abstracted from all party purpose and political speculation; not on words, but on facts. You, my Lords, will hear me, I conjure, by those rights which it is your best privilege to preserve; by that fame which it is your best pleasure to inherit; by all those feelings which refer to the first term in the series of existence, the original compact of our nature, our controlling rank in the creation. This is the call on all to administer to truth and equity, as they would satisfy the laws and satisfy themselves, with the most exalted bliss possible or conceivable for our nature; the self-approving consciousness of virtue, when the condemnation we look for will be one of the most ample mercies accomplished for mankind since the creation of the world! My Lords, I have done.

WILLIAM PITT

1759–1806

Declaration of War

William Pitt is a good example of a man in high office who compelled a divided House of Commons to follow his policy, not because of the eloquence and grandeur of his speeches but by the orderly, systematic way in which he presented the facts and drew the conclusions. In the struggle with Napoleon all Europe saw in Pitt the supreme leader of the opposition to Napoleon. In the House of Commons Charles James Fox was frequently a better orator than Pitt, yet in the long run the opinions of Pitt prevailed and not those of Fox.

William Pitt, the son of the Earl of Chatham, became Prime Minister in 1783. He was only twenty-four years of age. The reputation of Britain was at a low ebb. No man desired peace more ardently than Pitt. He needed a period of quiet in order to restore the fortunes of his country. From the very beginning he showed that he had an acute financial sense, a swift, accurate mind and both patience and courage in abundance. The Revolt of the American Colonies made a deep impression upon him, and he was determined that there should be no repetition in Canada, India or, nearer at home, in Ireland, of what had happened across the Atlantic.

Six years after he took office the French Revolution broke out. The Bastille, the notorious prison, was stormed by the Paris mob on 14th July, 1789. Pitt's attitude to the Revolution was not opposition, like that of Burke; on the other hand he did not hail it as a praiseworthy event, as men like Fox and the poet Wordsworth did:—he recognized that an abuse of power in France made revolution almost inevitable, but he was wise enough to know that when mighty forces are set in motion, unexpected consequences can follow. For three years he held tenaciously to a policy of neutrality.

The September Massacres of 1792 in France caused many people who supported the French Revolution to have grave doubts as to the outcome.

DECLARATION OF WAR

On 21st January, 1793, Louis XVI went to the scaffold. On 1st February France declared war on Britain and Holland.

This speech shows Pitt's reaction to this declaration of war. The man of peace was preparing the nation for war. It was delivered in March, 1793.

I AM not desirous to draw a sanguine picture. I was careful to state none of these encouragements to a war in any of the previous discussions. I considered that we ought then to determine solely on the merits of the case; and that, if we considered a war as necessary, we were bound to meet it, even to its utmost extent. There is no part which we ought not to be prepared to sacrifice for the preservation of the whole. This is a war in which, not merely adopting empty professions, but speaking the language of our hearts and fulfilling the impressions of our duty, we are ready to sacrifice our lives and fortunes for the safety of the country, the security of Europe, and in the cause of justice, humanity, and religion. I will not do such injustice to any one as to suppose, that, in such a cause, they are not ready to go the greatest length, and to make every sacrifice that may be required. I will here barely touch upon the contrast which the present situation of the country offers to the flourishing state during the last session with regard to revenue. That contrast no man feels more severely than I do. No man can more deeply regret any interruption of the prosperous state of the revenue, the object of my most anxious attention and my most favourite wishes; but if they consider the situation of the neighbouring and hostile State with respect to revenue, they have no reason to despond. Instead of giving way to feelings of useless regret upon that occasion, I trust you are influenced by far different sentiments.

Many are the motives which have induced us to enter into the war. I have heard of wars of honour; and such, too, have been deemed wars of prudence and policy. On the present occasion, whatever can raise the feelings, or animate the exertions of a people, concurs to prompt us to the contest. The contempt which the French have shown for a neutrality, on our part most strictly observed; the violations of their solemn and plighted faith; their presumptuous attempts to interfere in the government of this country, and to arm our subjects against ourselves; to vilify a monarch, the object of our gratitude, reverence, and affection; and to separate the Court from the people, by representing them as influenced by different motives, and acting from different interests. After provocation so wanton, so often repeated, and so highly aggravated, does not this become, on our part, a war of honour; a war necessary to assert the spirit of the nation, and the dignity of the British name? I have heard of wars undertaken for the general security of Europe; was it ever so threatened as by the progress of the French arms, and the system of ambition and aggrandizement which they have discovered? I have heard of wars for the defence of the Protestant religion: our enemies in this instance are equally the enemies of all religion—of Lutheranism, of Calvinism; and desirous to propagate, everywhere, by the force of their arms, that system of infidelity which they avow in their principles. I have heard of wars undertaken in defence of the lawful succession; but now we fight in defence of our hereditary monarchy. We are at war with those who would destroy the whole fabric of our constitution. When I look at these things, they afford me encouragement and consolation; and support me in discharging the painful task to which I am now called by my duty. The retrospect to that flourishing state in which we were placed previous to this war, ought to teach us to know the value of the present order of things; and to resist the malignant and envious attempts of those who would deprive us of that happiness which they despair themselves to attain. We ought to remember, that that very prosperous situation at the present crisis supplies us with the exertions, and furnishes us with the means, which our exigencies demand. In such a cause as that in which we are now engaged, I trust that our exertions will terminate only with our lives. On this ground I have brought forward the resolutions which I am now to propose; and on this ground I now trust for your support.

The Defence of Britain

The war with France did not start well for Britain. An ill-fated expedition was sent to the West Indies. Only at sea were British successes registered. The state of mind in the country, too, was by no means united. Fox was a redoubtable opponent of the war. In addition Pitt found it necessary to punish with severity anybody who advocated measures of reform or social betterment in the country. Some of these measures strike us today as being extremely harsh. Nevertheless they show the determination of the man to pursue the war with vigour.

The emergence of Napoleon out of the confusion in France gave a new turn to the struggle. In a series of quick, dramatic moves, Napoleon made himself virtually a military dictator of France, and from that basis he embarked upon his scheme of world conquest. At first he was regarded as a liberator. Beethoven's Emperor Concerto is dedicated to Napoleon as a liberator. Many people in England regarded Napoleon in the same light, but Pitt was not deceived. With a clear vision he saw that Napoleon was a tyrant, and that unless he was checked Britain would be in mortal danger.

The war with Napoleon went badly on land for Britain and her allies. At sea, however, it was a different matter. Pitt had discovered a young English Admiral, Horatio Nelson, and his victory at the Nile prevented Napoleon's eastward march to India. Pitt may have made mistakes in the conduct of the war on land, but, like his father before him, he knew what command of the seas meant.

In 1800 the Act of Union was signed with Ireland. During the negotiations Pitt promised that Catholics would sit in the Parliament at Westminster. King George III refused to allow this, and Pitt resigned in 1801. Addington, a former Speaker of the House of Commons, became Prime Minister.

The threat of invasion still hung over the country, and the following speech was made by Pitt on 18th July, 1803, when he was out of office, in support of the measures necessary for the defence of the country.

I FEEL sincerely happy that this measure has been at length brought before the House, as it affords a prospect of that vigour which is necessary in the present conjuncture. I approve of its principle and object. It indeed is founded on the principles of the plan which, unconnected as I am with His Majesty's Government, I have thought it my duty to intimate to ministers. I have been always decidedly of opinion that such a measure was essentially necessary, in addition to our regular force, in order to put the question as to our domestic security entirely beyond all doubt. I am not now disposed, because, indeed, I do not think it necessary, to enter into any investigation of the degree of danger which the country has to apprehend, though I am aware it is material that the danger should not be underrated.

But to return to the measure before the House. I rejoice in its introduction as the most congenial in its spirit to the constitution of this country, and in its execution not at all likely to meet any obstacle from the character or disposition of the people. In its structure there is nothing new to our history; in its tendency there is nothing ungrateful to our habits; it embraces the interests, it avails itself of the energies, and it promises to establish the security of the country. It imposes no burthens, nor does it propose any arrangement of which it can be in the power of any class of the community to complain. Its object is the safety of all, without containing anything in its provisions offensive to any. It is perfectly agreeable to the best institutions of civilized society, and has for its basis the rudiments of constitutional history.

It is obvious that, unless we make efforts adequate to the crisis in which we are placed, the country is insecure, and if those efforts cannot be effectual without compulsion, I trust no man can entertain a doubt of the propriety of resorting to it: but I have a confident expectation that compulsion will be unnecessary; that the number of voluntary offers will be sufficient to obviate the necessity of that disagreeable alternative. It is, however, an alternative of which I hope no man will disapprove, should the necessity arise, and least of all my right honourable friend,[1] who has not, on a former occasion, hesitated to recommend that compulsion. By His Majesty's prerogative he has it in his power, at any time that the country is threatened with invasion, to call out all his subjects for its defence; and the object of the measure before the House is, that the people, when called out, should be prepared to second his views, should be trained to military evolutions, should be ready to act with promptitude in any quarter where their services might be required, should be capable of conforming to orders without confusion or delay, of collecting with celerity and acting with decision. Such a plan is highly desirable; for it would be unwise to leave the defence of the country placed on our naval force, however superior, or in our regular army, however gallant and well disciplined, or even in the people armed *en masse*, unless previously drilled in military manœuvres and subject to the directions of Government, who, by the measure before the House, are to be invested with ample powers of rendering the application of this

[1] Windham.

force effectual, and of directing it to the several branches of public service which circumstances may call for.

The training of the people, however, should be prompt. No delay should be suffered, for there is not room to allow it. The efforts of those to be entrusted with the execution of this important duty should be unremitted, and indeed of all public and private individuals, until the country shall be completely secure against any attacks of the enemy. This security is certain, if every man will be active in his station; and of that activity I have not the least doubt, if Government will give proper stimulus.

With respect to the observations of my noble friend[1] upon the sentiments of my right honourable friend[2] as to the dangers of invasion, the noble lord seems to have quite mistaken his meaning; for my right honourable friend did not at all describe the danger in such a way as to damp the spirit of the country, but rather to excite its caution and energy, by removing the idea that an invasion is impracticable; and as soon as that delusive notion shall cease to prevail, I am quite certain that the whole tenor of my right honourable friend's remarks will be to produce confidence of security in the public mind, at the time when that feeling of confidence ought to exist, either with reference to the safety of the State or of individuals. The amount of our danger, therefore, it would be impolitic to conceal from the people. It was the first duty of ministers to make it known, and after doing so, it should have been their study to provide against it, and to point out the means of the country by which it might be averted. It is quite impossible that a people will make adequate efforts to resist a danger, of the nature and extent of which they are studiously kept in ignorance. Upon those grounds I disapprove of the outcry so often raised against my right honourable friend and others, who have endeavoured by their speeches to rouse the energies of the country in the most effectual way, namely, by pointing out the necessity which existed for employing those energies. After, however, the grounds of apprehension shall have been extinguished, I have little doubt that the exertions of my right honourable friend will be to point the attention of ministers to such means of annoying the enemy as his ingenuity can suggest; and that those grounds will be removed with proper attention and activity on the part of ministers, I can have no

[1] Lord Hawkesbury.
[2] Windham.

doubt; for who can fear for the event, when millions of Englishmen are to be opposed to the detachment of the instruments of French ambition? And whatever the number of our invaders may be, they cannot, comparatively with the force I trust we shall have to oppose them, be more than a mere detachment.

I have not understood from the words of my right honourable friend that he had any fear as to the event, but that he wished solely to urge the adoption of such measures as might tend to give an effective direction to our natural strength. My right honourable friend has appeared to me very little to indulge in those gloomy presages which are ascribed to him by those of whose sluggishness, supineness, and inactivity he has been long in the habit of complaining. But I feel the most sincere gladness that the charge of supineness can no longer apply. His Majesty's ministers seem now determined upon rousing the spirit of the country, and upon giving that spirit a just and powerful direction. I hail, for the sake of my country, the appearance of this resolution. This is an auspicious day, though I cannot help expressing my surprise that this measure has not been submitted to the consideration of the House long ago: but even now I hope it will answer its purpose, that it will meet the approbation of Parliament, and that the people will promptly come forward to second its object. After the precise views of this country shall be made known, and after its dangers shall be fully understood, I am sure that no man will shrink from the calls of his country in this hour of peril, unless from motives such as he dare not avow.

Whether ministers ought sooner to have proposed this measure is a question into which I shall not now enter at large, but I will merely observe that, if it becomes necessary from a knowledge of the enemy's views, I believe no knowledge of that kind has been recently obtained—none of which ministers and the public were not aware at the time that war was declared, and even before. Why then was this important measure delayed? The danger to be looked for has been apprehended for a considerable time back, and upon the contingency of it my noble friend admits that, even during peace, a very large and expensive establishment was kept up. I cannot conceive any excuse that can be alleged for such procrastination. It did not proceed, I suppose, from the desire of ministers to consider the scale and measure of our dangers, or from an opinion on their part, that it was better they should be tardy and gradual in their measures against the gigantic efforts of the enemy. This cannot have been the reason, and really I see no difference in the state of Europe, nor in the relative situation of this country with respect to France, from what it was at the commencement of the war. I am, therefore, at a loss to divine the motives which have influenced the conduct of ministers, and why this measure was not brought forward long since. If there was no necessity to be active, if there was leisure for slow deliberation, then of course the period is not such, in their estimation, as to call for any extraordinary promptitude of exertion, as to call aught to excite alarm; but, in truth, if there was any particular measure which claimed precedency, it was that now under consideration, which could not interfere with any other military arrangements. The question simply is this—was it prudent to postpone the introduction of a measure which had for its object to prepare the people for a general armament, and which preparation must necessarily consume some time before it could be efficient? Yet, in the wisdom of ministers, this is the particular measure which is to be delayed to the last.

METHODS OF TRAINING

I will not, however, stop to inquire into the time which has been already lost; but I shall express my earnest hope that no time will be wasted hereafter—that every instant will be actively engaged until the country be completely safe. I think that some arrangements should be made to connect the different departments of the executive authority, so that, upon orders issued from Government to the Lords-Lieutenant of counties, the people might be immediately set in motion; so that, without interfering with agriculture, which should not by any means be disturbed, the several classes might be disciplined, to attend the drill at least two days in each week, to assemble in particular places throughout the country; the limitation of distance from the residence of each man to the place of assembly, to be about six miles, the time of attendance to be not less than half a day. The distance I propose is not more than the stout English peasantry are in the habit of going, when led to a cricket match or any rural amusement. These men, in my conception, might be disciplined by soldiers on furlough, who, on being called back to their regiment, when danger should actually reach our shores, might be enabled to bring with them one hundred sturdy recruits, prepared for military action through their means.

With regard to the motion before the House, I must say that it is not liable to the objections advanced by my right honourable friend, on the ground that it would have a compulsory operation, for in fact it does not propose to resort to compulsion, if the object can be attained by voluntary offers; and I am of opinion that the purposes may be so effected. These voluntary offers may be promoted considerably by the presence of the nobility and gentry in their respective districts, and on that account, I rejoice in the prospect that we are soon to separate, not only with reference to this, but to the other measures which have passed the House, and to the execution of which the presence I have alluded to must materially contribute. The great men of the country to animate by their example, to countenance by their authority, and to assist by their advice the operations of the people, have it in their power to achieve the most important good, to excite a zeal and devotion to the public cause, and to diffuse their own spirit through all ranks of the community.

With a view to those desirable advantages, I wish that the session may be short; and I hope that as little time as possible may be lost in examining and arranging the details of this important measure, and that, whatever reasons we may have to look for voluntary offers, we shall not rely on those offers altogether; for, as the representatives of the people, we are bound to provide for their safety, and to provide a sufficient force. Though they may not be disposed to take care of themselves, it is our duty to take care of them. If, therefore, voluntary offers shall not be adequate to the purpose, we must of course resort to compulsory proceedings.

The drilling of the men is, as I have already observed, the principal object to be attended to; but I beg it to be understood that, in my opinion, the poorer classes should be remunerated for the time they may be engaged in discipline. I hope it is so intended, though I have not heard anything of the kind mentioned by my right honourable friend in the opening. The man who is taken from his labour for the public safety, ought certainly to be paid for his time; and this would serve to reconcile such persons to a practice which, otherwise, would be justly considered a very great hardship.

As to the trouble that the nobility and gentry may be called upon to submit to, in this general armament, I cannot do them the injustice of supposing that they would not submit to it with alacrity, or that questions of mere personal convenience would, in such a crisis as the present, have any weight with them.

In the execution of this measure, I do not like the idea of waiting for the slow progress of a ballot. I think that unless the volunteers should, within a certain date, comply with the condition prescribed, their consent should not be waited for. In those parishes where the voluntary offers should not be promptly made, the compulsory levy should be promptly enforced. This compulsion, however, would not, according to my apprehension, be in any instance necessary, if the Lords-Lieutenant of counties, with the deputies and other persons of respectability, would go round from house to house in their respective districts, and solicit the people to come forward. This I know I am not too sanguine in believing would effectually accomplish, within one month, the ends we have in view without any compulsion whatever, particularly when they are apprised fully of the necessity for their service; when they are encouraged by the advice of their superiors; and when they have deemed their country's danger demands it.

Much has been said of the danger of arming the people. I confess that there was a time when that fear would have had some weight; but there never was a time when there could have been any fear of arming the whole people of England, and particularly not under the present circumstances. I never, indeed, entertained any apprehensions from a patriot army regularly officered, according to the manner specified in the measure before the House, however I might hesitate to permit the assemblage of a tumultuary army otherwise constituted. From an army to consist of the round bulk of the people, no man who knows the British character could have the least fear—if it even were to include the disaffected; for they would bear so small a proportion of the whole, as to be incapable of doing mischief, however mischievously disposed. There was indeed a time when associations of traitors, systematically organized, excited an apprehension of the consequences of a sudden armament of the populace: but that time is no more, and the probability is now, as occurred in the case of the volunteers, that, if there are still any material number of disaffected, by mixing them with the loyal part of the community, the same patriotic zeal, the same submission to just authority, will be soon found to pervade the whole body, and that all will be equally anxious to defend their country or perish in the attempt; that the good and the loyal will correct the vicious disposition of the disaffected, will rectify their errors, and set right their misguided judgments. We may thus enlist those among our friends who would otherwise, perhaps, become the auxiliaries of our enemy.

Last Speech

In the spring of 1804 *the Addington ministry fell, and Pitt returned to power. He now bent all his energies to the formation of another coalition against Napoleon. He persuaded Austria and Russia to join together in opposing Napoleon on the mainland of Europe. But this took time. The threat of invasion was greater than ever. Napoleon concentrated his forces for the invasion of Britain. But so long as Nelson held command of the seas the invasion was impossible. The threat was removed once and for all by Nelson's victory at Trafalgar, when the French and Spanish fleets were destroyed.*

At the Lord Mayor's Banquet on 9th November, 1805, *Pitt gave his last speech. He was ill and weary. It is one of the shortest speeches on record, yet it is a classic.*

I RETURN you many thanks for the honour you have done me: but Europe is not to be saved by any single man. England has saved herself by her exertions, and will, as I trust, save Europe by her example.

Pitt's cherished coalition collapsed on the battlefields of Ulm and Austerlitz. Although the French had been shattered on the seas and the threat of invasion had passed, Napoleon was still the master of the mainland of Europe. On 23rd January, 1806, *Pitt died. His last words were: 'My country. How I leave my country!'*

Pitt is not so great an orator as Burke. Yet his speeches must be studied by all who hope to master the art of persuasion. He succeeded in an age of greater orators than he by the orderly presentation of his material, and the force of his character which shone through his speeches like a beacon, illuminating and comforting. He never tried to compete in the oratorical field with Fox. Perhaps he realized that his speeches were the more effective because of the contrast which they offered to those of his great adversary. Speeches must never be judged in vacuo *but in relation to the circumstances in which they are given.*

CHARLES JAMES FOX

1749–1806

The Liberty of the Subject

*In the history of the House of Commons the rivalry between William Pitt
and Charles James Fox is of lasting interest. The two men were not only
opposite in opinion, but also in character. Pitt was prudent in action and
restrained in utterance. Fox was reckless in action and passionate in utterance. Fox had a tremendous zest for life. He was always in difficulties but
he was well-beloved. He always responded to the needs of the oppressed.
Tyranny in any form was to him an intolerable affront to the dignity of
mankind. Therefore he disagreed with Pitt's policy towards the liberal and
radical elements in the country.*

*He felt that the measures which Pitt deemed necessary to curb the liberty
of those who disagreed with government policy were far too severe.*

*These speeches are reported in the third person. In this speech Fox pleads
for the liberty of the subject.*

IT was of consequence to the House to see what they were doing. They
were told that what they had done was enough; and that even this might
not be enough. What was to be done after this? Under the colour of
pretended alarms, were they to go on to an unlimited infringement and
demolition of all the strongest and most beautiful parts of the constitution? The right honourable gentleman was offended at the comparison that had been made between the conduct of ministers and their
adherents and the conduct of the present rulers in France, and he had
with great felicity quoted from Captain Fluellan the comparison between
the river in Macedon and the river in Monmouth, because there was
salmon in both. But with all respect for his wit, the right honourable

gentleman must be content to incur the imputation of similarity when his own conduct and that of the rulers of France were so similar.

They had taken great pains to throw odium on the pretended designs of a convention on account of the word convention. Let gentlemen look at their own conduct, and see if it was not in substance the same as that of the present rulers in France. What was the conduct of those rulers? From day to day they circulated stories of alarms and plots and conspiracies and insurrections among the people, to inflame and agitate their minds, and to spread panic and terror over the whole country that they might take advantage of their fears and obtain unlimited power, to be exercised in carrying on and confirming that very terror. They inspired the double alarm of danger from conspiracy and danger from the exercise of their own unlimited power, exerted as it every day was in the most shocking murders, with hardly the aspect of form of judicial trial. What was the conduct of the ministers here? Precisely in the same manner they circulated stories of alarms and conspiracies to fill the public mind with fear and, to use the jargon of the French, to make terror the order of the day.

By spreading these false and idle alarms they succeeded in obtaining powers destructive of the constitution, which, as in France, were to be exercised with such inhuman rigour as to keep the country in double awe and, by fostering indignation and discontent, give rise again to new jealousies which would afford occasion for still further stretches of power. Thus they followed the example set them by the men whose doctrines they pretended to abhor with the most shocking fidelity. Every part of their conduct was built on the French model, and he dreaded that it would be productive too certainly of the same effects.

The precise question for the House was to compare the danger with the remedy. The pretended danger was, as we might collect from the documents that had been laid upon the table—documents that everyone had seen published in the newspapers—that there was in certain societies a tendency to a convention. Whether the word convention was a bugbear that was to be held up to terrify their imaginations he knew not; but it was of consequence to inquire a little over the nature of the thing, and not to be startled at names. A convention, he supposed, meant no other than a meeting of the people; and if that meeting was for the discussion of any subject of general interest in a legal and peaceable way, there certainly was nothing in such meeting that could call either for or justify any such measure as the present. To a convention that had for its purpose to overawe the legislature, and to obtain any object, either of universal suffrage or other wild and impracticable theory, he should certainly not choose to give his countenance. But if there was a convention either of individuals for themselves, or of delegates of towns and districts, for the purpose of striving, by petitions and addresses to the three branches of the legislature, to put an end to the present most ruinous and unprovoked war, he should certainly neither be ashamed nor afraid—at least not until after the present bill had passed into a law —to attend, and be a member of such convention.

But what was to be dreaded from even the convention that was threatened which the laws of the country were not of themselves sufficient to check? If they meant, by their intended convention, to overawe the government of this country at a moment of such unprecedented strength as the government now possessed, he would say that they were fit for Bedlam, and for Bedlam only. So perfectly and entirely was it possible for magistrates, in every part of the kingdom, to execute the laws that he would venture to say that if any man, or men, at such convention committed any illegal act, he or they might be sent to prison and tried for the offence as securely as if no convention existed.

The danger, then, called for no remedy; and it was not because any such remedy was necessary that the present bill was introduced. It was to keep alive the passions of the people; it was to agitate and alarm their minds, to put them under the dominion of terror, and take from them the exercise of their rational faculties. Ministers knew well the dangerous predicament in which they stood: they had weakly and, as he thought, wickedly involved the country in a most disastrous war; every day plunged them deeper and deeper in the fatality which they had brought upon their country; they saw no hopes of extricating the nation from it with honour, nor of proceeding in it with success, and they dreaded all reflection on the subject: they knew that they had no safety but in depriving the people of response; they knew that if the alarm should be suspended for a moment, and if men were allowed time and leisure for the exercise of their understandings, the war, and the principles on which it was undertaken, would be scrutinized and discussed. They dreaded to encounter so hazardous a trial, and all their measures had been directed to keep alive an incessant commotion, so as to suspend every operation of the public intellect. For this reason a subscription had been set on foot; he said 'for this reason', because ministers had been open enough to acknowledge that it was not for money. It was, they had declared, to excite the zeal of the people. Zeal was one of those fervent emotions which would be favourable to their views, and which, while it lasted, would keep them from examining the objects of it. But the subscription, he supposed, had not succeeded to the hoped-for extent; that zeal which they had aroused was not equal, apparently, to the occasion, and they now strove to awaken a more powerful emotion, that of terror.

In short, it was a government of passion, a government in which ministers strove to lull asleep all the sober operations of the mind, and to awaken only the fears and terrors of the heart. Reason they dreaded, for reason was their enemy. It was well said by a philosopher of great character that all men dreaded reason who acted against reason; and certainly it was natural and in the order of things that animals, which by their practice counteracted the natural course and dictates of reason, should shrink and dread as their enemy those who seemed to be guided by its wisdom.

THAT GRAND AND BEAUTIFUL FABRIC

It had been said that the secret committee had been spoken of in terms not the most respectful. He, for one, certainly could not speak of some members of that committee without expressing his high respect and regard for them. He was not among those who gave up their personal friendships on account of differences in political opinion. A noble lord near him (Lord George Cavendish) had, in very affecting terms, deplored the circumstance that in the present moment he differed from men so near and dear to his heart as to make him feel it like differing from himself; so he might say that for some of those persons, though he had not ties of consanguinity, he felt so sincere a regard and so poignant a regret at differing from them as to make it like a parting from himself. His early habits of respect, his warm affections, all led him to this feeling; but the present was not a time to compliment men, or to shrink from the severe duties which conscience imposed, from recollections of tenderness and esteem. He must say, then, however highly he regarded some individuals of that committee, that it was made up of two characters; men who were dupes themselves, or men who were willing to dupe others. Their whole report was trifling and inconsequential; it told nothing which every man did not know before; for the last assertion about arming, the right honourable gentleman had said, was merely supplemental, and was not to be taken as a component part of the report.

Then what did the report consist of? Of a collection of papers which had all been seen by the public and which, if they did contain any danger, was not a danger of that day. It was known by everyone, and steps might have been taken on the subject months ago. Their avowed intention was to procure a system of universal suffrage; and this the right honourable gentleman said was what had destroyed France. However freely he might be disposed to agree with him as to the wildness and impracticability of universal suffrage, he must doubt of the fact of its having been the cause of the destruction of France. On the contrary, universal suffrage was to be considered rather as the effect than the cause; for the book[1] of the right honourable gentleman [Mr Burke], which had produced such enormous and fatal effects in England, had charged upon the French that they had not acted upon their own principles, but had narrowed the suffrage in a way totally inconsistent with their own doctrine. But were we to argue theoretically or practically from the example of France which the right honourable gentleman so incessantly presented to them? Was every man who had liberty in his mouth to be considered as a traitor, merely because liberty had been abused in France, and had been carried to the most shocking licentiousness?

He would venture to say that if this was to be the consequence, fatal indeed would it be for England! If the love of liberty was not to be maintained in England; if the warm admiration of it was not to be cherished in the hearts of the people; if the maintenance of liberty was not to be inculcated as a duty; if it was not to be reverenced as our chief good, as our boast and pride and richest inheritance;—what else had we worthy of our care? Liberty was the essence of the British constitution. King, lords, commons and courts of judicature were but the forms; the basis of the constitution was liberty, that grand and beautiful fabric, the first principle of which was government by law, and which this day they were going to suspend.

[1] *Reflections on the French Revolution.*

On Peace with France

Fox was a vehement opponent of the war with France. Time and time again he advocated a policy of conciliation. In this powerful speech delivered in 1794 he shows the force and passion of his convictions.

Fox was a master of irony. Notice the sentences beginning 'Submit to what? Submit to the French having a bad government? Have we not submitted to this for more than a century?'

When one compares the speeches of Pitt and Fox one can contrast the characters of the two men. But in the attitude towards Napoleon, Pitt was right and Fox was wrong. It is one of the great virtues of British parliamentary life that unpopular and mistaken views can be expressed; and these are sometimes expressed more powerfully than popular and correct views. Anyone who wishes to study the art of irony in public speaking will find many examples in the speeches of Charles James Fox.

It is tempting to speculate on what history would have been like if Fox and Pitt had been friends. But English literature would have been the poorer. The one was necessary for the other in order to bring out the quality of each.

No period in Fox's life became him better than its last year. He had always fought the cause of the oppressed. The plight of the negro slave filled him with horror. In 1807 shortly before his death he introduced the Act which abolished the slave trade. That was his greatest political achievement.

WHEN he formerly made a motion in that House for peace, he found no want of zeal for war, no want of zeal to cry down any man who had the hardiness to oppose it; at least he found enough, and knew not to what greater length it could have gone unless they had expelled him the House or declared him a traitor, as they seemed to think a laudable practice in other places towards any man who opposed the will of the majority. What was the cause of that zeal? Contempt for the enemy and confidence in their own strength; and the cause being gone, the effect had ceased. Such would ever be the case with zeal founded on false principles. Why were the zeal and exertions of the French less affected by ill-success than ours? Ministers would answer: 'They force every man into the field who is capable of serving, they strip every other man of whatever they want for the service of the army, and amid misery, wretchedness and death they produce an unnatural exertion by means of tyranny and terror.' At the call of necessity even such means must be resorted to.

Were a French army to land in this country, declaring that they would make no peace with us till we renounced our constitution and accepted a form of government according to their fancy, who would deny that every man capable of serving against them ought to be compelled to service, and that every sacrifice must be made by individuals to repel the common danger? Such acts in such cases, instead of tyranny, became a virtue; and he was surprised to hear men of correct minds deducing arguments from them of which they ought to be ashamed. 'Would we submit,' it was asked, 'to treat with the present government of France?' Submit to what? Submit to the French having a bad government? Had we not submitted to this for more than a century? Had we ever found ourselves uneasy under our submission to Persia having a bad government? Had we not submitted to all the injustice, cruelty, and slaughter perpetrated in Poland? Then it was asked, 'Would we submit to propose peace?' If all nations were to stand upon this point no war could ever be concluded but by the extermination of one or other of the contending parties, for one or other must submit to propose peace. But to propose peace was no submission, no degradation. Peace had often been proposed by the victorious party, and this had always been deemed an act of wisdom and magnanimity, not of concession. What were all the other degradations and submissions but lofty words and unmeaning phrases?

We had once said that we would never treat with the present government of France. Take away this impediment to peace, and every advantage we obtained afterwards, if the war must be continued, would be something in our favour; whereas, while that remained, our successes would only stimulate the enemy to fresh exertions, by fresh sufferings and fresh sacrifices; for it was impossible to suppose that the French government would ever negotiate for its own destruction. Would not this give a clear sanction of justice to the war? Would it not produce unanimity with greater zeal and exertion at home by convincing every man that we were not at war for unreasonable or impracticable objects, but to bring an unreasonable enemy to equitable terms of peace?

But what might it not be expected to produce in France, where, as ministers said, the government was perpetually changing from hand to hand, and the loss of power marked the period of life? Ministers were always speculating on the internal affairs of France; why not try a little of this speculation? The convention, they said, deluded the people by telling them that they were waging a war of extermination. To offer to treat would put an end to the delusion, the people would open their eyes, and the convention must give them peace or meet the extermination which they were said to denounce against others.

The present state of the war was calamitous beyond example. We had gained Martinique, Guadaloupe, St. Lucia and part of St. Domingo in the West Indies, with Corsica in the Mediterranean. Our allies had lost all he had enumerated in the former part of his speech. If these astonishing exertions of the enemy by land had impeded their exertions by sea, it would be something; but, unfortunately, the prediction in one of the King's speeches, that their navy had received an irrecoverable blow at Toulon, was already falsified. Was it not true that a fleet had already sailed from the port superior in point of number to our fleet in the Mediterranean? Their naval exertions at Brest had afforded Lord Howe one of the most glorious triumphs in the annals of our history. If their navy had been such as ministers represented it at the commencement of the war, viz., a navy only upon paper, Lord Howe would not have had the glory of beating an enemy of superior force. But even that blow proved not to be irreparable, for they had now a fleet at sea which it is doubtful whether we could immediately collect a sufficient force to drive from the English Channel. These circumstances were matter of very serious consideration to every man who felt for the honour and safety of his country.

If the war should go on, must we not expect, from what we had seen, that the enemy would again dispute with us the superiority at sea? The skill and courage of our navy he confided in as unmatched by any nation in the world; but skill and courage could not always compensate for inequality of force, and as our chance of victory was greater, so was our stake. The defeat of the French fleet, as we had so lately experienced, would be of little consequence to the general issue of the campaign, while the defeat of our fleet would be little short of absolute destruction. Why, then, expose us to such unequal risk? It was admitted, however, that when disaster had subdued obstinacy and extinguished hope, we must make peace even with the French republic. Then, indeed, all that was now imagined of humiliating and degrading would be true; we must throw ourselves at the feet of those we had condemned and reviled, perhaps exasperated, and submit to whatever terms they thought fit to impose. Why expose ourselves to the bare possibility of such ruin? Why not renounce the visionary project of overturning the present government of France?

If after that they abused the peace we made with them we should do as we had done with France before, contend for superiority with the same stake and the same exertion. If asked what terms of peace he would advise, he would answer that to adjust the terms was the business of ministers, who alone possessed the necessary information. Let them propose such terms as, on a consideration of all the circumstances of the relative strength of the contending parties, of what might be gained and what lost on either side, they should judge to be fair and equitable; and if these were refused we should be in a better situation than before, because both parties would know what they were fighting for, and how much the attainment of it was worth.

LORD ERSKINE

1750–1823

The Liberty of the Press

(Defence of Paine)

In the long and honourable history of English law one of the great names is that of Lord Erskine. After leaving Edinburgh Academy he entered the Navy, but he left after a short period of service and turned to the study of the law.

Erskine's great period as an advocate was reached shortly after the outbreak of the French Revolution. The repressive measures of Pitt denied the right of free speech and discussion, and Erskine was often briefed for the defence of those accused of what in those days was alleged to be treason. One of the greatest of his cases was the defence of Tom Paine. In his famous book, The Rights of Man, *Paine claimed that hereditary government, whether by kings or by lords, was 'an imposition on mankind'. He argued that all power rested ultimately in the people and that representative government should be established. In the development of this argument he advocated that the monarchy should be abolished.*

These opinions were regarded as highly dangerous, and Paine was charged with treason. In the first of the following speeches an extract is given from Erskine's defence of Tom Paine. In the event Paine was acquitted. Thereafter Erskine defended many other men of radical views, including Walker, who was indicted for treason and conspiracy, and Hardy, who was the secretary of the Corresponding Society—a well-known group of radicals.

Erskine's combination of logic and eloquence won him acquittals in all these cases. He became a universal idol.

Erskine holds an honoured place among those who, in times of danger, upheld liberty. When Parliament was using its powers to oppress, Erskine bravely maintained the sanctity of the law. His conduct and his practice established once and for all the principle that although Members of Parliament might make the laws of the land, the Judges, after hearing arguments by members of the Bar, interpret the laws.

Also he established the principle that every barrister has the duty to defend his clients to the utmost of his ability no matter how strong the prima facie *evidence against the accused might be.*

GENTLEMEN, I say, in the name of Thomas Paine, and in his words as author of *The Rights of Man*, as written in the very volume that is charged with seeking the destruction of property—

'The end of all political associations is the preservation of the rights of man, which rights are liberty, property, and security; that the nation is the source of all sovereignty derived from it; the right of property being secured and inviolable, no one ought to be deprived of it, except in cases of evident public necessity, legally ascertained, and on condition of a previous just indemnity.'

These are undoubtedly the rights of man—the rights for which all governments are established—and the only rights Mr Paine contends for; but which he thinks (no matter whether right or wrong) are better to be secured by a republican constitution than by the forms of the English government. He instructs me to admit that, when government is once constituted, no individuals, without rebellion, can withdraw their obedience from it; that all attempts to excite them to it are highly criminal for the most obvious reasons of policy and justice; that nothing short of the will of a WHOLE PEOPLE can change or affect the rule by which a nation is to be governed; and that no private opinion, however honestly inimical to the forms or substance of the law, can justify resistance to its authority, while it remains in force. The author of *The Rights of Man* not only admits the truth of all this doctrine, but he consents to be convicted, and I also consent for him, unless his work shall be found studiously and painfully to inculcate those great principles of government which it is charged to have been written to destroy.

Let me not, therefore, be suspected to be contending that it is lawful to write a book pointing out defects in the English government, and exciting individuals to destroy its sanctions, and to refuse obedience. But, on the other hand, I do contend that it is lawful to address the

English nation on these momentous subjects; for had it not been for this inalienable right (thanks be to God and our fathers for establishing it!), how should we have had this constitution which we so loudly boast of? If, in the march of the human mind, no man could have gone before the establishments of the time he lived in, how could our establishment, by reiterated changes, have become what it is? If no man could have awakened the public mind to errors and abuses in our government, how could it have passed on from stage to stage, through reformation and revolution, so as to have arrived from barbarism to such a pitch of happiness and perfection, that the Attorney-General considers it as profanation to touch it further, or to look for any further amendment.

In this manner power has reasoned in every age; government, in its own estimation, has been at all times a system of perfection; but a free press has examined and detected its errors, and the people have from time to time reformed them. This freedom has alone made our government what it is; this freedom alone can preserve it; and therefore, under the banners of that freedom, today I stand up to defend Thomas Paine. But how, alas! shall this task be accomplished? How may I expect from you what human nature has not made man for the performance of? How am I to address your reasons, or ask them to pause, amidst the torrent of prejudice which has hurried away the public mind on the subject you are to judge. Gentlemen, I have but a few more words to trouble you with: take my leave of you with declaring that all this freedom which I have been endeavouring to assert is no more than the ancient freedom which belongs to our own inbred constitution. I have not asked you to acquit Thomas Paine upon any new lights, or upon any principle but that of the law, which you are sworn to administer;— my great object has been to inculcate that wisdom and policy, which are the parents of the government of Great Britain, forbid this jealous eye over her subjects; and that, on the contrary, they cry aloud in the language of the poet, adverted to by Lord Chatham on the memorable subject of America, unfortunately without effect—

> 'Be to their faults a little blind,
> Be to their virtues very kind,
> Let all their thoughts be unconfined,
> And clap your padlock on the mind.'

Engage the people by their affections—convince their reason—and
they will be loyal from the only principle that can make loyalty sincere,
vigorous, or rational—a conviction that it is their truest interest, and
that their government is for their good. Constraint is the natural parent
of resistance, and a pregnant proof that reason is not on the side of
those who use it. You must all remember Lucian's pleasant story:
Jupiter and a countryman were walking together, conversing with
great freedom and familiarity upon the subject of heaven and earth.
The countryman listened with attention and acquiescence, while Jupiter
strove only to convince him; but happening to hint a doubt, Jupiter
turned hastily round and threatened him with his thunder. 'Ah, ah!'
says the countryman, 'now, Jupiter, I know that you are wrong; you are
always wrong when you appeal to your thunder.'

This is the case with me—I can reason with the people of England,
but I cannot fight against the thunder of authority.

Unjust Prosecution

(Defence of Walker)

UNJUST prosecutions lead to the ruin of all governments. Whoever
will look back to the history of the world in general, and of our own
particular country, will be convinced that exactly as prosecutions have
been cruel and oppressive and maintained by inadequate and un-
righteous evidence, in the same proportion and by the same means,
their authors have been destroyed instead of being supported by them;
as often as the principles of our ancient laws have been departed from in
weak and wicked times, so often the governments that have violated
them have been suddenly crumbled into dust; and therefore wishing, as
I most sincerely do, the preservation and prosperity of our happy
constitution, I desire to enter my protest against its being supported by
means that are likely to destroy it. Violent proceedings bring on the
bitterness of retaliation, until all justice and moderation are tramped
down and subverted. Witness those sanguinary prosecutions previous

to the awful period in the last century, when Charles I fell. That unfortunate Prince lived to lament those vindictive judgments by which his impolitic, infatuated followers thought they were supporting his throne; he lived to see how they destroyed it; his throne, undermined by violence, sunk under him, and those who shook it were guilty in their turn (such is the natural order of injustice), not only of similar, but of worse and more violent wrongs. Witness the fate of the unhappy Earl of Strafford, who, when he could not be reached by the ordinary laws, was impeached in the House of Commons, and who, when still beyond the consequence of that judical proceeding, was at last destroyed by the arbitrary and wicked mandate of the legislature.

I cannot tell how others feel upon these subjects, but I do know how it is their interest to feel concerning them. We ought to be persuaded that the only way by which government can be honourably or safely supported, is by cultivating the love and affection of the people, by showing them the value of the constitution by its protection, by making them understand its principles by the practical benefits derived from them, and above all in letting them feel their security in the administration of law and justice.

Put yourselves, gentlemen, in the place of the defendants, and let me ask: If you were brought before your country upon a charge supported by no other evidence than that which you have heard today, and encountered by that which I have stated to you, what would you say, or your children after you, if you were touched in your persons or your properties by a conviction? May you never be put to such reflections, nor the country to such disgrace! The best service we can render to the public is that we should live like one harmonious family, that we should banish all animosities, jealousies and suspicions of one another; and that, living under the protection of a mild and impartial justice, we should endeavour with one heart, according to our best judgments, to advance the freedom and maintain the security of Great Britain.

Trial by Equals

(Defence of Hardy)

BEFORE I advance to the regular consideration of this great cause, either as it regards the evidence or the law, I wish first to put aside all that I find in the speech of my learned friend, the Attorney-General, which is either collateral to the merits or in which I can agree with him. First, then, in the name of the prisoner and speaking his sentiments, which are well known to be my own also, I concur in the eulogium which you have heard upon the constitution of our wise forefathers. But before this eulogium can have any just or useful application, we ought to reflect upon what it is which entitles this constitution to the praise so justly bestowed upon it. To say nothing at present of its most essential excellence, or rather the very soul of it, viz., the share the people ought to have in their government, by a pure representation, for the assertion of which the prisoner stands arraigned as a traitor before you.

What is it that distinguishes the government of England from the most despotic monarchies? What but the security which the subject enjoys in a trial and judgment by his equals; rendered doubly secure as being part of a system of law which no expediency can warp and which no power can abuse with impunity? . . . If this prosecution has been commenced—as it is asserted—to avert from Great Britain the calamities incident to civil confusion, leading in its issues to the deplorable condition of France, I call upon you, gentlemen, to avert such a calamity from falling upon my client, and through his side upon yourselves and upon our country. Let not *him* suffer under vague expositions of tyrannical laws, more tyrannically executed. Let not him be hurried away to pre-doomed execution from an honest enthusiasm for the public safety. I ask for him a trial by this applauded constitution of our country. I call upon you to administer the law to him, according to our wholesome institutions, by its strict and rigid letter; however you may eventually disapprove of any part of his conduct, or, viewing it through a false medium, may think it even wicked, I claim for him, as a subject of England, that the law shall decide upon its criminal denomination. I protest in his name against all appeals to speculations concerning consequences, when the law commands us to look to intentions. If the State be threatened with evils, let Parliament administer a prospective remedy, but let the prisoner hold his life under the law.

Gentlemen, I ask this solemnly of the Court whose justice I am persuaded will afford it to me. I ask it more emphatically of you, the jury, who are called, upon your oaths, to make a true deliverance of your countryman from this charge. But lastly, and chiefly, I implore it of Him in Whose hands are all the issues of life; Whose humane and merciful eye expands itself over all the transactions of mankind, at Whose command nations rise and fall and are regenerated.

LORD MACAULAY

1800–1859

Speech on Literature

No man epitomized the aspirations of the Victorian age more than Lord Macaulay. He touched life at many points. He was a writer, a historian and a politician. From his earliest years he was a wide and omnivorous reader, and his memory retained most of what he read. It is said that he would recite by heart many of the plays of Shakespeare, and most of Paradise Lost. By temperament he was sanguine and hopeful, and, above all, sure of himself.

His Essays *and his* History of England *were read by a wide public, and his speeches commanded immediate attention. This speech, which he gave to the Edinburgh Philosophical Institution, shows Macaulay's qualities and characteristics. He was a master of the short sentence and the combination of short sentences. The resources of his well-stored mind were always at his disposal for the apt illustration and the ready comparison. In this speech delivered in 1846 also there is illustrated Macaulay's belief that the times in which he lived were the best of all possible times and that the future might indeed hold still greater advantages in store for mankind.*

I THANK you, gentlemen, for this cordial reception. I have thought it right to steal a short time from duties not unimportant for the purpose of lending my aid to an undertaking calculated, as I think, to raise the credit and to promote the best interests of the city which has so many claims on my gratitude.

The Directors of our Institution have requested me to propose to you as a toast the Literature of Britain. They could not have assigned to me a more agreeable duty. The chief object of this Institution is, I conceive, to impart knowledge through the medium of our own language. Edinburgh is already rich in libraries worthy of her fame as a seat of literature and a seat of jurisprudence. A man of letters can here without difficulty obtain access to repositories filled with the wisdom of many ages and of many nations. But something was still wanting. We still wanted a library open to that large, that important, that respectable class which, though by no means destitute of liberal curiosity or of sensibility to literary pleasures, is yet forced to be content with what is written in our own tongue. For that class especially, I do not say exclusively, this library is intended. Our directors, I hope, will not be satisfied, I, as a member, shall certainly not be satisfied, till we possess a noble and complete collection of English books, till it is impossible to seek in vain on our shelves for a single English book which is valuable either on account of matter or on account of manner, which throws any light on our civil, ecclesiastical, intellectual, or social history, which, in short, can afford either useful instruction or harmless amusement.

From such a collection, placed within the reach of that large and valuable class which I have mentioned, I am disposed to expect great good. And when I say this, I do not take into the account those rare cases to which my valued friend, the Lord Provost,[1] so happily alluded. It is indeed not impossible that some man of genius who may enrich our literature with imperishable eloquence and song, or who may extend the empire of our race over matter, may feel in our reading room, for the first time, the consciousness of powers yet undeveloped. It is not impossible that our volumes may suggest the first thought of something great to some future Burns, or Watt, or Arkwright.

But I do not speak of these extraordinary cases. What I confidently anticipate is that, through the whole of that class whose benefit we have peculiarly in view, there will be a moral and an intellectual improvement; that many hours, which might otherwise be wasted in folly or in vice, will be employed in pursuits which, while they afford the highest and most lasting pleasure, are not only harmless, but purifying and elevating. My own experience, my own observation, justifies me in entertaining this hope. I have had opportunities, both in this and in other countries, of forming some estimate of the effect which is likely to be produced by a good collection of books on a society of young men. There is, I will venture to say, no judicious commanding officer of a regiment who will

[1] Mr Adam Black.

not tell you that the vicinity of a valuable library will improve perceptibly the whole character of a mess. I well knew one eminent military servant of the East India Company, a man of great and various accomplishments, a man honourably distinguished both in war and in diplomacy, a man who enjoyed the confidence of some of the greatest generals and statesmen of our time. When I asked him, how, having left his country while still a boy, and having passed his youth at military stations in India, he had been able to educate himself, his answer was, that he had been stationed in the neighbourhood of an excellent library, that he had been allowed free access to the books, and that they had, at the most critical time of his life, decided his character, and saved him from being a mere smoking, card-playing, punch-drinking lounger.

Some of the objections which have been made to such institutions as ours have been happily and completely refuted by my friend the Lord Provost, and by the Most Reverend Prelate who has honoured us with his presence this evening,[1] that it would be idle to say again what has been so well said. There is, however, one objection which, with your permission, I will notice. Some men, of whom I wish to speak with great respect, are haunted, as it seems to me, with an unreasonable fear of what they call superficial knowledge. Knowledge, they say, which really deserves the name, is a great blessing to mankind, the ally of virtue, the harbinger of freedom. But such knowledge must be profound. A crowd of people who have a smattering of mathematics, a smattering of astronomy, a smattering of chemistry, who have read a little poetry and a little history, is dangerous to the commonwealth. Such half knowledge is worse than ignorance. And then the authority of Pope is vouched. Drink deep or taste not; shallow draughts intoxicate: drink largely and that will sober you.

I must confess that the danger which alarms these gentlemen never seemed to me very serious: and my reason is this; that I never could prevail on any person who pronounced superficial knowledge a curse, and profound knowledge a blessing, to tell me what was his standard of profundity. The argument proceeds on the supposition that there is some line between profound and superficial knowledge similar to that which separates truth from falsehood. I know of no such line. When we talk of men of deep science, do we mean that they have got to the bottom or near the bottom of science? Do we mean that they know all

[1] Archbishop Whateley.

that is capable of being known? Do we mean even that they know, in their own especial department, all that the smatterers of the next generation will know? Why, if we compare the little truth that we know with the infinite mass of truth which we do not know, we are all shallow together; and the greatest philosophers that ever lived would be the first to confess their shallowness. If we could call up the first of human beings, if we could call up Newton, and ask him whether, even in those sciences in which he had no rival, he considered himself as profoundly knowing, he would have told us that he was but a smatterer like ourselves, and that the difference between his knowledge and ours vanished, when compared with the quantity of truth still undiscovered, just as the distance between a person at the foot of Ben Lomond and at the top of Ben Lomond vanishes when compared with the distance of the fixed stars.

It is evident then that those who are afraid of superficial knowledge do not mean by superficial knowledge, knowledge which is superficial when compared with the whole quantity of truth capable of being known. For, in that sense, all human knowledge is, and always has been, and always must be, superficial. What then is the standard? Is it the same two years together in any country? Is it the same, at the same moment, in any two countries? Is it not notorious that the profundity of one age is the shallowness of the next; that the profundity of one nation is the shallowness of a neighbouring nation? Ramohun Roy passed, among Hindoos, for a man of profound Western learning; but he would have been but a very superficial member of this institute. Strabo was justly entitled to be called a profound geographer eighteen hundred years ago. But a teacher of geography, who had never heard of America, would now be laughed at by the girls of a boarding-school. What would now be thought of the greatest chemist of 1746, or of the greatest geologist of 1746? The truth is that, in all experimental science, mankind is, of necessity, constantly advancing. Every generation, of course, has its front rank and its rear rank; but the rear rank of a later generation occupies the ground which was occupied by the front rank of a former generation.

You remember Gulliver's adventures. First he is shipwrecked in a country of little men; and he is a Colossus among them. He strides over the walls of their capital; he stands higher than the cupola of their great temple: he tugs after him a royal fleet: he stretches his legs; and a royal army, with drums beating and colours flying, marches through the gigantic arch: he devours a whole granary for breakfast, eats a herd of cattle for dinner, and washes down his meal with all the hogsheads of a cellar. In his next voyage he is among men sixty feet high. He who, in Lilliput, used to take people up in his hand in order that he might be able to hear them, is himself taken up in the hands and held to the ears of his masters. It is all that he can do to defend himself with his hanger against the rats and mice. The court ladies amuse themselves with seeing him fight wasps and frogs: the monkey runs off with him to the chimney top: the dwarf drops him into the cream jug and leaves him to swim for his life. Now, was Gulliver a tall or a short man? Why in his own house at Rotherhithe, he was thought a man of the ordinary stature. Take him to Lilliput; and he is Quinbus Flestrin, the Man Mountain. Take him to Brobdingnag, and he is Grildrig, the little Manikin. It is the same in science. The pigmies of one society would have passed for giants in another.

JOHN HENRY NEWMAN
1801–1890

The Work of the Christian

John Henry Newman was an Anglican clergyman who was caught up in the Oxford Movement and who was received into the Roman Catholic Church in 1845. The Oxford Movement was one of the great ecclesiastical movements of the nineteenth century. Three men were outstandingly identified with the Movement—Keble, Froude and Newman. It has been said that Keble inspired it, Froude gave it impetus, but it was Newman who took up the work. He became a Cardinal in the Roman Catholic Church.

Cardinal Newman had a sense of man's personal relationship with God. He had great sincerity and sympathy. He believed that it was by imagination rather than reason that man attained truth. He was a most popular preacher and attracted congregations who were genuinely interested in the ideas thrown up by the Oxford Movement, and who appreciated his gifts as a preacher.

Of his sermons, it has been well said that they were simple in diction, sinuous, graceful and exquisitely cadenced. This sermon delivered at St. Mary's, Oxford, shows these qualities.

'Man goeth forth to his work and to his labour until the evening.' Ps. civ. 23.

THOUGH God created the heavens and the earth in six days, and then rested, yet He rested only to begin a work of another kind; for our Lord says, 'My Father worketh hitherto,' and He adds, 'and I work.' And at another time He says, concerning Himself more expressly, 'I must work the works of Him that sent Me, while it is day: the night cometh, when no man can work.' And when that night came, He said, 'I have finished the work which Thou gavest Me to do.' 'It is finished.' And in the text we are told generally of all men, 'Man goeth forth to his work and to his labour until the evening.' The Creator wrought till the Sabbath came; the Redeemer wrought till the sun was darkened, and it was night. 'The sun ariseth,' and 'man goeth forth,' and works 'till the evening'; when 'the keepers of the house tremble, and the strong man bow themselves, and those that look out at the windows are darkened, and desire fails, because man goeth to his long home, and the mourners go about the streets'; when 'the silver cord is loosed, and the golden bowl is broken, and the dust returns to the earth as it was, and the spirit returns unto God who gave it'. In the evening man returns to God, and his works, whether good or whether evil, do follow him.

This solemn truth, that we are sent here to do a work, is in various ways set before us in the Service appointed for this day. First, we read, in the beginning of Genesis, of Almighty God's work in the creation of the world, which is the archetype of all works which His creatures are able to do through His grace unto His glory. Then we read of Adam, placed in Paradise, the garden in Eden, 'to dress it and to keep it'. Soon alas, did he fall, and become subject to heavier toil, the earth being cursed for his sake, and bringing forth unto him thorns and thistles. God, however, in His mercy, did not desert him; and, accordingly, we read in the Gospel of the householder going out from morning till evening 'to hire labourers into his vineyard'. He went out early, and then about the third hour, and about the sixth and ninth, nor stopped till the eleventh.

Such were His dealings with the race of man till the fullness of time was come, and in the last days, even at the eleventh hour, He sent His Son to gather together labourers for His work from all parts of the earth. And the history of those fresh Gospel labourers is presented to us in today's Epistle, in the pattern of St. Paul who 'went a warfare'; who planted a vineyard; who ploughed and thrashed, and trod out the corn; for necessity was laid upon him, and it was woe unto him if he preached not the Gospel. Nay, moreover, who kept under his body, and brought it into subjection, lest after he had preached to others, the end should come, and he should be a castaway.

Thus the Service for this day carries us from the creation of all things to the judgment, and that with this one thought—the work which is put upon us to do. Adam had to dress Paradise; fallen man to 'eat bread' from the blighted ground 'in the sweat of his face'; the labourers worked in the vineyard, some through the 'heat of the day', others in the eventide; and the Apostles and their followers ploughed, and sowed, and planted, in a different field, but still in their Master's service, as it was at the beginning. Thus the lesson put before us today contrasts with that of the Epiphany. We have ended the feast of grace, and are now come to the work days, and therefore we read of man going forth to his work and to his labour from sun-rising unto the evening. Or we may connect these two seasons with Lent, which is to follow; and whereas our Lord, in His Sermon on the Mount, speaks of three great duties of religion, prayer, alms-giving, and fasting—our duties towards God, our neighbour, and ourselves—we may consider the Epiphany to remind us of worship in the temple, Septuagesima of good works, and Lent of self-denial and self-discipline.

Now the lesson set before us today needs insisting on, because in these latter times men have arisen, speaking heresy, making much of the free grace of the Gospel but denying that it enjoined a work, as well as conferred a blessing; or, rather, that it gave grace in order that it might enjoin a work. Christmas comes first, and Septuagesima afterwards: we must have grace before we work in order to work; but as surely as grace is conferred on us, so surely is a work enjoined. It has been pretended by these teachers that works were only required under the Law, and grace comes instead under the Gospel: but the true account of the matter is this, that the Law enjoined works, and the grace of the Gospel fulfils them; the Law commanded, but gave no power; the Gospel bestows the power. Thus the Gospel is the counterpart of the Law. Christ says, 'I am not come to destroy, but to fulfil.' The Gospel does not abrogate works, but provides for them. 'Man goeth forth to his work and to his labour' from the morning of the world to its evening. All dispensations are one and the same here. Adam in Paradise, Adam fallen, Noah in the morning, Abraham at the third hour, the chosen people at the sixth and ninth, and Christians at the eleventh—all, so far as this, have one religion.

And thus, says St. Paul, 'Do we then make void the law through faith? God forbid. Yes, we establish the law.' Again, he tells us 'that as sin hath reigned unto death, even so' grace reigns 'through righteousness', not without righteousness, 'unto eternal life.' And again, 'the righteousness of the law is fulfilled in us, who walk not after the flesh, but after the Spirit.' And to the Ephesians, 'we are His workmanship, created in Christ Jesus unto good works.' And to the Philippians, 'work out your own salvation with fear and trembling; for it is God which worketh in you, both to will and to do of His good pleasure.'

But here an objection may be drawn from the parable of the labourers which requires notice. It may be said that the labourers, who represent the Jews, complain that those who were called in the evening, that is Christians, had worked but a short time, and in the cool of the day. 'They murmured against the good man of the house, saying, These last have wrought but one hour, and Thou hast made them equal unto us which have borne the burden and heat of the day.' Hence it may be argued, that Christians have no irksome or continued toil, but are saved, without their trouble, by grace. Now it is true, we are of those who have been called when the day was drawing to a close; but this neither proves that we have a slight task to do, nor a short time to labour, as a few words will show.

THE BURDEN AND HEAT OF THE DAY

For what is meant by 'the burden and heat of the day'? I have explained it already. It means that religion pressed heavily on the Jews as a burden, because they were unequal to it; and it was as the midday heat, overpowering them with its intensity, because they had no protection against it. 'The sun,' says the Psalmist, 'goes forth from the uttermost part of the heaven, and runneth about unto the end of it again, and there is nothing hid from the heat thereof.' And he continues: 'The law of the Lord is an undefiled law, converting the soul; the testimony of the Lord is sure, and giveth wisdom unto the simple.' What is so bright and glorious as the sun? Yet what so overpowering to the feeble? What so pure and keen as the Law of the Lord? Yet what so searching and awful to the sinner? 'The work of God,' says the Apostle, 'is quick and powerful, and sharper than any two-edged sword'; and therefore it did but probe and wound those who were unprepared for it, and they could but cry out: 'O wretched man that I am, who shall deliver me from the body of this death.'

This was the burden and heat of the day: to have a perfect law, and an unregenerate heart; the thunders of Sinai, yet the sovereignty of the flesh; Moses with the tables of stone, and the people setting up the golden calf. At best they could confess: 'The law is spiritual, but I am carnal, sold under sin; for that which I do, I allow not: for what I would, that do I not; but what I hate, that do I.' But for us, on the other hand, Christ hath redeemed us from the burden and heat, and the curse of the law, by being made a curse for us; and we henceforth may say, with the Apostle: 'What things were gain to me, those I counted loss for Christ; not as though I had already attained, either were already perfect; but this one thing I do, forgetting those things which are behind, and reaching forth unto those things which are before, I press toward the mark, for the prize of the high calling of God in Christ Jesus.'

Do you wish to see how little the Christian is saved from toil by his being saved from 'the burden and heat of the day'? Then consider the Epistle for this Sunday, and the whole chapter of which it is part. It is one of those passages in which St. Paul speaks of himself and his brother labourers in the vineyard; and from this instance you will be able to decide how little Christ has saved those whom He loves from toil and trouble. Christ, we know, is the second Adam, and has restored us to a better paradise. He, for that river which divided into four heads and watered the garden, has given us 'a pure river of water of life, clear as crystal, proceeding out of the throne of God and of the Lamb'; and for 'every tree of the garden' of which Adam might eat freely, has He given 'the tree of life, which beareth twelve manner of fruits, and yieldeth her fruit every month, and the leaves of the tree are for the healing of the nations.' Yet compare the state of Adam in the second chapter of Genesis with that of St. Paul in the ninth chapter of his first Epistle to the Corinthians, and it will be plain that our blessedness under the Gospel is not the removal of labour, but the gift of strength; that the original paradise is not yet restored to us with its repose and security, and that our duties still are not those of Adam innocent, but of Adam fallen.

Adam, for instance, was surrounded by his subject brutes, but had no duties towards them; he was lord of the creation, and they ministered to him. God Almighty brought them to him, and he gave them names; and he was free to accept their homage, or to dispense with it, as pleased him, ranging through the trees of the garden at his will. But what says the blessed Apostle? He makes himself one of those who are even like the brute oxen that treadeth out the corn, and only claim that their mouths be not muzzled, but their hire secured to them. He speaks of himself as an Apostle, or one sent unto his brethren; as ministering about holy things; as having necessity laid upon him; and as making himself 'servant unto all, that he might gain the more.' 'And unto the Jews,' he says, 'I became as a Jew, that I might gain the Jews; to them that are under the law as under the law, that I might gain them that are under the law; to them that are without law, as without law . . . that I might gain them that are without law. To the weak became I as weak, that I might gain the weak: I am made all things to all men, that I might by all means save some.'

Adam, though in a state of quiet and contemplation, was not solitary; for when there was no help-meet for him, 'the Lord God caused a deep sleep to fall on Adam, and he slept; and He took one of his ribs, and closed up the flesh instead thereof; and the rib which the Lord God had taken from man, made He a woman, and brought her unto the man.' But St. Paul tells us, that he reversed in his own case this ordinance of God. 'Mine answer to them which do examine me is this, Have we not power to eat and to drink? Have we not power to lead about a sister, a wife, as well as other Apostles, and as the brethren of the Lord, and Cephas?' He might have been as Adam, and he would not be. And Adam's task was to dress the garden, no heavy labour in Eden; to subdue the ground, which needed not much discipline, but obeyed without effort. But what was St. Paul's culture? What was the ground on which he worked? And did he treat it gently, or was he severe with it, to bring it unto subjection? Did he indulge in its flowers and fruits, or did he watch against thorns and thistles, and subjugate it in the sweat of his brow? Hear his own account of it. 'Every man that striveth for the mastery is temperate in all things: now they do it to obtain a corruptible crown, but we an incorruptible. I therefore so run, not as uncertainly; so fight I, not as one that beateth the air: But I keep under my body, and bring it unto subjection: lest that by any means, when I have preached to others, I myself should be a castaway.' It cannot be said, then, that we have returned to Paradise, because we have not to bear the burden and the heat of the day. It is not that our work is lighter, but our strength is greater.

LET US TURN FROM SHADOWS

Nor, secondly, can we argue that our work is shorter from the labourers' complaint, 'These have wrought but one hour.' For we are called, as is evident, in the world's evening, not in our own. We are called in our own morning: we are called from infancy. By the eleventh hour is not meant that Christians have little to do, but that the time is short; that it is the last time; that there is a 'present distress'; that they have much to do in a little time; that 'the night cometh when no man can work'; that their Lord is at hand, and that they have to wait for Him. 'This I say, brethren,' says St. Paul, 'the time is short; it remaineth that both they that have wives be as though they had none; and they that weep, as though they wept not; and they that rejoice, as though they rejoiced not; and they that buy, as though they possessed not; and they that use this world, as not abusing it, for the fashion of this world passeth away.'

It was otherwise with the Jews; they had a grant of this world; they entered the vineyard in the morning; they had time before them; they might reckon the future. They were bid: 'Go their way, eat their bread with joy, and drink their wine with a merry heart, and let their garments be always white, and let their head lack no ointment, and live joyfully with the wife whom they loved all the days of the life of their vanity . . . for that was their portion in this life, and in their labour which they took under the sun.'

But it is otherwise with us. Earth and sky are ever failing; Christ is ever coming; Christians are ever lifting up their heads and looking out, and therefore it is the evening. We may not set our hearts on things present; we may not say to our soul: 'Thou hast much goods laid up for many years, take thine ease, eat, drink, and be merry': and therefore it is the evening. We may not think of home, or brethren or sister, or father, or mother, or wife, or children, or land; and therefore it is the evening. The evening is long and the day was short; for the first shall be last, and the last first. What seems vigorous perishes; what seems ever expiring is carried on; and this last age, though ever failing, has lasted longer than the ages before it, and Christians have more time for a greater work than if they had been hired in the morning.

Oh may we ever bear in mind that we are not sent into this world to stand all day idle, but to go forth to our work and to our labour until the evening. Until the evening, not in the evening only of life, but serving God from our youth, and not waiting till our years fail us. Until the evening, not in the day-time only, lest we begin to run well, but fall away before our course is ended. Let us 'give glory to the Lord our

God, before He cause darkness, and before our feet stumble upon the dark mountains'; and having turned to Him, let us see that our goodness be not 'as the morning cloud, and as the early dew which passeth away'. The end is the proof of the matter. When the sun shines, this earth pleases; but let us look towards that eventide and the cool of the day, when the Lord of the vineyard will walk amid the trees of His garden, and say unto His steward: 'Call the labourers, and give them their hire, beginning from the last unto the first.' That evening will be the trial; when the heat, and fever, and noise of the noontide are over, and the light fades, and the prospect saddens, and the shades lengthen, and the busy world is still, and 'the door shall be shut in the streets, and the daughters of music shall be brought low, and fears shall be in the way, and the almond tree shall flourish, and the grasshopper shall be a burden, and desire shall fail', and 'the pitcher shall be broken at the fountain, and the wheel broken at the cistern'; then, when it is 'vanity of vanities, all is vanity', and the Lord shall come, 'who both will bring to light the hidden things of darkness, and will make manifest the counsels of the hearts'; then shall we 'discern between the righteous and the wicked, between him that serveth God and him that serveth Him not'.

May the day and that hour ever be in our thoughts, when we rise, when we lie down; when we speak, when we are silent; when we act, and when we rest: whether we eat or drink, or whatever we do, may we never forget that 'for all these things God will bring us into judgment!' For 'He cometh quickly, and His reward is with Him, to give every man according to His work shall be.'

'Blessed are they that do His Commandments, that they may have right to the tree of life, and may enter in through the gates into the city.' Blessed will they be then, and only they, who, with the Apostle, have ever had on their lips, and in their hearts, the question, 'Lord what wilt Thou have me to do?' whose soul, 'hath broken out for the very fervent desire that it hath alway unto His judgments'; who have 'made haste and prolonged not the time to keep His commandments'; who have not waited to be hired, nor run uncertainly, nor beaten the air, nor taken darkness for light, and light for darkness, nor contented themselves with knowing what is right, nor taken comfort in feeling what is good, nor prided themselves in their privileges, but set themselves vigorously to do God's will.

Let us turn from shadows of all kinds—shadows of sense, or shadows of argument and disputation, or shadows addressed to our imagination and tastes. Let us attempt, through God's grace, to advance and sanctify the inward man. We cannot be wrong here. Whatever is right, whatever is wrong, in this perplexing world, we must be right in doing justly, in living mercy, in walking humbly with our God; in denying our wills, in ruling our tongues, in softening and sweetening our tempers, in mortifying our lusts; in learning patience, meekness, purity, forgiveness of injuries, and continuance in well-doing.

RICHARD COBDEN

1804–1865

Protection in Agriculture

Richard Cobden was the directing mind of the Anti-Corn Law League. It was Cobden who induced John Bright to enter politics. The eloquence and ideas of these two men brought about the repeal of the Corn Laws in 1846.

Today many of Cobden's ideas seem curiously dated while others are very up-to-date. In his advocacy of arbitration and disarmament among nations he was very much in advance of his time.

This extract is taken from his great speech on 13th March, 1845. Sir Robert Peel, who was Prime Minister, was expected to reply. It is said that when he heard Cobden's speech he crumpled up his notes and, turning to his friend, Sidney Herbert, he said: 'You may answer this, for I cannot.'

Richard Cobden was one of the great radicals of the nineteenth century.

I HOLD that the landed proprietors are the parties who are responsible if the labourers have not employment. You have absolute power; there is no doubt about that. You can, if you please, legislate for the labourers, or yourselves. Whatever you may have done besides, your legislation has been adverse to the labourer, and you have no right to call upon the farmers to remedy the evils which you have caused. Will not this evil—if evil you call it—press on you more and more every year? What can you do to remedy the mischief? I only appear here now because you have proposed nothing. We all know your system of allotments, and we are all aware of its failure. What other remedy have you? For, mark you, that is worse than a plaything, if you were allowed to carry out your own views. Aye, it is well enough for some of you that there are wiser heads than your own to lead you, or you would be conducting yourselves into precisely the same condition in which they are in Ireland, but with this difference—this increased difficulty—that there they do manage to maintain the rights of property by the aid of the English Exchequer and 20,000 bayonets; but divide your own country into small allotments, and where would be the rights of property? What do you propose to do now? That is the question. Nothing has been brought forward this year, which I have heard, having for its object to benefit the great mass of the English population; nothing I have heard suggested which has at all tended to alleviate their condition.

You admit that the farmer's capital is sinking from under him, and that he is in a worse state than ever. Have you distinctly provided some plan to give confidence to the farmer, to cause an influx of capital to be expended upon his land, and so bring increased employment to the labourer? How is this to be met? I cannot believe you are going to make this a political game. You must set up some specific object to benefit the agricultural interest. It is well said that the last election was an agricultural triumph. There are two hundred county members sitting behind the Prime Minister who prove that it was so.

What, then, is your plan for this distressing state of things? That is what I want to ask you. Do not, as you have done before, quarrel with me because I have imperfectly stated my case; I have done my best, and I again ask you what you have to propose? I tell you that this 'Protection', as it has been called, is a failure. It was so when you had the prohibition up to 80s. You know the state of your farming tenantry in 1821. It was a failure when you had a protection price of 60s., for you know what was the condition of your farm tenantry in 1835. It is a failure now with your last amendment, for you have admitted and proclaimed it to us; and what is the condition of your agricultural population at this time?

I ask, what is your plan? I hope it is not a pretence—a mere political game that has been played throughout the last election, and that you have not all come up here as mere politicians. There are politicians in the House—men who look with an ambition—probably a justifiable one—to the honours of office. There may be men who—with thirty years of continuous service, having been pressed into a groove from which they can neither escape nor retreat—may be holding office, high office, maintained there probably at the expense of their present convictions which do not harmonize very well with their early opinions. I make allowances for them; but the great body of the honourable gentlemen opposite came up to this House, not as politicians, but as the farmers' friends, and protectors of the agricultural interests. Well, what do you propose to do? You have heard the Prime Minister declare that, if he could restore all the protection which you have had, that protection would not benefit agriculturists. Is that your belief? If so, why not proclaim it? And if it is not your conviction, you will have falsified your mission in this House by following the right honourable baronet out into the lobby, and opposing inquiry into the condition of the very men who sent you here.

The Spirit of the Age

With mere politicians I have no right to expect to succeed in this motion. But I have no hesitation in telling you that, if you give me a committee of this House, I will explode the delusion of agricultural protection! I will bring forward such a mass of evidence, and give you such a preponderance of talent and of authority, that when the blue book is published and sent forth to the world, as we can now send it, by our vehicles of information, your system of protection shall not live in public opinion for two years afterward. Politicians do not want that. This cry of protection has been a very convenient handle for politicians. The cry of protection carried the counties at the last election, and politicians gained honours, emoluments, and place by it. But is that old tattered flag of protection, tarnished and torn as it is already, to be kept hoisted still in the counties for the benefit of politicians; or will you come forward honestly and fairly to inquire into this question? I cannot believe that the gentry of England will be made mere drum-heads to be sounded upon by a Prime Minister, to give forth unmeaning and empty sounds, and to have no articulate voice of their own. No! You are the gentry of England who represent the counties. You are the aristocracy of England. Your fathers led our fathers; you may lead us if you will go the right way. But, although you have retained your influence with this country longer than any other aristocracy, it has not been by opposing popular opinion, or by setting yourselves against the spirit of the age.

In other days, when the battle and the hunting-fields were the tests of manly vigour, your fathers were first and foremost there. The aristocracy of England were not like the noblesse of France, the mere minions of a court; nor were they like the hidalgos of Madrid, who dwindled into pigmies. You have been Englishmen. You have not shown a want of courage and firmness when any call has been made upon you. This is a new era. It is the age of improvement; it is the age of social advancement, not the age for war or for feudal sports. You live in a mercantile age, when the whole wealth of the world is poured into your lap. You cannot have the advantages of commercial rents and feudal privileges; but you may be what you always have been, if you will identify yourselves with the spirit of the age. The English people look to the gentry and aristocracy of their country as their leaders. I, who am not one of you, have no hesitation in telling you that there is a deep-rooted, an hereditary prejudice, if I may so call it, in your favour in this country. But you never got it, and you will not keep it, by obstructing the spirit of the age. If you are indifferent to enlightened means of finding employment for your own peasantry; if you are found obstructing that advance which is calculated to knit nations more together in the bonds of peace by means of commercial intercourse; if you are found fighting against the discoveries which have almost given breath and life to material nature, and setting up yourselves as obstructives of that which destiny has decreed shall go on—why, then, you will be the gentry of England no longer, and others will be found to take your place.

And I have no hesitation in saying that you stand just now in a very critical position. There is a wide-spread suspicion that you have been tampering with the best feelings and with the honest confidence of your constituents in this cause. Everywhere you are doubted and suspected. Read your own organs, and you will see that this is the case. Well, then, this is the time to show that you are not the mere party politicians which you are said to be. I have said that we shall be opposed in this measure by politicians; they do not want inquiry. But I ask you to go into this committee with me. I will give you a majority of county members. You shall have a majority of the Central Society in that committee. I ask you only to go into a fair inquiry as to the causes of the distress of your own population. I only ask that this matter may be fairly examined. Whether you establish my principle or yours, good will come out of the inquiry; and I do, therefore, beg and entreat the honourable independent country gentlemen of this House that they will not refuse, on this occasion, to go into a fair, a full, and an impartial inquiry.

JOHN BRIGHT

1811–1889

Free Trade

John Bright, like his friend Richard Cobden, came from the middle classes. Until the middle of the nineteenth century government in Britain had been largely carried on by members of the land-owning classes. But the character of Britain was changing. It was no longer primarily an agricultural country. The inventions of half a dozen men of genius were now making Britain the workshop of the world.

The government of Sir Robert Peel, which came into power in 1841, recognized some of the changes which were taking place. The tariff system was reformed and Customs duties greatly reduced, but a high import duty still remained on corn. If the price of bread was too high this meant misery for the working classes. The landowners on their part were unwilling to allow cheap corn to come in from abroad, and this class—which was strongly represented in Parliament—bitterly opposed any attempt at repeal of the Corn Laws.

The Anti-Corn Law League had many supporters, not only among the masses but among the new class of manufacturers and industrialists, of which Cobden and Bright were members. Cobden supplied the organization, Bright the inspiration. It is interesting to note that the Penny Post, which had been introduced in 1840, helped the League. The pamphlets were sent all over the country at the new cheap rates. Picked teams of speakers toured the length and breadth of the land urging repeal. Cobden even persuaded townspeople who had money to do so, to buy forty-shilling freeholds in county constituencies so that they could have a double vote.

The speech which follows is part of one which was given by John Bright in Covent Garden Theatre in 1845. The agitation was then at its height. The potato crop in Ireland had failed; famine stared the masses in the face.

Peel could wait no longer. The landowners, however, fought to the last.
By the narrowest of majorities the Corn Laws were repealed in 1846. Peel's
government fell shortly afterwards. Peel's action split the Tory Party. It
is interesting to note that one of the men who attacked Peel most strongly
was a young Jew named Benjamin Disraeli.

Lord Salisbury said of Bright's speeches that they were robust, powerful,
and vigorous. There is a fearlessness about his speeches which, even after a
lapse of over a hundred years, reveals the man.

THEY sometimes think we are hard upon the aristocracy. They think
that the vast populations of Lancashire and Yorkshire are democratic
and turbulent. But there are no elements there, except that of great
numbers, which are to be compared in their dangerous character with
the elements of disaffection and insubordination which exist round
about the halls and castles of this proud and arrogant aristocracy. You
have seen in the papers, within the last fortnight, that the foul and
frightful crime of incendiarism has again appeared. It always shows
itself when we have had for some short time a high price of bread.
The Corn Law is as great a robbery of the man who follows the plough
as it is of him who minds the loom, with this difference, that the man
who follows the plough is, of the two, nearest the earth, and it takes less
power to press him into it. Mr Benett, one of the Members for Wiltshire,
at an agricultural meeting held not long since, made a very long speech,
in which he said some remarkable things—the most remarkable being,
that if he had again to come into the world, and had the option of
choosing the particular rank or class in society to which he would belong,
after reviewing, I believe, a period of about seventy years, he confessed
that he would choose to be an agricultural labourer. Now, this sentiment is certainly of a very novel character; and it is one worth examining, coming, as it did, from a man who had at one time, I am told, a
property of eight or ten thousand a year in land.

Now, what is the condition of this agricultural labourer, for whom
they tell us Protection is necessary? He lives in a parish whose owner,
it may be, has deeply mortgaged it. The estate is let to farmers without
capital, whose land grows almost as much rushes as wheat. The bad
cultivation of the land provides scarcely any employment for the
labourers, who become more and more numerous in the parish; the

competition which there is amongst these labourers for the little employment to be had, bringing down the wages to the very lowest point at which their lives can be kept in them. They are heart-broken, spirit-broken, despairing men. They have been accustomed to this from their youth, and they see nothing in the future which affords a single ray of hope. We have attended meetings in those districts, and have been received with the utmost enthusiasm by these round-frocked labourers. They would have carried us from the carriage which we had travelled in, to the hustings; and if a silly squire or a foolish farmer attempted any disturbance or improper interference, these round-frocked men were all around us in an instant, ready to defend us; and I have seen them hustle many a powerful man from the field in which the meeting was being held.

If there be one view of this question which stimulates me to harder work in this cause than another, it is the fearful sufferings which I know to exist amongst the rural labourers in almost every part of this kingdom. How can they be men under the circumstances in which they live? During the period of their growing up to manhood, they are employed at odd jobs about the farm or the farm-yard, for wages which are merely those of little children in Lancashire. Every man who marries is considered an enemy to the parish; every child who is born into the world, instead of being a subject of rejoicing to its parents and to the community, is considered as an intruder come to compete for the little work and the small quantity of food which is left to the population. And then comes toil, year after year, long years of labour, with little remuneration; but perhaps at sixty or seventy, a gift of 20s and a coat, or of £2, from the Agricultural Society, because they have brought up a large family, and have not committed that worst of all sins, taken money from the parochial rates. One of their own poets has well expressed their condition:

> 'A blessed prospect—
> To slave while there is strength—in age the workhouse,
> A parish shell at last, and the little bell
> Toll'd hastily for a pauper's funeral!'

But the crowning offence of the system of legislation under which we have been living is, that a law has been enacted, in which it is altogether unavoidable that these industrious and deserving men should be brought down to so helpless and despairing a condition. By withdrawing the stimulus of competition, the law prevents the good cultivation of the land of our country, and therefore diminishes the supply of food which we might derive from it. It prevents, at the same time, the importation of foreign food from abroad, and it also prevents the growth of supplies abroad, so that when we are forced to go there for them they are not to be found. The law is, in fact, a law of the most ingeniously malignant character. It is fenced about in every possible way. The most demoniacal ingenuity could not have invented a scheme more calculated to bring millions of the working classes of this country to a state of pauperism, suffering, discontent, and insubordination than the Corn Law which we are now opposing.

And then a fat and sleek dean, a dignitary of the church and a great philosopher, recommends for the consumption of the people—he did not read a paper about the supplies that were to be had in the great valley of the Mississippi, but he said that there were Swede turnips and mangel-wurzel—and the Hereditary Earl Marshal of England, as if to out-herod Herod himself, recommends hot water and a pinch of curry-powder. I was rejoiced, not for the sake of the Duke of Norfolk; for I pitied him, but still I was in my heart rejoiced when I saw the speech which he had made in Sussex. The people of England have not, even under thirty years of Corn Law influence, been sunk so low as to submit tamely to this insult and wrong. It is enough that a law should have been passed to make your toil valueless, to make your skill and labour unavailing to procure for you a fair supply of the common necessaries of life—but when to this grievous iniquity they add the insult of telling you to go, like beasts that perish, to mangel-wurzel, or to something which even the beasts themselves cannot eat, then I believe the people of England will rise, and with one voice proclaim the downfall of this odious system.

THE PORTAL OF DELIVERANCE

This law is the parent of many of those grievous fluctuations in trade under which so much suffering is created in this commercial kingdom. There is a period coming—it may be as bad or worse than the last— when many a man, now feeling himself independent and comfortable in his circumstances, will find himself swept away by the torrent, and his goodly ship made a complete wreck. Capital avails almost nothing; fluctuations in trade we have, such as no prudence can guard against. We are in despair one year, and in a state of great excitement in the next. At one time ruin stares us in the face, at another we fancy that we are getting rich in a moment. Not only is trade sacrificed, but the moral character of the country is injured by the violent fluctuations created by this law. And now have we a scarcity coming or not? They say that to be forewarned is to be forearmed, and that a famine foretold never comes. And so this famine could not have come if the moment we saw it to be coming we had had power to relieve ourselves by supplies of food from abroad. The reason why a famine foretold never comes, is because when it is foreseen and foretold, men prepare for it, and thus it never comes. But here, though it has been both foreseen and foretold, there is a law passed by a paternal legislature remaining on the statute-book, which says to twenty-seven millions of people, 'Scramble for what there is, and if the poorest and the weakest starve, foreign supplies shall not come in for fear some injury should be done to the mortgaged land-owners.'

Well, if this class of whom I have spoken have maintained this law for thirty years—if they continued it from 1838 to 1842—be assured that no feeling of mercy, no relenting, no sympathy for the sufferings of the people, will weigh one atom in the scale of making them give up the law now. They have no one to whom they can look for a promise to maintain it; but we have some one to whom to look for a promise to repeal it. But the promises of Lord John Russell, or any other minister, are entirely conditional. He knows that he alone can repeal the Corn Law. I had almost said that the overturning of the monarchy would be a trifle compared with the touching of the pockets of the squires. Lord John Russell himself has said that it can only be done by the unequivocal expression of the public will. How is this expression to be made? By meeting such as this, and by the meetings which myself and others have seen in all parts of the kingdom; and also by preparations of the most active character for that general election which, in all human probability, is near upon us.

I believe you have heard that we had a meeting in Manchester the other day, which was attended by more of the wealth and influence of that district than I have ever seen assembled at a meeting of the same numbers before. It was resolved on Tuesday to have a general meeting

of all those who are wishful to support the League in this great and
final struggle. It has been announced that the Council of the League
are calling upon their friends throughout the country to raise a fund
of £250,000 for the purpose of being ready in any emergency, and for
the sake of maintaining before the ranks of the Protectionists, at least,
as bold and resolute a character as we have maintained for the past
seven years. Now, that money will be subscribed as it is required, and
that large sums will be paid, and I can promise this meeting and the
country that it will be honestly and judiciously applied to carry out the
great national object for which the League has been established. If the
Protectionists like to defer the settlement of this question till the warm
weather comes, we will not trouble our friends to tear themselves half
to pieces in getting within the walls of this theatre, but we will ask them
to meet here, in Manchester, Leeds, Glasgow, Sheffield, Birmingham,
and other towns, in numbers so great, in unanimity so remarkable, and
in resolution so undaunted, that the aristocracy of this country, with
all their pride of ancestry and their boasted valour, will quail before
the demonstration that will then be made.

Two centuries ago the people of this country were engaged in a fearful
conflict with the Crown. A despotic and treacherous monarch assumed
to himself the right to levy taxes without the consent of Parliament
and the people. That assumption was resisted. This fair island became
a battle-field, the kingdom was convulsed, and an ancient throne over-
turned. And, if our forefathers two hundred years ago resisted that
attempt—if they refused to be the bondmen of a king, shall we be the
born thralls of an aristocracy like ours? Shall we, who struck the lion
down, shall we pay the wolf homage? or shall we not, by a manly and
united expression of public opinion, at once, and for ever, put an end
to this giant wrong?

Our cause is at least as good as theirs. We stand on higher vantage-
point; we have large numbers at our back; we have more wealth,
intelligence, union, and knowledge of the political rights and the true
interests of the country; and, what is more than all this—we have a
weapon, a power, and machinery, which is a thousand times better than
that of force, were it employed—I refer to the registration, and especially to the forty shillings freehold, for that is the great constitutional
weapon which we intend to wield, and by means of which we are sure
to conquer, our laurels being gained, not in bloody fields, but upon

the hustings and in the registration courts. Now, I hope, that if this law be repealed within the next six months, and if it should then be necessary that this League should disperse, I do trust that the people of England will bear in mind how great a panic has been created among the monopolist rulers by this small weapon, which we have discovered hid in the Reform Act, and in the constitution of the country. I would implore the middle and working classes to regard it as the portal of their deliverance, as the strong and irresistible weapon before which the domination of this hereditary peerage must at length be laid in the dust.

The Angel of Death

Bright opposed the Crimean War because, in his opinion, it was unnecessary. The conduct of the war was incompetent in the extreme. It is often said that Britain enters wars with the ideas and equipment of the previous war. This was certainly so in the Crimean War with Russia. The equipment, the weapons and the training of the soldiers were founded on the lessons of Waterloo. Yet, strangely enough, it was from this war, with all its incompetency and its horror, that the Red Cross movement started. The work of Florence Nightingale led directly to this movement.

Miss Nightingale was in advance of her time in another way. Mid-Victorian England was very much of a man's world. She gave a new status to women. She had succeeded where men had failed.

This speech is one of the most famous speeches ever given in the House of Commons. It was delivered by John Bright on 7th June, 1855, less than a year before the Treaty of Paris, which ended the war in 1856. In it he makes a powerful plea for peace. His reference to the Angel of Death caused a great sensation at the time. A speech of this kind, with its lofty idealism and aspirations, is not an easy one to make. Yet there is not a false note anywhere. It is the speech of a man who can merge poetry with passion.

THERE is one subject upon which I should like to put a question to the noble Lord at the head of the government. I shall not say one word here about the state of the army in the Crimea, or one word about its numbers or its condition. Every Member of this House, every inhabitant of this country, has been sufficiently harrowed with details regarding it. To my solemn belief, thousands—nay, scores of thousands of persons—have retired to rest, night after night, whose slumbers have been disturbed or whose dreams have been based upon the sufferings and agonies of our soldiers in the Crimea. I should like to ask the noble Lord at the head of the government—although I am not sure if he will feel that he can or ought to answer the question—whether the noble Lord the Member for London has power, after discussions have commenced, and as soon as there shall be established good grounds for believing that the negotiations for peace will prove successful, to enter into any armistice? ['No! No!']

I know not, Sir, who it is that says 'No, no,' but I should like to see any man get up and say that the destruction of 200,000 human lives lost on all sides during the course of this unhappy conflict is not a sufficient sacrifice. You are not pretending to conquer territory— you are not pretending to hold fortified or unfortified towns; you have offered terms of peace which, as I understand them, I do not say are not moderate; and breathes there a man in this House or in this country whose appetite for blood is so insatiable that, even when terms of peace have been offered and accepted, he pines for that assault in which of Russian, Turk, French and English, as sure as one man dies, 20,000 corpses will strew the streets of Sebastopol? I say I should like to ask the noble Lord—and I am sure that he will feel, and that this House will feel, that I am speaking in no unfriendly manner towards the government of which he is at the head—I should like to know, and I venture to hope that it is so, if the noble Lord the Member for London has power, at the earliest stage of these proceedings at Vienna, at which it can properly be done—and I should think that it might properly be done at a very early stage—to adopt a course by which all further waste of human life may be put an end to, and further animosity between three great nations be, as far as possible, prevented?

I appeal to the noble Lord at the head of the government and to this House; I am not now complaining of the war—I am not now complaining of the terms of peace, nor, indeed, of anything that has been done—but I wish to suggest to this House what, I believe, thousands and tens of thousands of the most educated and of the most

Christian portion of the people of this country are feeling upon this subject, although, indeed, in the midst of a certain clamour in the country, they do not give public expression to their feelings. Your country is not in an advantageous state at this moment; from one end of the kingdom to the other there is a general collapse of industry. Those Members of this House not intimately acquainted with the trade and commerce of the country do not fully comprehend our position as to the diminution of employment and the lessening of wages. An increase in the cost of living is finding its way to the homes and hearts of a vast number of the labouring population.

At the same time there is growing up—and, notwithstanding what some hon. Members of this House may think of me, no man regrets it more than I do—a bitter and angry feeling against that class which has for a long period conducted the public affairs of this country. I like political changes when such changes are made as the result, not of passion, but of deliberation and reason. Changes so made are safe, but changes made under the influence of violent exaggeration or of the violent passions of public meetings, are not changes usually approved by this House or advantageous to the country. I cannot but notice, in speaking to gentlemen who sit on either side of this House, or in speaking to any one I meet between this House and any of those localities we frequent when this House is up—I cannot, I say, but notice that an uneasy feeling exists as to the news which may arrive by the very next mail from the East. I do not suppose that your troops are to be beaten in actual conflict with the foe, or that they will be driven into the sea; but I am certain that many homes in England in which there now exists a fond hope that the distant one may return—many such homes may be rendered desolate when the next mail shall arrive. The Angel of Death has been abroad throughout the land; you may almost hear the beatings of his wings. There is no one, as when the first-born were slain of old, to sprinkle with blood the lintel and the two sideposts of our doors, that he may spare and pass on; he takes his victims from the castle of the noble, the mansion of the wealthy, and the cottage of the poor and the lowly, and it is on behalf of all these classes that I make this solemn appeal.

BENJAMIN DISRAELI, EARL OF BEACONSFIELD

1804–1881

Peace with Honour

The history of British politics in the latter half of the nineteenth century is dominated by two men: Benjamin Disraeli (later Earl of Beaconsfield) and William Ewart Gladstone.

Disraeli first came into prominence by his opposition to his leader, Sir Robert Peel. The Tory Party was split, and for the next twenty years—except for two short spells of office—it was in opposition. But Disraeli did not waste these years. In his novel Sybil *he pointed out that there were two classes in Britain. As a politician he did not overlook what he had depicted as a writer. In his political life he worked towards the fusion of the classes. He did not fear, as many of his party feared, the extension of the franchise, and it is worth noting that he was responsible for the Franchise Act of 1867.*

His greatest period was during his Premiership of 1874–80. Although he was over seventy and not in good health, he persisted in his idea of a Tory democracy. To do this he had to convince the electorate, now increased by his own Franchise Act of 1867, and also his ultra-Conservative colleagues. With both he was brilliantly successful.

In 1876 trouble broke out in the Balkans. The people of this region groaned under Turkish rule. Slavs, Rumanians and Greeks looked to Russia as their liberator. In 1877 war broke out between Turkey and Russia. In 1878 a Russian army was threatening Constantinople. The Treaty of San Stefano signed in March of that year gave Russia control of the Balkans.

This was unacceptable to Britain. The Congress of Berlin was called, at which Britain was represented by Disraeli, now Earl of Beaconsfield, and the new German Empire by Bismarck. As a result Russia was induced to return much of what she had gained at San Stefano. Russian infiltration into the Balkans was halted.

Beaconsfield returned home claiming that he had brought 'peace with honour'. The country shared these sentiments. He was described as 'the greatest conqueror who had conquered war and brought us back peace'.

Beaconsfield made a speech at the Mansion House, from which this extract is taken. As a speaker, he was detached and often cynical, the master of the literary phrase and the barbed attack. One of his phrases in the second last paragraph of this extract has passed into everyday currency.

WHEN I study the catalogue of congratulatory regrets with attention, the Convention of Constantinople appears to be the ground on which a great assault is to be made on the government. It is said that we have increased, and dangerously increased, our responsibilities as a nation by that Convention. In the first place, I deny that we have increased our responsibilities by that Convention. I maintain that by that Convention we have lessened our responsibilities. Suppose now, for example, the settlement of Europe had not included the Convention of Constantinople and the occupation of the isle of Cyprus; suppose it had been limited to the mere Treaty of Berlin; what, under all probable circumstances, might then have occurred? In ten, fifteen, it might be in twenty, years, the power and resources of Russia having revived, some quarrel would again have occurred, Bulgarian or otherwise, and in all probability the armies of Russia would have been assailing the Ottoman dominions both in Europe and Asia, and enveloping and enclosing the city of Constantinople and its all-powerful position.

Now, what would be the probable conduct, under these circumstances, of the government of this country, whoever the ministers might be, whatever party might be in power? I fear there might be hesitation for a time—a want of decision—a want of firmness; but no one doubts that ultimately England would have said: 'This will never do; we must prevent the conquest of Asia Minor; we must interfere in this matter, and arrest the course of Russia.' No one, I am sure, in this country who impartially considers this question can for a moment doubt what, under any circumstances, would have been the course of this country.

Well, then, that being the case, I say it is extremely important that this country should take a step beforehand which should indicate what the policy of England would be; that you should not have your Ministers meeting in a Council Chamber, hesitating and doubting and considering contingencies, and then acting at last, but perhaps acting too late. I say, therefore, that the responsibilities of this country have not been increased; the responsibilities already existed, though I for one would never shrink from increasing the responsibilities of this country, if they are responsibilities which ought to be undertaken. The responsibilities of this country are practically diminished by the course we have taken.

My lords and gentlemen, one of the results of my attending the Congress of Berlin has been to prove, what I always suspected to be the absolute fact, that neither the Crimean war, nor this horrible devastating war which has just terminated, would have taken place, if England had spoken with the necessary firmness.

Russia has complaints to make against this country that neither in the case of the Crimean war nor on this occasion—and I do not shrink from my share of the responsibility in this matter—was the voice of England so clear and decided as to exercise a due share in the guidance of European opinion.

Suppose, gentlemen, that my noble friend and I had come back with the Treaty of Berlin, and had not taken the step which is to be questioned within the next eight-and-forty hours, could we with any self-respect, have met our countrymen when they asked, what securities have you made for the peace of Europe? How far have you diminished the chance of perpetually recurring war on this question of the East by the Treaty of Berlin? Why, they could say, all we have gained by the Treaty of Berlin is probably the peace of a few years, and at the end of that time the same phenomenon will arise and the Ministers of England must patch up the affair as well as they could.

That was not the idea of public duty entertained by my noble friend and myself. We thought the time had come when we ought to take steps which would produce some order out of the anarchy and chaos that had so long prevailed. We asked ourselves, was it absolutely a necessity that the fairest provinces of the world should be the most devastated and most ill-used, and for this reason that there is no security for life or property so long as that country is in perpetual fear of invasion and aggression?

It was under these circumstances that we recommended the course we have taken; and I believe that the consequences of that policy will tend to and even secure peace and order in a portion of the globe which hither to has seldom been blessed by these celestial visitants.

I hold that we have laid the foundation of a state of affairs which may open a new continent to the civilization of Europe, and that the welfare of the world and the wealth of the world may be increased by availing ourselves of that tranquillity and order which the more intimate connection of England with that country will now produce.

But I am sorry to say that though we taxed our brains and our thought to establish a policy which might be beneficial to the country, we have not satisfied those who are our critics.

I was astonished to learn that the Convention of the fourth of June has been described as 'an insane convention'. It is a strong epithet. I do not myself pretend to be as competent a judge of insanity as my right honourable opponent. I would put this issue to an English jury—Which do you believe the most likely to enter into an insane convention—a body of English gentlemen honoured by the favour of their Sovereign and the confidence of their fellow-subjects, managing your affairs for five years, I hope with prudence, and not altogether without success, or a sophisticated rhetorician, inebriated with the exuberance of his own verbosity, and gifted with an egotistical imagination that can at all times command an interminable and inconsistent series of arguments to malign an opponent and to glorify himself?

My lords and gentlemen, I leave the decision upon that Convention to the Parliament and people of England. I believe that in that policy are deeply laid the seeds of future welfare not merely to England, but to Europe and Asia; and confident that the policy we have recommended is one that will be supported by the country, I and those that act with me can endure these attacks.

WILLIAM EWART GLADSTONE

1809–1898

Speech at Edinburgh, 1879

*William Ewart Gladstone, the Liberal, was the complete antithesis of
Disraeli, the Tory. With his resonant voice and his hawk-like eye he stood
in contrast to the slender, dandified Disraeli. Where Disraeli was cynical
and aloof Gladstone was the embodiment of moral indignation and high
principle. No friendship existed between the two men. Disraeli described
Gladstone as an 'unprincipled maniac'; Gladstone described Disraeli
as 'a man more false than his doctrine'.*

*Yet, between them, they revolutionized English political life and created
the pattern of parliamentary and party government that we know today.
Both men saw that the extension of the franchise had created a new electorate. The new masters were the new voters and legislation had to be
fashioned to meet their needs. In some ways Disraeli the Tory was more
prescient than Gladstone the Liberal.*

*In his direct appeals to the public Gladstone was in advance of Disraeli.
His Midlothian Campaign of 1880 was the first great example of a party
leader explaining his policies to the people. Many were shocked at this.
Queen Victoria herself thought it quite inappropriate that foreign policy
should be expounded from the window of a railway carriage. But Gladstone
realized that the reforms of both Disraeli and himself had produced people
better educated and therefore more fitted to consider the issue of party
politics.*

*In these speeches Gladstone did not underestimate the capacity of the
masses for thought and feeling. His audiences loved him; he was the 'Grand
Old Man'. His photograph was to be found in the majority of Liberal homes.*

*This speech, which was delivered at Edinburgh, marked the start of his
Midlothian Campaign. It is a good example of his style. Here we see the*

*long sentences, the complete certainty of the rightness of his cause and his
moral fervour. At the same time the speech shows how many of Gladstone's
opponents could regard him as being hypocritical.*

MY Lords and Gentlemen—All will feel who are present and all who,
being absent, give any heed to the proceedings of today will feel that
this is not an ordinary occasion. It is not an ordinary occasion which
brings you and me together—me as a candidate for your parliamentary
suffrages, and you, I will not say as solicited by me, for by me you
have not been solicited—but you as the spontaneous and gracious
offerers to me of a trust which I deem it a high duty under these
circumstances to seek, and which I shall deem it the highest honour to
receive. It is not an ordinary occasion, gentlemen, because, as we all
know, the ordinary rule is that in county representation it is customary,
though not invariably the rule—it is customary to choose someone who,
by residence, by property, by constant intercourse, is identified with
the county that he is asked to represent. In these respects I come
among you as a stranger. It is not the first time that such a combination
has been known. On the contrary, it has been, I may say, not unfre-
quent for important counties, and especially for metropolitan counties,
to select those who, in that sense, are strangers to their immediate
locality to be their candidates or to be their representatives in Parliament, but always with a special purpose in view, and that purpose has
been the rendering of some emphatic testimony to some important
public principle. It is not, gentlemen, for the purpose of gratuitously
disturbing your county that I am come among you, for before I could
think it my duty to entertain the wishes so kindly pressed upon me,
I used the very best exertions in my own power, and called in the very
best and most experienced advice at my command, in order that I
might be assured that I was not guilty of creating that wanton disturbance—in truth, that I was to come among you not as an intruder,
not as a voluntary provoker of unnecessary strife, but as the person
who, according to every reasonable principle of evidence, was designated
by the desire of the decided majority of electors as their future representative.

Then, my lords and gentlemen, neither am I here, as I can truly and
cheerfully say, for the purpose of any personal conflict. I will begin

this campaign, if so it is to be called—and a campaign, and an earnest campaign I trust it will be—I will begin by avowing my personal respect for my noble opponent and for the distinguished family to which he belongs. Gentlemen, I have had the honour—for an honour I consider it—to sit as a colleague with the Duke of Buccleuch in the Cabinet of Sir Robert Peel. This is now nearly forty years ago. Since that time I frankly avow that I have changed various opinions; I should say that I have learned various lessons. But I must say, and express it as my distinct and decided conviction, that that noble Duke, who was then my colleague under Sir Robert Peel,[1] has changed like myself, but in an opposite direction, and I believe that on this great occasion he is farther from his old position than I am. Let me, gentlemen, in the face of you who are Liberals, and determined Liberals, let me render this tribute to the memory of Sir Robert Peel. I never knew a more conscientious public man; I never knew—in far the greater portion of questions that concerned the public interest—a more enlightened statesman. And this opinion I give with confidence, in the face of the world, founded upon many years of intimate communication with him upon every subject of public interest; that, could his valuable life have been prolonged to this moment, could he have been called upon to take part, as we are now called upon to take part, in the great struggle which is commencing in this country, Sir Robert Peel would have been found contending along with you against the principles which now specially place you in determined opposition to the government of the day. I render to the Duke of Buccleuch as freely as to Lord Dalkeith this tribute, that he—given and presupposed the misfortune of his false political opinions—is in all respects what a British nobleman ought to be, and sets to us all an example in the active and conscientious discharge of duty, such as he believes duty to be, which we shall do well, from our very different point of view, to follow.

And now I hope I have spoken intelligibly upon that subject, and I will pass on to another which is far less agreeable. I thought when the invitation of the electors of Midlothian was sent to me, that the matter in controversy was one of sufficient breadth and complication, and I then was not aware that it would become still more enhanced and still more entangled by a question which, in its first aspect, was local, but which, in its ulterior aspect, is of the deepest importance, embraces in

---

[1] Gladstone started his political career as a Tory.

its scope the whole country, and descends to the root of our institutions. I thought that in one thing at least my noble opponent and myself were agreed—that is to say, that we were agreed in making a common appeal to the true and legitimate electors of Midlothian. I am grieved to find that that is not to be the case; that, mistrusting the body to whom the constitution and the law had given the power of choice between candidates for Midlothian, an attempt has been made to import into the county a body of strangers, having no natural interest in the county, gifted with colourable qualifications invented by the chicanery of law, and that it is on this body that reliance is placed, in order, perchance, to realize some faint hope of overbearing the true majority of the constituency. I won't dilate, gentlemen, upon that subject—I won't now expatiate upon it—but this I must say, that if anything was wanting to make me feel it more than ever a duty to endeavour to fight the battle with energy and determination, this most unfortunate act was the very thing destined for that purpose. Why, gentlemen, quite apart from every question of principle, nothing, I venture to say, can be so grossly imprudent as that which is familiarly known in homely but most accurate phrase as the manufacture of faggot votes. Those who manufacture faggot votes provoke investigation into the whole state of the law, and of those provisions of the law which at the present moment are framed with such liberality towards the possessors of property.

Why, sirs, is it not enough that the man who happens to have property in six or ten counties can give a vote in respect of that property, in conformity with the rules of the constitution, in every one of those counties? Is it not enough that he who, after all, has only the interests of a citizen in the wellbeing of the country, shall be permitted, by the free assent of all parties, without dishonour, without evasion, to multiply his own individual existence, and to contribute to the issue of six or ten electioneering contests, instead of one? Is not this enough? Is not this sufficiently liberal to the rich man as compared with the poor man, who hardly ever, though he may be a voter, can by possibility have more than a single vote? Ought not the Duke of Buccleuch and his friends to be satisfied with that state of law? Is it not the fact that in this country, although the law refuses to give a double vote in respect of a larger qualification, yet is it not the fact that it is the rarest thing in the world to meet a poor voter who has more than one vote, whereas it is the rarest thing in the world to meet a gentleman voter, as he is called, who has not got more than one vote? Why are they not content with that state of things? Why do they determine upon adding to that lawful multiplication of power, which, I must say, is based upon a remarkable liberality towards the possessors of property? Why, in addition to that, are they determined to aim at an unlawful multiplication of power, and to bring it upon you, the genuine voters of Midlothian, those guests, those foreigners—for foreigners they are— foreigners they are in respect of the concerns of this county—its political concerns—for the purpose of overbearing the genuine and true sense of the constituency? Gentlemen, my anticipation is that this extraordinary manœuvre will utterly, certainly and miserably fail of its purpose. I have not been surprised to be assured by those among you who have interested themselves specially in the affairs of the coming election, that we stand quite as well as we did, or better than we did, before the introduction of these faggot votes. We are divided into parties in this country, and the division is a healthy one. But there is always, at the same time, a certain margin of gentlemen who will have regard to other than party considerations, where they think that some great public principle is at stake; and my belief is that there will be, and must be, many in Midlothian who will not consent to compromise a principle more sacred and more important than any of the ordinary differences of party, namely this, that the representative of each county shall be chosen by the county itself, and shall not be chosen by importations of gentlemen from abroad, brought in to overbear its true and native sense.

THEY ARE NOT ANXIOUS

Well, gentlemen, I pass on from that subject, which you are very capable of handling, and which, I daresay, you will find a good deal to say upon before we have brought this business to a conclusion—I pass on to other matters, and I wish to say a word upon the subject— having thus far spoken of my own personal appearance and its grounds upon the subject of the time at which I appear before you. Why do I come here to trouble you at this time? Are we going to have a dissolution? There is a question of great interest. I won't pretend, gentlemen, to answer it. My belief is that there has been a good deal of consultation in high quarters upon that subject; and observe the reason why there should be, and why there must have been consultation. The reason is plain. It is this: we have arrived at the time wherein, according to the fixed and invariable practice, I think, of the entire century, nay, even of more than the entire century, there ought to be a dissolution. The rule, and the wise rule, of our governors in other times has been, that although the law allows a duration of seven years to Parliament, it should not sit to transact more than the regular business of six sessions. And you will see, gentlemen, the good sense, I think, of such a rule. It appears to be founded upon this, that the operations of the seventh session would be likely to descend as to their moral level below the standard of the earlier portions of a Parliament; that the interests of the country would be more liable to be compromised by personal inducements, and personal inducements not in relation to the country at large, but in relation to particular groups and cliques of persons—in relation to what are sometimes called harassed interests. And matters of that kind would be likely to bring about a bartering and trafficking in public interests for personal ends if it were made absolutely certain that in so many weeks, or in two or three months, the Parliament must be dissolved. Now, out of this has grown a rule; I am far from saying that rule is a rule mathematical or inflexible; for some great public or national reason it is perfectly justifiable to depart from it—but what is the public or national reason for departing from it now? None at all. I defy the most ingenious man to suggest to me any reason whatever for departing from this rule, which has been in use through the whole of our lifetime—I believe even through the lifetime of your fathers and grandfathers. I don't believe the wit of man can give a reason for departing from it except this, that it is thought to be upon the whole for the interests of Her Majesty's Government. That, I say at once, is not a legitimate reason for departing from the constitutional rule.

They have no right to take into view the interests of the government in respect to a question whether a Parliament shall be prolonged beyond the period fixed by long and unbroken usage. They are bound to decide that question upon national and imperial considerations, and if no national or imperial consideration dictates a departure from the rule, they are bound to adhere to the rule. Well, now we are told they mean to break the rule. I can't say I shall be surprised at their breaking the rule of usage, for this government, which delights in the title of Conservative, or rather which was not satisfied with the title of Conservative, but has always fallen back upon the title of Tory—this Tory government, from which we have the right to expect—I would almost say to exact—an extraordinary reverence for everything that was fixed—reverence which has been paid in many instances whether it is good or bad—yet this Tory government has undoubtedly created a greater number of innovations, broken away from a greater number of precedents, set a greater number of new-fangled examples to mislead and bewilder future generations, than any government which has existed in my time. Therefore I am not at all surprised that they should have broken away from a rule of this kind so far as regards the respect due to an established and, on the whole, a reasonable and a useful custom; but at the same time they would not break away without some reason—an illegitimate reason, because one connected with their interests; a strange reason because one would have thought that a government whose proceedings, as will be admitted on all hands, have been of so marked a character, ought to have been anxious at the earliest period permitted by usage to obtain the judgment of the country.

And why, gentlemen, are they not anxious to obtain the judgment of the country? It is surely plain that they are not anxious. If they were anxious, they would follow the rule, and dissolve the Parliament. It is plain, therefore, that they are not anxious. Why are they not anxious? Have they not told us all along that they possess the confidence of the people? Have they not boasted right and left that vast majorities of the nation are in the same sense with themselves? Oh, gentlemen, these are idle pretexts! It is an instinct lying far deeper than those professions that teach them that the country is against them. And it is because they know that the country is against them that they are unwilling to appeal to the country. Why, gentlemen, a dissolution, an appeal to the public judgment, when there is a knowledge beforehand on the part of those who make the appeal that the answer will be favourable, gives additional strength to those who make the appeal. If it be true, as they still say, that the country is in their favour, I say that after the favourable reply that they would receive to their appeal, they would come back to Parliament far stronger for the purpose of giving effect to the principles that they hold to be true, than they are at this moment. They know perfectly well that a favourable appeal would strengthen their hands; they know perfectly well that an unfavourable answer will be the end of their ministerial existence; and it therefore requires no great wit on our part to judge why, when they have reached the usual, and what I may almost call constitutional period, they don't choose to make an appeal at all.

There are some reasons, gentlemen, why they ought to make that appeal which bear on their own party interests. They will not have a very pleasant operation to perform when they produce their next Budget. I am not going to enter into that subject now. You must excuse me if I do not attempt on this occasion to cover the whole of the enormously wide field that is open before me; but I promise, especially as the Chancellor of the Exchequer says it is most agreeable to him that the question of finance should be discussed, and in fact, he has chosen the most extraordinary opportunity, for the first time that I can recollect, for discussing it—namely, at the Lord Mayor's dinner—but as he is so desirous it should be discussed, I, having every disposition to comply with his wishes as far as I can, will certainly endeavour to enter into that matter, and set out the main facts of the case as well as I am able. I do not think there is a great anxiety to produce that Budget; and this of itself would recommend a dissolution.

I tell you, gentlemen, what I think and that is what has led me to dwell at length on the subject of dissolution. It is because it is not a theoretical, but a practical consideration. It is this: we are told by 'whippers-in', and gentlemen who probably have an inspiration that sometimes flows from the higher quarters into those peculiar and favoured channels—we are told that they think there will not be a dissolution for twelve months. Twelve months, gentlemen. There is what is called a 'chapter of accidents', and by postponing the dissolution for twelve months, you get your twelve months of the exercise of power. Now, I am not going to impute to this government, or any government, sordid motives for the desire to retain power. In my opinion, imputations of that kind, which are incessantly made upon me, and incessantly made upon the Liberal Party generally, and especially upon the leaders of the Liberal Party—in my opinion, imputations of that kind are disgraceful only to those who make them.

LORD RUSSELL OF KILLOWEN

1832–1900

The Impartiality of the Law

Charles Russell, who lived to become Lord Russell of Killowen and Lord Chief Justice of England, was born in Ireland. After practising for a short time in Ireland he came to England, where very soon he established himself as one of the leading barristers of the day.

He was a genius in cross-examination, and he could state a case forcibly to a jury. He did not indulge in high-flown oratory, as did so many barristers, and particularly Irish barristers, of the day. He believed that juries were composed of people with common-sense who would base their conclusion on a combination of fact and principle. The following extract, which is taken from his speech made in 1889 *defending Mrs Maybrick on a murder charge, illustrates his methods.*

GENTLEMEN—I have said all that occurs to me to say on this matter. There is nothing of which the people of this island have a greater right to be proud than that settled order of the people and the respect for the law and administration of the law which the people honestly and heartily entertain—which they entertain because they believe the law to be just, because they believe the law to be honestly administered. And there is no more striking scene to the reflective mind than that which is presented on the trial of a criminal case where the charge is a grave one—a judge who tries with certain hands fairly to hold the scales of justice, and a jury, calm, honest, dispassionate, with no desire except to do justice in the case according to their conscientious belief. To this has to be added the fact that the Crown, representing the law in its executive character, conduct their prosecutions in recent years without exception, not as if a great effort was made, as in private litigation, to wrest a verdict, but only so as to lay, as is the duty of those who represent the prosecution, fully and completely and fairly before the jury all the grounds upon which the opinion of the jury should be asked in determining the grave question of guilt or innocence.

In the language of the officer of this Court giving the prisoner in charge to you, he informed you that the prisoner at the bar had put herself upon her country, which country you are. You are in number large enough to prevent—forgive me for suggesting it—the individual views and prejudices or prepossessions of one from affecting all, but in number small enough, limited enough, to preserve to each one of you the undivided sense of individual responsibility. The verdict is to be the verdict of each of you and the verdict of you all. I am not making in this case—let it be clearly understood—an appeal for mercy. You are administering a law which is merciful; you are administering a law which forbids you to pronounce a verdict of guilty unless all other reasonable hypotheses of innocence can be excluded.

Now I end, as I began, by asking you, each one of you, in the perplexities, in the doubts, in the mystery, in the difficulties which surround this case, in view of the contrariety of things and opinions presented to you, upon some points more or less important, can you, can any of you, with satisfied judgment and with safe conscience, say that this woman is guilty? If your duty compels you to do it, you will do it, you must do it. But you cannot, you will not, you must not, unless the whole burthen and facts and weight of the case, fairly and fully considered with honest and impartial minds, drive you, drive you irresistibly to that conclusion.

LORD ROSEBERY

1847-1929

The Freedom of the Press

Lord Rosebery is an example of the thoughtful, scholarly man who was not quite fitted for the rough and tumble of political life. He was Prime Minister for a short period in 1894-5, but political events were too much for him and for his government. Yet Lord Rosebery's speeches are worthy of study. He will always be remembered as the inventor of the word 'Commonwealth' to describe the relationship of Britain with the Dominions overseas.

This speech on the freedom of the Press is a good example of that mixture of charm and thought—and indeed, prophecy—which is characteristic of so many of Lord Rosebery's speeches. It is worth noting that he gave this speech in the year 1913. In 1914 the First World War broke out. In that war the British Press not only maintained its traditions but created new standards of truth and accuracy for the future. One cannot help feeling that Lord Rosebery seemed to know that a new challenge to the Press was imminent.

I HAVE become so rusty in the art of speaking that I feel tonight as though I were delivering my maiden speech. I had indeed hoped to have done with speaking, but remember that years ago your club honoured me with an invitation at the time when I owned a residence near Naples, and I was guiltily conscious of the fact that I preferred going to Naples to attending the dinner. I therefore felt that, if you wished to claim it, you had a mortgage upon my services. Nevertheless, I don't feel in high spirits when approaching an audience which I regard as by far the most difficult that I have ever addressed—a collection of the

cream (if that were not a confusion of metaphor) of that great con-
fraternity, that great freemasonry, which is called the Press, and which
is composed of the most critical, almost cynical (if that adjective were
not offensive), and the most blasé listeners to speeches of which any
audience is composed.

My only comfort is this—that, owing to circumstances, I occupy a
humble place on the slope of the mountain of onlookers of which you
occupy the top. You are critical, you are dispassionate; you sound
occasionally the bugle notes of war and strife from the top of the
mountain, but in the secluded spot which I occupy I have no wish to
stir up strife, and I observe the whole drama in an atmosphere to which
you cannot aspire. During the Crimean War, while fighting took place
on the heights of Alma, it was stated that a hermit lived near the foot
and was totally unconscious for a long time that any war had been
going on. While those present inspired and conducted the contending
forces I am the hermit. It is all very well to be a hermit, but it does not
make the position the less formidable when one has to address an
audience of journalists.

One terror at any rate has been removed. The great terror of every
public speaker in his time has been the reporter. So far as I can make
out, the reporter has largely disappeared. He has ceased to report the
speeches to which it was understood the whole community were looking
forward with breathless interest. He had turned his pencil into a
ploughshare; what he has done with it, I do not exactly know. At any
rate, he has ceased to be that terror to public speakers that he was in
my time; and he no longer reports—except the great lions of the Front
Benches, every wag of whose tail it is necessary for every citizen to
observe.

But at present, outside the proceedings of those great men, reports
have ceased, to the infinite relief, if I may say so, of the speakers. I
speak with feeling as a speaker. No conscientious speaker ever rose in
the morning and read his morning newspaper without having a feeling
of pain, to see in it, reported verbatim, with agonizing conscientiousness, things which he would rather not have said, and things which he
thought ought not to bear repetition. The agonizing conscientiousness
of the reporter caused a reaction in the speaker which no words can
describe, except the testimony of one who had experienced it. Then let
me take the point of view of the reader, which is now my only point of

view. Does any reader of the last twenty years ever read the speeches that are reported? I have no doubt that those whose duty it is to criticize, laud, or rebuke the speakers of the public Press feel it their painful duty to read the speeches. But does anybody else? Does any impartial reader of the newspapers, the man who buys a paper on his way to the City in the morning, and an evening paper in the evening—does he ever read the speeches? I can conscientiously say, having been a speaker myself, that I never could find anybody who read my speeches. It was quite different in the time when I was young, when practically the whole family sat down after breakfast and read the whole debate through. But the present age is in too great a hurry for that. They take the abstract; they may possibly read the abstract of speeches; but I appeal to an intelligent audience when I assert with confidence that not one man in a hundred ever read the speeches which were so largely reported in the Press. Their removal from the Press gave space to other matters of greater interest, and is one of the greatest reliefs the newspaper reader ever experienced.

I always find it a little difficult to know what to say, because the Press, like a great steam engine, is a little sensitive in relation to itself. If the Press were not sensitive it would not have the sympathy of the public— it could not speak with the voice of the nation. Those who would speak to journalists have only one safe course; they must adhere to certain principles. They must assert the power of the Press, they must assert the potentiality of the Press, they must assert the responsibility of the Press, and, fourthly, they must assert in the strongest language possible that the British Press is the best and cleanest in the world. To all those four principles I give my conscientious adherence. I believe in the power of the Press. I believe in the potentiality of the Press even more. I believe even more in the responsibility of the Press: and I believe most of all that the British Press is the best and cleanest in the world. But I am not quite sure that that covers the whole ground. There are two other things to be observed. One is (and it is no new one) the enormous monopoly which is now exercised by the Press. The great daily newspapers have such a monopoly, owing to the enormous cost of founding new ones, which is obvious to you all. I do not know what the cost is, but I have heard it put at from a half to three-quarters of a million, and even then with indifferent chances of success. Owing to the monopoly which is possessed and exercised by the principal daily newspapers of this country, their responsibility is greater than that of the newspaper of forty or fifty years ago.

THE DEVELOPMENT OF THE PRESS

Secondly, I would point out the great development of the Press. As far as I have been able to trace the origin of the Press, it dates from the threat of the Spanish Armada in 1588. It was then a mere fly-sheet, but it showed what was necessary or interesting to the people of this country. Now, every day journalists produce, not a newspaper, but a library, a huge production of information and knowledge upon every kind of subject. It may not be invidious to refer to one particular newspaper, though I know it will be a thorny subject. Take *The Times*, when it issued its South American Supplement. It was a weighty business—I have not perused it myself, but it contains, I imagine, every possible act that could ever be known about South America. It weighed about one hundredweight. That is an extreme case, but it appealed to me on more than one occasion. If you consider that prodigious mass of information, that huge concretion of knowledge, launched upon the British public as a newspaper—and that is what the British public now expects—and just contrast that with anything that was known before these days, and I think it involves a great responsibility, that Niagara of information which is poured upon the British public every day, as well as conferring some benefit. The Press enables us to know, as far as it is possible, everything about everybody and everywhere. Let me take my point about the responsibility of the Press with regard to its omniscience. We hear a great deal about the apathy of the population about great questions. I think it is perfectly true. There is a profound apathy. People have no time to bother about anything except their own concerns and the last football match.

But is not that due to the prodigious amount of news, startling news very often, which the Press affords every inhabitant of these islands who buys a newspaper? Is it not the fact that it must be so—one feels that it must—that if a great number of impressions are hastily and successively made on the receptivity of the brain, those impressions are blunted, until the mental constitution becomes apathetic about other pieces of news? Do you not yourselves feel that, except, possibly, the blowing up of the Tower of London, there is hardly anything in the world tonight that could make you feel that anything great had occurred? How is it possible that a population, nurtured and fed on that perfect journalism, should have the slightest interest in any possible event that might occur on the morrow?

A hundred years ago there were two wars, one a great war and the other not so great, but very galling—the one with the United States of America and the other the great struggle to try to beat down the super-man Napoleon. Then the public had no interest in the world, nothing reported, except with regard to those two wars. I think that if we realized the difference between the journalism of those days and the journalism of the present day we should feel that the responsibility for the apathy of the country as regards public questions is largely due to the perfection to which journalism has been brought. In those far-off days there was the meagre sheet, which was issued two or three times a week, and the demands of war had practically shut three continents out from our purview altogether, whereas now we hear daily and hourly every item of news about every country and every person all over the world. Therefore, I say that the responsibility for the apathy of our people about public events must rest largely with the perfection of the Press. That being the case, at any rate this could be done—the influence of the great newspapers of this country could be made the best and most beneficent for the people who receive them.

Gentlemen, I do not wish to detain you, but it is perhaps the last time I shall address an assembly of journalists—or perhaps any assembly at all. I do not think I should choose an assembly of journalists, with that critical eye, for the one I should habitually address, but I wish to say one word more, in case I should never have again an opportunity to address an assembly of journalists. I speak very warmly and very sincerely when I say that your power and potentialities appeal to me more than anything else with regard to journalism. Your power is obviously enormous and you must wish to exercise it with that con-scientiousness and honour, as I believe you do exercise it; but the potentiality is something which I am not sure that even you always realize. I take it in regard to one question, the question of peace and war.

In some respects I do not suppose you have so much influence as Parliament; I do not suppose you have so much influence as Ministers. There was a famous saying attributed to a notable Scotsman[1] two

[1] Andrew Fletcher of Saltoun.

hundred years ago, that he knew a wise man who said that if they would let him have the writing of the ballads of the country he did not very much care who made the laws. Well, ballads do not matter much, but newspapers do, and I should agree with that sentiment if you substituted the word 'newspapers' for 'ballads'. Your power is enormous. As you give to the people you receive back from the people mutual electricity, which gives you your power.

All that is a commonplace. But with regard to peace and war there is no commonplace. With regard to legislation and so forth, you probably have not so much power as Ministers or Members of Parliament, except when you embody the unmistakable voice of the people. With regard to peace and war, upon those issues you have paramount influence—far greater than any Member of Parliament, as great as any Minister of the Crown himself. When critical occasions arise you can either magnify them or minimize them. I pray you in issues which involve peace and war diminish them as much as possible. Think what an awful responsibility is on you!

I think you have the power more than any other body of men to promote or to avert the horrors of war. I am quite sure that my humble advice is not needed by men who know their business so much better than I can know it, but they may sometimes, in the hurry of journalism —because it is a hurried profession—forget the great principles which must be inherent in the journalist. As they write, they may on impulse of the moment, in defence against the aggressive journalism from abroad, forget their obligation to their own country. And I would ask them in these few last words, when any such issue may occur, and God knows the atmosphere is electrical enough at this moment, not to say a word that may unnecessarily, or except in defence, bring about to their fellow-countrymen the innumerable catastrophes of war.

LORD OXFORD AND ASQUITH

1852–1928

A Call to Arms

At the outbreak of the First World War in August, 1914, Mr H. H. Asquith (later Lord Oxford and Asquith) was Prime Minister. Upon him and his Foreign Secretary, Sir Edward Grey, lay the terrible responsibility of entering upon the war with Germany.

Asquith, the leader of the Liberal Party, was a classical scholar of high attainment. His speeches show the influence of his classical education. They all have the Latin quality of 'gravitas'. They are carefully constructed upon the models of Greece and Rome.

One of the characteristics of Asquith's severely classical style is the manner in which he adds point after point in a long sentence, ending in a climax. The last sentence of the first paragraph is a good example of this. Also it is worth noting the way in which he balances one idea against another: 'silent witness' and 'willing accomplice'; 'triumph of force over law' and 'brutality over freedom'; 'honour and dishonour' and 'treachery and good faith'.

Asquith made no concessions to his audience. He spoke in this severely classical style because his mind could imagine no other. This speech, which was delivered at the Mansion House, London, a month after the outbreak of the First World War, shows the virtues—and the limitations—of the classical style of oratory in the modern world.

IT is three and a half years since I last had the honour of addressing in this hall a gathering of the citizens. We were then meeting under the presidency of one of your predecessors men of all creeds and parties, to celebrate and approve the joint declaration of the two great English speaking States that for the future any differences between them should be settled, if not by agreement, at least by judicial inquiry and arbitration, and never in any circumstances by war. Those of us who hailed that great eirenicon between the United States and ourselves as a landmark on the road of progress were not sanguine enough to think, or even to hope, that the era of war was drawing to a close. But still less were we prepared to anticipate the terrible spectacle which now confronts us—a contest, which for the number and importance of the Powers engaged, the scale of their armaments and armies, the width of the theatre of conflict, the outpouring of blood and loss of life, the incalculable toll of suffering levied upon non-combatants, the material and moral loss accumulating day by day to the higher interests of civilized mankind—a contest which in every one of these aspects is without precedent in the annals of the world.

We were very confident three years ago in the rightness of our position when we welcomed the new securites for peace. We are equally confident in it today, when reluctantly, and against our will, but with clear judgment and a clean conscience, we find ourselves involved with the whole strength of this Empire in this bloody arbitrament between might and right. The issue has passed out of the domain of argument into another field. But let me ask you, and through you the world outside, what would have been our condition as a nation today, if through timidity, or through a perverted calculation of self-interest, or through a paralysis of the sense of honour and duty, we had been base enough to be false to our word, and faithless to our friends? Our eyes would have been turned at this moment with those of the whole civilized world to Belgium, a small State, which has lived for more than seventy years under a several and collective guarantee to which we, in common with Prussia and Austria, were parties. We should have seen, at the instance and by the action of two of those guaranteeing Powers, her neutrality violated, her independence strangled, her territory made use of as affording the easiest and most convenient road to a war of unprovoked aggression against France. We, the British people, should at this moment have been standing by, with folded arms and with such countenance as we could command, while this small and unprotected State, in defence of her vital liberties, made a heroic stand against overweening and overwhelming force. We should have been admiring as detached spectators the siege of Liège, the steady and manful resistance of a small army, the occupation of Brussels with all its splendid traditions and memories, the gradual forcing back of the patriotic defenders of their fatherland to the ramparts of Antwerp, countless outrages suffered by them, buccaneering levies exacted from the unoffending civil population, and, finally, the greatest crime committed against civilization and culture since the Thirty Years' War, the sack of Louvain, with its buildings, its pictures, its unique library, its unrivalled associations, a shameless holocaust of irreparable treasures, lit up by blind barbarian vengeance. What account could we, the government and the people of this country, have been able to render to the tribunal of our national conscience and sense of honour, if, in defiance of our plighted and solemn obligations, we had endured, and had not done our best to prevent, yes, to avenge, these intolerable wrongs? For my part, I say that sooner than be a silent witness, which means in effect a willing accomplice, to this tragic triumph of force over law, and brutality over freedom, I would see this country of ours blotted out of the pages of history.

That is only a phase, a lurid and illuminating phase, in the contest into which we have been called by the mandate of duty and of honour to bear our part. The cynical violation of the neutrality of Belgium was not the whole, but a step, a first step, in a deliberate policy of which, if not the immediate, the ultimate and not far distant aim was to crush the independence and the autonomy of the Free States of Europe. First Belgium, then Holland and Switzerland, countries like our own, imbued and sustained with the spirit of liberty, were, one after another, to be bent to the yoke. And these ambitions were fed and fostered by a body of new doctrine, a new philosophy, preached by professors and learned men. The free and full self-development which to these small States, to ourselves, to our great and growing Dominions over the seas, to our kinsmen across the Atlantic, is the well-spring and life-breath of national existence, that free self-development is the one capital offence in the code of those who have made force their supreme divinity, and upon its altars they are prepared to sacrifice both the gathered fruits and the potential germs of the unfettered human spirit. I use this language advisedly. This is not merely a material, it is also a spiritual conflict. Upon its issue everything that contains the promise of hope, that leads to emancipation and a fuller liberty for the millions who make up the mass of mankind, will be found sooner or later to depend.

Let me now turn for a moment to the actual situation in Europe. How do we stand? For the last ten years by what I believe to be happy and well-considered diplomatic arrangements we have established friendly and increasingly intimate relations with the two Powers, France and Russia, with whom in days gone by we have had in various parts of the world occasion for constant friction, and now and again for possible conflict. These new and better relations, based in the first instance upon business principles of give and take, matured into a settled temper of confidence and goodwill. They were never in any sense or at any time, as I have frequently stated in this hall, directed against other Powers.

One Power and One Power Only

No man in the history of the world has ever laboured more strenuously or more successfully than my right hon. friend Sir Edward Grey for that which is the supreme interest of the modern world—a general and abiding peace. It is, I venture to think, a very superficial criticism which suggests that under his guidance the policy of this country has ignored, still less that it has counteracted and hampered, the Concert of Europe. It is little more than a year ago when under the stress and strain of the Balkan crisis, the Ambassadors of the Great Powers met here day after day and week after week, curtailing the area of possible differences, reconciling, warning ambitions and aims, and preserving against almost incalculable odds the general harmony, and it was in the same spirit and with the same purpose when a few weeks ago Austria delivered her ultimatum to Serbia that the Foreign Secretary—for it was he—put forward the proposal for a mediating conference between the four Powers not directly concerned, Germany, France, Italy, and ourselves. If that proposal had been accepted the actual controversy would have been settled with honour to everybody, and the whole of this terrible welter would have been avoided. And with whom does the responsibility rest for its refusal and for all the illimitable sufferings which now confront the world? One Power, and one Power only, and that Power is Germany. There is the foundation and origin of this world-wide catastrophe. We persevered to the end, and no one who has not been confronted, as we were, with the responsibility, which unless you had been face to face with it you could not possibly measure, the responsibility of determining the issues of peace and war—no one who has not been in that position can realize the strength, energy, and persistence with which we laboured for peace. We persevered by every expedient that diplomacy could suggest—straining almost to the breaking point our most cherished friendships and obligations—even to the last moment making effort upon effort, and indulging hope against hope. Then, and only then, when we were at last compelled to realize that the choice lay between honour and dishonour, between treachery and good faith—when we at last reached the dividing line which makes or mars a nation worthy of the name, it was then only that we declared for war.

Is there anyone in this hall, or in this United Kingdom, or in the vast Empire of which we here stand in the capital and centre, who blames us or repents our decision? If not, as I believe there is not, we must steel ourselves to the task, and, in the spirit which animated our forefathers in their struggle against the dominion of Napoleon, we must, and we shall, persevere to the end.

I say nothing more, because I think we should bear in mind, all of us, that we are at present watching the fluctuation of fortune only in the early stages of what is going to be a protracted struggle. We must learn to take long views and to cultivate above all other qualities—those of patience, endurance, and steadfastness.

Meanwhile, let us go, each one of us, to his or her appropriate part in the great common task.

Never had a people more or richer sources of encouragement and inspiration. Let us realize, first of all, that we are fighting as a United Empire, in a cause worthy of the highest traditions of our race. Let us keep in mind the patient and indomitable seamen who never relax for a moment, night or day, their stern vigil on the lonely sea. Let us keep in mind our gallant troops, who today, after a fortnight's continuous fighting under conditions which would try the mettle of the best army that ever took the field, maintain not only an undefeated but an unbroken front.

Finally, let us recall the memories of the great men and the great deeds of the past, commemorated some of them in the monuments which we see around us on these walls, not forgetting the dying message of the younger Pitt—his last public utterance, made at the table of your predecessor, my Lord Mayor, in this very hall, 'England has saved herself by her exertions and will, as I trust, save Europe by her example'. The England of those days gave a noble answer to his appeal and did not sheathe the sword until after nearly twenty years of fighting the freedom of Europe was secured. Let us go and do likewise.

EARL LLOYD GEORGE

1863-1945

An Appeal to the Nation

Mr David Lloyd George (later Earl Lloyd George) was Chancellor of the Exchequer in Asquith's government at the outbreak of the First World War. As the war continued it was felt that Asquith's conduct of the war was not vigorous enough, and in 1916 Lloyd George became Prime Minister in a Coalition Government.

Lloyd George was the complete antithesis of Asquith. He was energetic and bustling where Mr Asquith was slow and deliberate; he was witty and humorous where Mr Asquith was grave and serious; he was attentive to public opinion where Mr Asquith was indifferent to it.

There is no doubt that Lloyd George was a great war leader. Pitt, Lloyd George and Churchill are the supreme examples of men who, working through the machinery of Parliament, directed and controlled the resources of their country in the successful prosecution of a great war.

Lloyd George's speeches are of interest to the student of oratory. In literary quality they are not so good as those of Asquith. There is nothing of classical restraint and reticence in them. They are vivid and sometimes flamboyant. He realized, as Asquith failed to realize, that the conduct of a war in which all sections of the community were involved, and where the casualties were appalling, required that ordinary people should be sustained and encouraged. The emergence of the popular Press meant that speeches were reported, and, in consequence, read by a wider audience than the audience who actually heard the speech. Lloyd George also realized that the caption and the headline which break up columns of type would be remembered when the speech was forgotten. In all his war-time speeches we find short, sharp, pithy remarks which were often headlined.

It would be wrong to dismiss some of his tricks of expression and manner as the tricks of the demagogue. In his speeches, bridges are always being built, the light is always seen at the end of dark tunnels and clouds are for ever rolling away. He himself believed that these things were happening, and in a war, where, until the closing months, defeat and disaster were ever-present possibilities, it says much for his buoyancy of spirit and his boundless courage that he could speak with such hope.

The first speech, delivered at Queen's Hall, London, was in September, 1914, while he was still Chancellor of the Exchequer. Note the homely illustrations which he uses to make his points, and the peroration in which he recalls his boyhood in North Wales.

THERE is no man in this room who has always regarded the prospect of engaging in a great war with greater reluctance and with greater repugnance than I have done throughout the whole of my political life. There is no man either inside or outside this room more convinced that we could not have avoided it without national dishonour. I am fully alive to the fact that every nation that has ever engaged in war has always invoked the sacred name of honour. Many a crime has been committed in its name; there are some being committed now. All the same, national honour is a reality, and any nation that disregards it is doomed. Why is our honour as a country involved in this war? Because, in the first instance, we are bound by honourable obligations to defend the independence, the liberty, the integrity, of a small neighbour that has always lived peaceably. She could not have compelled us; she was weak; but the man who declines to discharge his duty because his creditor is too poor to enforce it is a blackguard. We entered into a treaty—a solemn treaty—two treaties—to defend Belgium and her integrity. Our signatures are attached to the documents. Our signatures do not stand there alone; this country was not the only country that undertook to defend the integrity of Belgium. Russia, France, Austria, Prussia—they are all there. Why are Austria and Prussia not performing the obligations of their bond? It is suggested that when we quote this treaty it is purely an excuse on our part—it is our low craft and cunning to cloak our jealousy of a superior civilization—that we are attempting to destroy.

It is the interest of Prussia to break the treaty, and she has done it. She avows it with cynical contempt for every principle of justice. She says, 'Treaties only bind you when it is your interest to keep them.' 'What is a treaty?' says the German Chancellor. 'A scrap of paper.' Have you any £5 notes about you? I am not calling for them. Have you any of those neat little Treasury £1 notes? If you have, burn them; they are only scraps of paper. What are they made of? Rags. What are they worth? The whole credit of the British Empire. Scraps of paper! I have been dealing with scraps of paper within the last month. One suddenly found the commerce of the world coming to a standstill. The machine had stopped. Why? I will tell you. We discovered—many of us for the first time, for I do not pretend that I do not know much more about the machinery of commerce today than I did six weeks ago, and there are many others like me—we discovered that the machinery of commerce was moved by bills of exchange. I have seen some of them—wretched, crinkled, scrawled over, blotched, frowsy, and yet those wretched little scraps of paper move great ships laden with thousands of tons of precious cargo from one end of the world to the other. What is the motive power behind them? The honour of commercial men.

Treaties are the currency of international statesmanship. Let us be fair: German merchants, German traders, have the reputation of being as upright and straightforward as any traders in the world but if the currency of German commerce is to be debased to the level of that of her statesmanship, no trader from Shanghai to Valparaiso will ever look at a German signature again. This doctrine of the scrap of paper, this doctrine which is proclaimed by Bernhardi, that treaties only bind a nation as long as it is to its interest, goes under the root of all public law. It is the straight road to barbarism. It is as if you were to remove the Magnetic Pole because it was in the way of a German cruiser. The whole navigation of the seas would become dangerous, difficult and impossible; and the whole machinery of civilization will break down if this doctrine wins in this way. We are fighting against barbarism and there is one way of putting it right. If there are nations that say they will only respect treaties when it is to their interest to do so, we must make it to their interest to do so for the future.

They think we cannot beat them. It will not be easy. It will be a long job; it will be a terrible war; but in the end we shall march through terror to triumph. We shall need all our qualities—every quality that Britain and its people possess—prudence in counsel, daring in action, tenacity in purpose, courage in defeat, moderation in victory; in all things faith.

A Sheltered Valley

The people will gain more by this struggle in all lands than they comprehend at the present moment. It is true they will be free of the greatest menace to their freedom. That is not all. There is something infinitely greater and more enduring which is emerging already out of this great conflict—a new patriotism, richer, nobler, and more exalted than the old. I see amongst all classes, high and low, shedding themselves of selfishness, a new recognition that the honour of the country does not depend merely on the maintenance of its glory in the stricken field, but also in protecting its homes from distress. It is bringing a new outlook for all classes. The great flood of luxury and sloth which had submerged the land is receding, and a new Britain is appearing. We can see for the first time the fundamental things that matter in life, and that have been obscured from our vision by the tropical growth of prosperity.

May I tell you in a simple parable what I think this war is doing for us? I know a valley in North Wales, between the mountains and the sea. It is a beautiful valley, snug, comfortable, sheltered by the mountains from all the bitter blasts. But it is very enervating, and I remember how the boys were in the habit of climbing the hill above the village to have a glimpse of the great mountains in the distance, and to be stimulated and freshened by the breezes which came from the hilltops, and by the great spectacle of their grandeur. We have been living in a sheltered valley for generations. We have been too comfortable and too indulgent—many, perhaps, too selfish—and the stern hand of Fate has scourged us to an elevation where we can see the great everlasting things that matter for a nation—the great peaks we had forgotten, of Honour, Duty, Patriotism, and, clad in glittering white, the great pinnacle of Sacrifice pointing like a rugged finger to Heaven. We shall descend into the valleys again; but as long as the men and women of this generation last, they will carry in their hearts the image of those great mountain peaks whose foundations are not shaken, though Europe rock and sway in the convulsions of a great war.

The New World

The following speech illustrates the qualities which made Lloyd George a great war leader. It was delivered in London on 14th December, 1917.

The date is worth noting. The year 1917 had been a critical year for Great Britain and her allies. On the Western Front there had been a near-mutiny in the French Army. The great battle of Passchendaele had fought itself to a standstill in mud and blood. The casualties in the British Army had been enormous. On the Eastern Front, Germany had defeated Russia, and the German armies which had been engaged on that Front were now being re-deployed and re-equipped to do battle in the West. The only gleam of hope from the British point of view lay in the fact that in 1917 the United States of America had joined the allies in the struggle with Germany.

Everyone knew that 1918 would be a decisive year. Everyone knew that the German armies in their full strength would be hurled against the British and French lines. Would American reinforcements arrive in time? No certain answer could be given to that question, for America was quite unprepared to fight a European war.

As Prime Minister, Lloyd George knew the desperate straits in which Britain and her allies found themselves. He, more than anyone, knew the full extent of the disasters of 1917. Yet in this speech there is no hint of despondency or defeatism. It is a warning against over-optimism and also against pessimism. With the simple, homely illustration of the clock he tells the people, 'We must go through all the hours. . . .'

WE are laying surely the foundation of the bridge which, when it is complete, will carry us into the new world. The river is, for the moment, in spate, and some of the scaffolding has been carried away and much of the progress we have made seems submerged and hidden, and there are men who say: 'Let us abandon the enterprise altogether. It is too costly. It is impracticable of achievement. Let us rather build a pontoon bridge of new treaties, league of nations, understanding.' It might last you some time. It would always be shaky and uncertain. It would not bear much strain. It would not carry heavy traffic, and the first flood would sweep it away. Let us get along with the pile-driving and make a real solid permanent structure.

There are people who are too apt at one moment to get unduly elated at victories, which are but incidents in the great march of events, and the same people get unwholesomely depressed by defeats which again are nothing more than incidents. . . . They remind me of a clock I used to pass at one time in my life almost every day. It worried me a great deal, for whatever the time of day, it always pointed to twelve o'clock. If you trusted that clock you would have believed it was either noon or midnight. There are people of that type in this war who at one moment point to the high noon of triumph and the next to the black midnight of defeat or despair. There is no twilight. There is no morning. They can claim a certain consistency, for they are always at twelve; but you will find that their mainspring in this war is out of repair. We must go through all the hours, minute by minute, second by second, with a steady swing, and the hour of the dawn will in due time strike.

We have all been dreaming of a new world to appear when the deluge of war has subsided. Unless we achieve victory for the great cause for which we entered this war, the new world will simply be the old world with the heart out of it.

The old world, at least, believed in ideals. It believed that justice, fair play, liberty, righteousness must triumph in the end; that is, however you interpret the phrase, the old world believed in God, and it staked its existence on that belief. Millions of gallant young men volunteered to die for that divine faith. But if wrong emerged triumphant out of this conflict, the new world would feel in its soul that brute force alone counted in the government of man; and the hopelessness of the Dark Ages would once more fall on the earth like a cloud. To redeem Britain, to redeem Europe, to redeem the world from this doom must be the settled purpose of every man and woman who places duty above ease. This is the fateful hour of mankind. If we are worthy of the destiny with which it is charged, untold generations of men will thank God for the strength which He gave us to endure to the end.

SIR JAMES M. BARRIE

1860–1937

Courage

Sir James M. Barrie is best known today as the author of Peter Pan. *In 1922, as Lord Rector of St. Andrews University, he gave an address on 'Courage' which, at the time, was recognized in every way to be a great speech.*

Barrie's humour was whimsical and elfin. Although the theme of 'Courage' is a serious one, his delicate humour runs through the speech. He introduced a new character in M'Connachie. According to Barrie it was M'Connachie, his alter ego, who led him into authorship.

The speech is a good example of the literary speech. It is full of allusions to literature. There are many memorable phrases in it, e.g., the lovely virtue. It is carefully presented. One must also remember in reading a speech that sometimes an action can give an added effect. When this speech was delivered Barrie paused at the part beginning 'I should like to read you some passages of a letter'. He put his hand into a pocket and appeared to search for the letter. Then he held it up: 'I have the little filmy sheets here.' After another pause he described its long journey. Then, and only then, did he reveal that it was a letter sent to him by his personal friend Captain R. F. Scott, who, ten years previously, had perished in the Antarctic after his discovery of the South Pole.

You have had many Rectors here in St. Andrews who will continue in bloom long after the lowly ones such as I am, are dead and rotten and forgotten. They are the roses in December; you remember someone said that God gave us memory so that we might have roses in December. But I do not envy the great ones. In my experience—and you may find in the end it is yours also—the people I have cared for most and who have seemed most worth caring for—my December roses—have been very simple folk. Yet I wish that for this hour I could swell into someone of importance, so as to do you credit. I suppose you had a melting for me because I was hewn out of one of your own quarries, walked similar academic groves, and trudged the road on which you will soon set forth. I would that I could put into your hands a staff for that somewhat bloody march, for though there is much about myself that I conceal from other people, to help you I would expose every cranny of my mind.

But, alas, when the hour strikes for the Rector to answer to his call he is unable to become the undergraduate he used to be, and so the only door into you is closed. We, your elders, are much more interested in you than you are in us. We are not really important to you. I have utterly forgotten the address of the Rector of my time, and even who he was, but I recall vividly climbing up a statue to tie his colours round its neck and being hurled therefrom with contumely. We remember the important things. I cannot provide you with that staff for your journey; but perhaps I can tell you a little about it, how to use it and lose it and find it again, and cling to it more than ever. You shall cut it—so it is ordained—every one of you for himself, and its name is courage. You must excuse me if I talk a good deal about courage to you today. There is nothing else much worth speaking about to undergraduates or graduates or white-haired men and women. It is the lovely virtue—the rib of Himself that God sent down to His children.

My special difficulty is that though you have had literary Rectors here before, they were the big guns, the historians, the philosophers; you have had none, I think, who followed my more humble branch, which may be described as playing hide and seek with angels. My puppets seem more real to me than myself, and I could get on much more swingingly if I made one of them deliver this address. It is M'Connachie who has brought me to this pass. M'Connachie, I should explain, as I have undertaken to open the innermost doors, is the name I give to the unruly half of myself; the writing half. We are complement and supplement. I am the half that is dour and practical and canny, he is the fanciful half; my desire is to be the family solicitor, standing firm on my hearth rug among the harsh realities of the office furniture; while he prefers to fly around on one wing. I should not mind him doing that, but he drags me with him. I have sworn that M'Connachie shall not interfere with this address today, but there is no telling. I might have done things worth while if it had not been for M'Connachie, and my first piece of advice to you at any rate shall be sound: don't copy me. A good subject for a rectorial address would be the mess the Rector himself has made of life. I merely cast this forth as a suggestion, and leave the working of it out to my successor. I do not think it has been used yet.

My own theme is Courage, as you should use it in the great fight that seems to me to be coming between youth and their betters; by youth, meaning, of course, you, and by your betters, us. I want you to take up this position: That youth have for too long left exclusively in our hands the decisions in national matters that are more vital to them than to us. Things about the next war, for instance, and why the last one ever had a beginning. I use the word fight because it must, I think, begin with a challenge; for the aim is the reverse of antagonism, it is partnership. I want you to hold that the time has arrived for youth to demand a partnership, and to demand it courageously. That to gain courage is what you come to St. Andrews for; with some alarums into college life. That is what I propose, but, of course, the issue lies with M'Connachie.

You are already disturbing your betters considerably. I sometimes talk this over with M'Connachie, with whom, as you may guess, circumstances compel me to pass a good deal of my time. In our talks we agree that we, your betters, constantly find you forgetting that we are your betters. Your answer is that the war and other happenings have shown you that age is not necessarily another name for sapience; that our avoidance of frankness in life and in the arts is often, but not so often as you think, a cowardly way of shirking unpalatable truths, and that you have taken us off our pedestals because we look more natural on the ground. You who are at the rash age even accuse your elders, sometimes not without justification, of being more rash than yourselves. 'If Youth but only knew', we used to teach you to sing; but now, just because Youth has been to the war, it wants to change the next line into 'If Age had only to do'.

In so far as this attitude of yours is merely passive, sullen, negative, as it mainly is, despairing of our capacity and anticipating a future of gloom, it is no game for man or woman. It is certainly the opposite of that for which I plead. Do not stand aloof, despising, disbelieving, but come in and help—insist on coming in and helping. After all, we have shown a good deal of courage; and your part is to add a greater courage to it. There are glorious years lying ahead of you if you choose to make them glorious. God's in His Heaven still. So forward, brave hearts, to what adventures I cannot tell, but I know that your God is watching to see whether you are adventurous.

EXAMPLES OF COURAGE

If you want an example of courage try Henley, or Stevenson. I could tell you some stories about these two, but they would not be dull enough for a rectorial address. For courage, again, take Meredith, whose laugh was 'as broad as a thousand beeves at pasture'. Take, as I think, the greatest figure literature has still left to us, to be added today to the roll of St. Andrews' alumni, though it must be in absence. The pomp and circumstance of war will pass and all others now alive may fade from the scene, but I think the quiet figure of Hardy[1] will live on.

I seem to be taking all my examples from the calling I was lately pretending to despise. I should like to read you some passages of a letter from a man of another calling, which I think will hearten you. I have the little filmy sheets here. I thought you might like to see the actual letter; it has been a long journey; it has been to the South Pole. It is a letter to me from Captain Scott of the Antarctic, and was written in the tent you know of, where it was found long afterwards with his body and those of some other very gallant gentlemen, his comrades. The writing is in pencil, still quite clear, though towards the end some of the words trail away as into the great silence that was waiting for them. It begins: 'We are pegging out in a very comfortless spot. Hoping this letter may be found and sent to you, I write you a word of farewell. I want you to think well of me and my end.' (After some private instructions too intimate to read, he goes on): 'Good-bye—I am not at all afraid of the end, but sad to miss many a simple pleasure which I had planned for the future in our long marches. . . . We are in a desperate state—feet frozen, etc., no fuel, and a long way from food, but it would do your

---

[1] Thomas Hardy, the poet and novelist, was invested with the honorary degree of LL.D. by St. Andrews University.

heart good to be in our tent, to hear our songs and our cheery conversation. . . .' Later—(it is here that the words become difficult)—'We are very near the end . . . We did intend to finish ourselves when things proved like this, but we have decided to die naturally without.'

I think it may uplift you all to stand for a moment by that tent and listen, as he says, to their songs and cheery conversation. When I think of Scott I remember the strange Alpine story of the youth who fell down a glacier and was lost, and of how a scientific companion, one of several who accompanied him, all young, computed that the body would again appear at a certain date and place many years afterwards. When that time came round some of the survivors returned to the glacier to see if the prediction would be fulfilled; all old men now; and the body reappeared as young as on the day he left them. So Scott and his comrades emerge out of the white immensities always young.

How comely a thing is affliction borne cheerfully, which is not beyond the reach of the humblest of us. What is beauty? It is these hard-bitten men singing courage to you from their tent; it is the waves of their island home crooning of their deeds to you who are to follow them. Sometimes beauty boils over and then spirits are abroad. Ages may pass as we look or listen, for time is annihilated. There is a very old legend told to me by Nansen the explorer—I like well to be in the company of explorers—the legend of a monk who had wandered into the fields and a lark began to sing. He had never heard a lark before, and he stood there entranced until the bird and its song had become part of the heavens. Then he went back to the monastery and found there a doorkeeper whom he did not know and who did not know him. Other monks came, and they were all strangers to him. He told them he was Father Anselm, but that was no help. Finally, they looked through the books of the monastery, and these revealed that there had been a Father Anselm there a hundred or more years before. Time had been blotted out while he listened to the lark.

That, I suppose, was a case of beauty boiling over, or a soul boiling over; perhaps the same thing. Then spirits walk.

Make merry while you may. Yet light-heartedness is not for ever and a day. At its best it is the gay companion of innocence; and when innocence goes—as go it must—they soon trip off together, looking for something younger. But courage comes all the way:

'Fight on, my men, says Sir Andrew Barton,
I am hurt, but I am not slaine;
I'll lie me down and bleed a-while,
And then I'll rise and fight againe.'

Another piece of advice; almost my last. For reasons you may guess I must give this in a low voice. Beware of M'Connachie. When I look in a mirror now it is his face I see. I speak with his voice. I once had a voice of my own, but nowadays I hear it from far away only, a melancholy, lonely, lost little pipe. I wanted to be an explorer, but he willed otherwise. You will all have your M'Connachies luring you off the high road. Unless you are constantly on the watch, you will find that he has slowly pushed you out of yourself and taken your place. He has rather done for me. I think in his youth he must somehow have guessed the future and been fleggit[1] by it, flichtered[2] from the nest like a bird, and so our eggs were left, cold. He has clung to me, less from mischief than for companionship; I half like him and his penny whistle; with all his faults he is as Scotch as peat; he whispered to me just now that you elected him, not me, as your Rector.

Well, we have at last come to an end. Some of you may remember when I began this address; we are all older now. I thank you for your patience. This is my first and last public appearance, and I never could or would have made it except to a gathering of Scottish students. If I have concealed my emotions in addressing you it is only the thrawn[3] national way that deceives everybody except Scotsmen. I have not been as dull as I could have wished to be; but looking at your glowing faces, cheerfulness and hope would keep breaking through. Despite the imperfections of your betters we leave you a great inheritance, for which others will one day call you to account. You come of a race of men the very wind of whose name has swept to the ultimate seas. Remember—

'Heaven doth with us as we with torches do,
Not light them for themselves . . .'

Mighty are the universities of Scotland, and they will prevail. But

[1] Frightened.
[2] Startled. A word commonly used in Barrie's native county of Angus.
[3] Awkward.

even in your highest exultations never forget that they are not four, but five. The greatest of them is the poor, proud homes you come out of, which said so long ago: 'There shall be education in this land.' She, not St. Andrews, is the oldest university in Scotland, and all the others are her whelps.

In bidding you good-bye, my last words must be of the lovely virtue. Courage, my children, and 'greet the unseen with a cheer'. 'Fight on, my men,' said Sir Andrew Barton. Fight on—you—for the old red gown till the whistle blows.

LORD BIRKENHEAD

1872–1929

Address to the American Bar Association

Of Lord Birkenhead it can be truly said that his gifts as an orator made his career possible. In the General Election of 1906 the Liberal Party was returned with a huge majority. One of the new Conservative members was a young man, Mr F. E. Smith, who had been elected for the Walton Division of Liverpool. On the evening of 12th March of that year he rose in a packed House of Commons to make his maiden speech. Usually maiden speeches are characterized by nervousness and extreme humility; but the speech of Mr F. E. Smith was neither. It was a masterpiece of invective and humour, delivered with ease, assurance, and sometimes insolence. Everyone who heard that speech knew that a great political career lay in store for the young Mr F. E. Smith. That speech marked the beginning of a career which led him to a peerage and the Lord Chancellorship.

In his lifetime Lord Birkenhead made many political speeches where the pattern of that first speech was repeated. But not all his great speeches were political. Perhaps the outstanding virtue of Lord Birkenhead was his loyalty to his friends and those institutions which had made his career possible. He had a great affection for his university—Oxford—and for the Inn of Court—Gray's Inn—which he had entered as a young, unknown barrister. This speech shows his affection for that Inn. He would have agreed with Francis Bacon, a former Lord Chancellor and also a member of Gray's Inn, when he said: 'I hold every man to be a debtor to his profession.'

The main characteristics of Lord Birkenhead's great speeches are his lucidity, the arrangement of his material, and his incisive humour. He had a sense of the continuity of the present with the past and with the future. He never regarded himself as standing in isolation. He was conscious of the great people and great events that had gone before and of the great people and great events that would assuredly follow.

ADDRESS TO THE AMERICAN BAR ASSOCIATION

In 1924 a group of American lawyers visited Gray's Inn. Lord Birkenhead,
as Treasurer of the Inn, gave a speech of welcome. This speech shows his
qualities as an orator: his clarity of expression, his affection for his pro-
fession and for his Inn, his regard for all that was best in the past and his
hopes for the future.

THE HISTORY OF GRAY'S INN

UNFORTUNATELY tonight we approach the last of the three occasions
upon which we of this ancient Society have been privileged to entertain
distinguished Canadian and American guests. For myself, I could wish,
if the resources of the human constitution, and, more important, the
resources of human rhetoric, permitted it, that this series of entertainments might indefinitely continue. Inasmuch as the Toast committed to
me in virtue of my office has been always the same, and must continue
in any series of such entertainments as I have contemplated to be the
same, inasmuch as unfortunately an official report of these poor contributions of mine is being preserved, I feel no small degree of delicacy
at any repetition of that which I have said before.

Unfortunately, my first task has always been, as the task of a Treasurer
of this Inn welcoming visitors from overseas must always be, to commend to them in some way the House in which we are privileged to
offer you hospitalities. But, so long, so varied is the story of this Society,
so innumerable has been the company of men, illustrious in the life and
history of this Inn, who have met, and banqueted, and conversed in this
Hall, that it is very easy to discourse upon that topic without incurring
the slightest risk of repetition.

I do not know whether many of you here know how old a part of
London you are sitting in at this moment. It is comparatively elevated
in relation to the Thames. If you had visited the site of this Inn at the
end of the thirteenth century you would have seen a lofty windmill.
It was part of the possessions, the country seat of one Reginald de Gray,
the member and the head of an ancient English family. London was
almost remote. He was outside what were called the Customs of the
City of London, and here he dwelt, not in title a nobleman, but in state
almost a nobleman, wealthy, and removed, as I have said, from the
jurisdiction of the City of London. His mansion was here, his farm was
here, his windmill was here.

If any of you find leisure during your visit in London to go into our old Chapel (older certainly in many of its features than the Hall), you will detect reasons for supposing that this Chapel was the very Chapel in which, towards the end of the thirteenth century, Reginald de Gray lived with almost patriarchal sway.

And then he parted with his inheritance—how or why I cannot tell you, for history preserves upon this point no authentic record—but he parted with it to a company of lawyers at a time when the legal profession began to associate itself into those Brotherhoods from which the Inns of Court ultimately developed, and a company of lawyers, for their comfort and ours, acquired this site. I cannot give you a definite date, because no historian can dogmatically pronounce upon this matter, but I should suppose it was about the middle of the fourteenth century that this Inn was acquired by lawyers; and it has thereafter been known as Gray's Inn, from the title of the noble family that lived here for so long.

From the fourteenth century onwards it has played a great part in the life of England. There has hardly been a time when it was not comparable in greatness and in influence with any of the other Inns of Court, and there have been at least two periods in which it has most conspicuously exceeded any of the other Inns of Court, or all of them put together, in the part which it has played in our national life and in the distinction of the men who have enriched our history.

Of all the men whom this Society has sent forth, the greatest is known to every one of you, perhaps the greatest brain which in any country of the world has ever been devoted to the study of the science of jurisprudence, I mean Francis Bacon, whose contemporary portrait is behind me as I speak. He was characteristically a Gray's Inn man. He was not merely a great man, a supreme genius who happened to be a member of Gray's Inn; he was a man who, if he ever set himself to disentangle the complicated threads of his complex life, would unquestionably have assigned his association with this Inn as one of the most memorable and unforgettable elements in the whole of that most important career. This Inn was proud of him in the moment of his supreme intellectual success, at the moment when, as the founder of the empiric principle of philosophy in England, he was winning the admiration of intellectual Europe; when, at the same moment, he was universally recognized, with the only possible exception of Coke, as the most unrivalled jurist in these islands. At the same time, by universal admission, he was an accomplished courtier and a sagacious statesman. At that moment it was easy for this or any other Society to remain faithful to so dazzling a light and ornament.

But it was not at that moment that this Society was tested. It was when, in the period of his disgrace, there were few so low to do him reverence; it was then that, with well-founded confidence and affection, he came back in the tiny Society to those who, in spite of all, reverenced and loved and cherished him. And you can still see the site of the rooms into which he crept here to spend the rest of his life, always sustained by the affection of this Society, and I like, in this connection, to recall the imperishable words, in this respect and dealing with this matter, of his will. He said: 'For my name and memory, I leave it to men's charitable speeches, and to foreign nations, and the next ages.'

No more valiant and confident appeal was ever wrung from a mind of genius. And the ages have sustained that appeal. Horace indeed wrote of himself and of his expectations, to be well justified in the event of immortality, *Exegi monumentum aere perennius*; but although we have from Horace his own admission upon the fact that *Militavi non sine gloria*, he had at least never pretended to be a soldier. Bacon, who made this supreme and confident and justified appeal to the balanced perspective of history, had been a judge and he knew well how far the strictures and the condemnation which rent him were well founded.

THE TRUSTEE OF CIVILIZATION

If time allowed me, I could dwell upon many other historical circumstances which I think would not fail to interest you. Queen Elizabeth, whose brilliant portrait confronts you there, was the great friend and patroness of this Inn, and she lived in a day in which it was not even improper to remark of a monarch that she was the protectress of this Inn; and if any of you have leisure tomorrow, or even tonight, to walk up the steps that lead to our Library you will see a picture, not without interest, though of somewhat recent production, which depicts Queen Elizabeth, with some charming maids of honour and attended by courtiers, walking up and down the paths of that garden in which many of you gave us the pleasure of your company either yesterday or today, and in the room which adjoins this you will find a chair of undoubted authenticity which was presented to this Society by Queen Elizabeth herself.

I cannot help hoping that many of you have had occasion to visit our gardens because one of the most delightful essays of Bacon was upon the subject of gardens. The phrase has been quoted a thousand times in publications in your country and in ours in which he spoke of gardening as the purest pleasure of all. Perhaps some of our guests do not know that that beautiful and even stately garden, secluded in the midst of the very business of London, was designed in its main elements by Bacon himself. If you read that essay again, and if you have studied our garden you will, I think, read with an added interest his recommendation that in every garden there should be a bank, not too steep, with perhaps a hedge upon it, perhaps six feet high.

You can go into Gray's Inn now, hundreds of years after all that was left of Bacon materially has become ashes, and you can still see that bank, that hedge and bank six feet high, which he commended in the famous essay. You will not indeed see the hedge upon the top of the bank, for, when he wrote, that which lay upon the other side of the hedge were the pleasant pastures of the English countryside of that day. The hedge has been succeeded by a row of iron railings, just as the pastures in which the sheep browsed in his day have been succeeded by a succession of streets which an unfavourable observer might even describe as slums. And therefore the hedge has given place to the iron railings. But the superiority of one who, whether he wrote Shakespeare or not—and being a Gray's Inn man he certainly ought to have done—at least reached in this essay a charming and delightful conception.

I would remind you of one other observation, because that again is perpetuated in the modern appearance of our garden. He said: 'I wish also, in the very middle . . . alleys, enough for four to walk abreast.' If you have seen our garden, you will see that there is today, as there was in Bacon's day, the same broad alley in the very middle, wide enough for four men to walk abreast.

I hope that these historical recollections of vital interest to us in this House will not prove too tedious for those whom we cannot hope to interest so vitally as we ourselves are interested in them; but I thought today that perhaps there was some lesson to be gleaned from that which I had the happiness of observing this afternoon.

As there are no reporters here, except those whom we can happily control, because the only reports are official ones, I may be allowed to say that I abandoned the attractions of the Garden Party at Buckingham Palace, in order that I might have the happiness of witnessing the assembly within these beautiful, historic gardens of a large number of American and English children, and I confess to me the afternoon was one of deep emotion.

I looked at those beautiful children of both countries abandoning themselves completely, as all childhood should, in the days of its vernal spring, to the pleasure and the enjoyment of the moment. I saw them, brothers and sisters, utterly unconscious of any historic difference, and utterly determined not to allow anyone to create any new historic difference. In their sweet and charming association I drew an augury happy and confident as to the future of these two peoples. We are not, I hope, to be instructed altogether by our children. They never heard of Lord North—I suppose they will have to one day. King George III did not disturb their enjoyment of the Punch and Judy exhibition, and I think they would have given a short shrift to anybody who had tried to intrude topics at once so alien and so antagonistic to the enjoyment of the present.

I cannot help thinking that we may perhaps draw more moral from that party afforded today to the youth of both countries. I am not sure that they have been given a chance up to the present; if they have not, it has certainly not been their fault. They have had textbooks thrust into their hands—thrust, I ought to say, into their unwilling hands—on which they were never consulted, and of which at least they can claim that they were not the authors. May we not throw far behind us the memories of far-gone unhappiness? May we not leave the dead past to bury its past and realize that the whole English-speaking community is the trustee of civilization and owes a responsibility, not to the past, but to the future?

If you take the length of time during which the Roman Empire exercised its matchless sway, it exceeded by some three centuries the period, not inconsiderable, in which the British Empire has exercised high influence. No one living is bold enough to place a temporal limit upon the period of time in which the United States of America must be among the greatest countries in the world. Are we, indeed—you with your thousand or two thousand or three thousand years in front of you; we, with we know not what undischarged span still to pass—are we for all time to be placed under the memory of things that took place two hundred years ago?

Let us devote our lives to the vital present and to the immensely important future. Let us do it in the spirit of men who say: 'We make no inquest into the dead past; we realize our responsibilities to the men who are alive today, who depend upon us for inspiration and advice and guidance, and to those future generations who may point either in their happiness or misery as a result of our acts or of our omissions.'

SIR WINSTON CHURCHILL
1874–

The Loaded Pause

Few men have had a more varied career than Sir Winston Churchill. He has fought in battle. He has been a prisoner of war, and is one of that select band of brave and resourceful men who managed to escape from captivity. He is a writer and a historian, whose works on modern history and on the history of the past will be read and studied by generations yet to come. He is a painter of distinction and his title of Royal Academician Extraordinary is no mere honorary title, but one which his genius as a painter richly merits. As a politician he has held most of the important offices of state, and during the Second World War, when Britain and the free world was threatened by monstrous tyranny, his was the inspiration and the driving force which united the allied forces for victory.

His career showed no orderly progression. Periods of great successes and achievement were followed by periods when he was in the doldrums. Yet, when the supreme call came to him in 1940 it seemed that in this curious past life of his nothing had been wasted and that, as he said himself: 'All my past life had been but a preparation for this hour and for this trial.' It is remarkable that a man who should have been concerned with mighty and dangerous events should have himself retained such a buoyancy of character, such a steadfastness of purpose, such a magnanimity of outlook and such an impish humour. The achievements of Sir Winston Churchill are many and varied but none is so great as the character of the man himself.

When Adolf Hitler seized supreme power in Germany in 1933 the great majority of people were unaware of what this meant to the rest of the world. From the very beginning Mr Winston Churchill, as he then was, saw the danger. The British government of those days turned a deaf ear to his warnings and his exhortations, yet he persisted. His attitude brought him no friends. Odium was heaped upon him from people in Britain who regarded him as a scaremonger and from people in Germany who accused him of being a warmonger. In later years Sir Winston Churchill described the Second World War as the unnecessary war. If Britain and the free world had listened to his warnings the career of Adolf Hitler could have been brought to an end without a world war.

The speech which follows was delivered in 1936 in the House of Commons. This is a good example of the kind of speeches which Sir Winston made at that time. We see set out the general principles of British foreign policy. We see the use he makes of parallels from history. We see also the repetition of ideas, which is a characteristic of his oratorical style. By constant repetition he hoped to persuade an unwilling House of Commons. From the point of view of content and style, this is a speech worth studying.

FOR four hundred years the foreign policy of England has been to oppose the strongest, most aggressive, most dominating Power on the Continent, and particularly to prevent the Low Countries falling into the hands of such a Power. Viewed in the light of history these four centuries of consistent purpose amid so many changes of names and facts, of circumstances and conditions, must rank as one of the most remarkable episodes which the records of any race, nation, State or people can show. Moreover, on all occasions England took the more difficult course. Faced by Philip II of Spain, against Louis XIV under William III and Marlborough, against Napoleon, against Wilhelm II of Germany, it would have been easy and must have been very tempting to join with the stronger and share the fruits of his conquest. However, we always took the harder course, joined with the less strong Powers, made a combination among them, and thus defeated and frustrated the continental military tyrant whoever he was, whatever nation he led. Thus we preserved the liberties of Europe, protected the growth of its vivacious and varied society, and emerged after four terrific struggles with an ever-growing fame and widening Empire, and with the Low Countries safely protected in their independence. Here is the wonderful unconscious tradition of British foreign policy. All our thoughts rest in that tradition today. I know of nothing which has occurred to alter or weaken the justice, wisdom, valour and prudence, upon which our ancestors acted. I know of nothing that has happened to human nature which in the slightest degree alters the validity of their conclusions. I know of nothing in military, political, economic or scientific fact which makes me feel that we are less capable. I know of nothing which makes me feel that we might not, or cannot, march along the same road. I venture to put this very general proposition before you because it seems to me that if it is accepted everything else becomes much more simple.

Observe that the policy of England takes no account of which nation it is that seeks the overlordship of Europe. The question is not whether it is Spain, or the French Monarchy, or the French Empire, or the German Empire, or the Hitler régime. It has nothing to do with rulers or nations, it is concerned solely with whoever is the strongest or the potentially dominating tyrant. Therefore we should not be afraid of being accused of being pro-French or anti-German. If the circumstances were reversed, we could equally be pro-German and anti-French. It is a law of public policy which we are following, and not a mere expedient dictated by accidental circumstances, or likes and dislikes, or any other sentiment.

The question therefore arises which is today the Power in Europe which is the strongest, and which seeks in a dangerous and oppressive sense to dominate. Today, for this year, probably for part of 1937, the French Army is the strongest in Europe. But no one is afraid of France. Everyone knows that France wants to be left alone, and that with her it is only a case of self-preservation. Everyone knows that the French are peaceful and overhung with fear. They are at once brave, resolute, peace-loving and weighted down by anxiety. They are a liberal nation with free parliamentary institutions.

Germany, on the other hand, fears no one. She is arming in a manner which has never been seen in German history. She is led by a handful of triumphant desperadoes. The money is running short, discontents are arising beneath these despotic rulers. Very soon they will have to choose on the one hand between economic and financial collapse or internal upheaval, and on the other, a war which could have no other object and which, if successful, can have no other result than a Germanized Europe under Nazi control. Therefore it seems to me that all the old conditions present themselves again, and that our national salvation depends upon our gathering once again all the forces of Europe to contain, to restrain, and if necessary to frustrate German domination. For believe me, if any of those other Powers, Spain, Louis XIV, Napoleon, Kaiser Wilhelm II, had with our aid become the absolute masters of Europe, they could have despoiled us, reduced us to insignificance and penury on the morrow of their victory. We ought to set the life and endurance of the British Empire and the greatness of this island very high in our duty, and not be led astray by illusions about an ideal world which only means that other and worse controls will step into our place, and that the future direction will belong to them.

THE LEAGUE OF NATIONS

It is at this stage that the spacious conception and extremely vital organization of the League of Nations presents itself as a prime factor. The League of Nations is, in a practical sense, a British conception, and it harmonizes perfectly with all our past methods and actions. Moreover, it harmonizes with those broad ideas of right and wrong, and of peace based upon controlling the major aggressor, which we have always followed. We wish for the reign of law and freedom among nations and within nations, and it was for that, and nothing less than that, that those bygone architects of our repute, magnitude and civilization fought, toiled and won. The dream of a reign of International Law and of the settlement of disputes by patient discussion, but still in accordance with what is lawful and just, is very dear to the British people. You must not underrate the force which these ideals exert upon the modern British democracy. One does not know how these seeds are planted by the winds of the centuries in the hearts of the working people. They are there, and just as strong as their love of liberty. We should not neglect them, because they are the essence of the genius of this island. Therefore we believe that in the fostering and fortifying of the League of Nations will be found the best means of defending our island security, as well as maintaining grand universal causes with which we have very often found our own interests in natural accord.

My three main propositions are: first, that we must oppose the would-be dominator or potential aggressor. Secondly, that Germany under its present Nazi régime and with its prodigious armaments, so swiftly developing, fills unmistakably that part. Thirdly, that the League of Nations rallies many countries, and unites our own people here at home in the most effective way to control the would-be aggressor. I venture most respectfully to submit these main themes to your consideration. Everything else will follow from them.

It is always more easy to discover and proclaim general principles than to apply them. First, we ought to count our effective association with France. That does not mean that we should develop a needlessly hostile mood against Germany. It is a part of our duty and our interest to keep the temperature low between these two countries. We shall not have any difficulty in this so far as France is concerned. Like us, they are a parliamentary democracy with tremendous inhibitions against war, and, like us, under considerable drawbacks in preparing their defence. Therefore I say we ought to regard our defensive association with France as fundamental. Everything else must be viewed in proper subordination now that the times have become so sharp and perilous. Those who are possessed of a definite body of doctrine and of deeply-rooted convictions upon it will be in a much better position to deal with the shifts and surprises of daily affairs than those who are merely taking short views, and indulging their natural impulses as they are evoked by what they read from day to day. The first thing is to decide where you want to go. For myself, I am for the armed League of all Nations, or as many as you can get, against the potential aggressor, with England and France as the core of it. Let us neglect nothing in our power to establish the great international framework. If that should prove to be beyond our strength, or if it breaks down through the weakness or wrong-doing of others, then at least let us make sure that England and France, the two surviving free great countries of Europe, can together ride out any storm that may blow with good and reasonable hopes of once again coming safely into port.

A Colossal Military Disaster

In September, 1939, the Second World War broke out. The Prime Minister of Great Britain, Mr Neville Chamberlain, invited Mr Churchill[1] to fill the post of First Lord of the Admiralty. Except at sea the first six months of the war saw little action, but on 9th April, 1940, this twilight war came to an end. On that day Germany attacked Denmark and Norway. A month later, on 10th May, the German Army and Air Force struck against the west. Holland and Belgium were invaded. The German armoured divisions roared along the roads and the German Air Force held mastery in the sky. On the evening of 10th May His Majesty King George VI sent for Mr Churchill and asked him to form a new government. He accepted, and the great war coalition of Conservative, Labour and Liberal members under the direction of Mr Churchill as Prime Minister and Minister of Defence came into being.

The position was dangerous in the extreme. The Western Front was crumbling. In his first speech as Prime Minister Mr Churchill did not conceal the gravity of the position. He said: 'I have nothing to offer but blood, toil, tears and sweat.'

By a miracle a large part of the British Expeditionary Force managed to escape back to England via Dunkirk during the closing days of May and the first few days of June. Mr Churchill explains in the speech which follows what happened. This was the first of his great speeches as Prime Minister. The disaster in France had not taken away his resolution. On the contrary it had strengthened it.

This speech is well worth serious study. Here we see that mastery of detail, that command of the unexpected word, the orderly presentation of material and, above all, that appeal to man's unconquerable mind. The conclusion is often quoted. Notice the orderly progression: 'We shall fight in France.' Then 'We shall fight in the seas and the oceans'. Later 'In the air'. Now he forecasts the possibility of invasion: 'We shall defend our island'. He goes on to further detail: first of all 'On the beaches.' Then, if retreat is necessary: 'On the landing grounds.' If still further retreat is

---

[1] Mr Churchill was created a Knight of the Garter in 1953. He delivered all the following speeches as Mr Churchill.

necessary: 'In the fields and in the streets'; and even if driven into the last redoubt 'In the hills'. Then there is a short, sharp statement—'We shall never surrender.'

Those who heard this speech can recall the effect which it had. Britain was in danger, but the British people were resolved to continue the struggle. In the Prime Minister's majestic phrases, this resolve was nobly expressed. His speeches were more than mere words. The British Broadcasting Corporation transmitted them from London into all the countries of the world, friend and foe alike. Because of the beauty and power of their language they sustained the brave, comforted the weary, encouraged the laggard and struck fear into the hearts of the enemy. The word and deed matched. The English language became a weapon, both of attack and defence.

HARD AND HEAVY TIDINGS

FROM the moment that the French defences at Sedan and on the Meuse were broken at the end of the second week of May, only a rapid retreat to Amiens and the south could have saved the British and French armies who had entered Belgium at the appeal of the Belgian King; but this strategic fact was not immediately realized. The French High Command hoped they would be able to close the gap, and the armies of the north were under their orders. Moreover, a retirement of this kind would have involved almost certainly the destruction of the fine Belgian Army of over twenty divisions and the abandonment of the whole of Belgium. Therefore, when the force and scope of the German penetration were realized and when a new French generalissimo, General Weygand, assumed command in place of General Gamelin, an effort was made by the French and British armies in Belgium to keep on holding the right hand of the Belgians and to give their own right hand to a newly created French Army which was to have advanced across the Somme in great strength to grasp it.

However, the German eruption swept like a sharp scythe around the right and rear of the armies of the north. Eight or nine armoured divisions, each of about four hundred armoured vehicles of different kinds, but carefully assorted to be complementary and divisible into small self-contained units, cut off all communications between us and the main French armies. It severed our own communications for food and ammunition, which ran first to Amiens and afterwards through

Abbeville, and it shore its way up the coast to Boulogne and Calais, and almost to Dunkirk. Behind this armoured and mechanized onslaught came a number of German divisions in lorries, and behind them again there plodded comparatively slowly the dull brute mass of the ordinary German Army and German people, always so ready to be led to the trampling down in other lands of liberties and comforts which they have never known in their own.

I have said this armoured scythe-stroke almost reached Dunkirk—almost but not quite. Boulogne and Calais were the scenes of desperate fighting. The Guards defended Boulogne for a while and were then withdrawn by orders from this country. The Rifle Brigade, the 60th Rifles, and the Queen Victoria's Rifles, with a battalion of British tanks and 1,000 Frenchmen, in all about 4,000 strong, defended Calais to the last. The British brigadier was given an hour to surrender. He spurned the offer, and four days of intense street fighting passed before silence reigned over Calais, which marked the end of a memorable resistance. Only thirty unwounded survivors were brought off by the Navy and we do not know the fate of their comrades. Their sacrifice, however, was not in vain. At least two armoured divisions, which otherwise would have been turned against the British Expeditionary Force, had to be sent to overcome them. They have added another page to the glories of the light divisions, and the time gained enabled the Graveline water-lines to be flooded and to be held by the French troops.

Thus it was that the port of Dunkirk was kept open. When it was found impossible for the armies of the north to reopen their communications to Amiens with the main French armies, only one choice remained. It seemed, indeed, forlorn. The Belgian, British and French armies were almost surrounded. Their sole line of retreat was to a single port and to its neighbouring beaches. They were pressed on every side by heavy attacks and far outnumbered in the air.

When a week ago today I asked the House to fix this afternoon as the occasion for a statement, I feared it would be my hard lot to announce the greatest military disaster in our long history. I thought—and some good judges agreed with me—that perhaps 20,000 or 30,000 men might be re-embarked. But it certainly seemed that the whole of the French First Army and the whole of the British Expeditionary Force north of the Amiens–Abbeville gap, would be broken up in the open field or else would have to capitulate for lack of food and ammunition. These were the hard and heavy tidings for which I called upon the House and the nation to prepare themselves a week ago. The whole root and core and brain of the British Army, on which and around which we were to build, and are to build, the great British armies in the later years of the war, seemed about to perish upon the field or to be led into an ignominious and starving captivity.

That was the prospect a week ago. But another blow which might well have proved final was yet to fall upon us. The King of the Belgians had called upon us to come to his aid. Had not this ruler and his government severed themselves from the allies, who rescued their country from extinction in the late war, and had they not sought refuge in what has proved to be a fatal neutrality, the French and British armies might well at the outset have saved not only Belgium but perhaps even Poland. Yet at the last moment when Belgium was already invaded, King Leopold called upon us to come to his aid, and even at the last moment we came. He and his brave, efficient army, nearly half a million strong, guarded our left flank and thus kept open our only line of retreat to the sea. Suddenly, without prior consultation, with the least possible notice, without the advice of his Ministers and upon his own personal act, he sent a plenipotentiary to the German Command, surrendered his army and exposed our whole flank and means of retreat.

I asked the House a week ago to suspend its judgment because the facts were not clear, but I do not feel that any reason now exists why we should not form our own opinions upon this pitiful episode. The surrender of the Belgian Army compelled the British at the shortest notice to cover a flank to the sea more than thirty miles in length. Otherwise all would have been cut off, and all would have shared the fate to which King Leopold had condemned the finest army his country had ever formed. So in doing this and in exposing this flank, as anyone who followed the operations on the map will see, contact was lost between the British and two out of the three corps forming the First French Army, who were still farther from the coast than we were, and it seemed impossible that any large number of allied troops could reach the coast.

VICTORY INSIDE DELIVERANCE

The enemy attacked on all sides with great strength and fierceness, and their main power, the power of their far more numerous air force, was thrown into the battle or else concentrated upon Dunkirk and the beaches. Pressing in upon the narrow exit, both from the east and from the west, the enemy began to fire with cannon upon the beaches by which alone the shipping could approach or depart. They sowed magnetic mines in the channels and seas; they sent repeated waves of hostile aircraft, sometimes more than a hundred strong in one formation, to cast their bombs upon the single pier that remained, and upon the sand dunes upon which the troops had their eyes for shelter. Their U-boats, one of which was sunk, and their motor launches took their toll of the vast traffic which now began. For four or five days an intense struggle reigned. All their armoured divisions—or what was left of them—together with great masses of infantry and artillery, hurled themselves in vain upon the ever-narrowing, ever-contracting appendix within which the British and French armies fought.

Meanwhile, the Royal Navy, with the willing help of countless merchant seamen, strained every nerve to embark the British and Allied troops; 220 light warships and 650 other vessels were engaged. They had to operate upon the difficult coast, often in adverse weather, under an almost ceaseless hail of bombs and an increasing concentration of artillery fire. Nor were the seas, as I have said, themselves free from mines and torpedoes. It was in conditions such as these that our men carried on, with little or no rest, for days and nights on end, making trip after trip across the dangerous waters, bringing with them always men whom they had rescued. The numbers they have brought back are the measure of their devotion and their courage. The hospital ships, which brought off many thousands of British and French wounded, being so plainly marked were a special target for Nazi bombs; but the men and women on board them never faltered in their duty.

Meanwhile, the Royal Air Force, which had already been intervening in the battle, so far as its range would allow, from home bases, now used part of its main metropolitan fighter strength, and struck at the German bombers, and at the fighters which in large numbers protected them. This struggle was protracted and fierce. Suddenly the scene has cleared, the crash and thunder has for the moment—but only for the moment—died away. A miracle of deliverance, achieved by valour, by perseverance, by perfect discipline, by faultless service, by resource, by skill, by unconquerable fidelity, is manifest to us all. The enemy was hurled back by the retreating British and French troops. He was so roughly handled that he did not harry their departure seriously. The Royal Air Force engaged the main strength of the German Air Force, and inflicted upon them losses of at least four to one; and the Navy, using nearly 1,000 ships of all kinds, carried over 335,000 men, French and British, out of the jaws of death and shame, to their native land and to the tasks which lie immediately ahead. We must be very careful not to assign to this deliverance the attributes of a victory. Wars are not won by evacuations. But there was a victory inside this deliverance, which should be noted. It was gained by the Air Force. Many of our soldiers coming back have not seen the Air Force at work; they saw only the bombers which escaped its protective attack. They underrate its achievements. I have heard much talk of this; that is why I go out of my way to say this. I will tell you about it.

This was a great trial of strength between the British and German Air Forces. Can you conceive a greater objective for the Germans in the air than to make evacuation from these beaches impossible, and to sink all these ships which were displayed, almost to the extent of thousands? Could there have been an objective of greater military importance and significance for the whole purpose of the war than this? They tried hard, and they were beaten back; they were frustrated in their task. We got the Army away; and they have paid fourfold for any losses which they have inflicted. Very large formations of German aeroplanes—and we know that they are a very brave race—have turned on several occasions from the attack of one-quarter of their number of the Royal Air Force, and have dispersed in different directions. Twelve aeroplanes have been hunted by two. One aeroplane was driven into the water and cast away, by the mere charge of a British aeroplane, which had no more ammunition. All of our types—the Hurricane, the Spitfire and the new Defiant—and all our pilots have been vindicated as superior to what they have at present to face.

When we consider how much greater would be our advantage in defending the air above this island against an overseas attack, I must say that I find in these facts a sure basis upon which practical and reassuring thoughts may rest. I will pay my tribute to these young airmen. The great French Army was very largely, for the time being, cast back and disturbed by the onrush of a few thousands of armoured vehicles. May it not also be that the cause of civilization itself will be defended by the skill and devotion of a few thousand airmen. There never had been, I suppose, in all the world, in all the history of war, such an opportunity for youth. The Knights of the Round Table, the Crusaders, all fall back into the past: not only distant but prosaic; these young men, going forth every morn to guard their native land and all that we stand for, holding in their hands these instruments of colossal and shattering power, of whom it may be said that

> *'Every morn brought forth a noble chance*
> *And every chance brought forth a noble knight'*

deserve our gratitude, as do all of the brave men who, in so many ways and on so many occasions, are ready, and continue ready, to give life and all for their native land.

I return to the Army. In the long series of very fierce battles, now on this front, now on that, fighting on three fronts at once, battles fought by two or three divisions against an equal or somewhat larger number of the enemy, and fought fiercely on some of the old grounds that so many of us knew so well, in these battles our losses in men have exceeded 30,000 killed, wounded and missing. I take occasion to express the sympathy of the House to all who have suffered bereavement or who are still anxious. The President of the Board of Trade[1] is not here today. His son has been killed, and many in the House have felt the pangs of affliction in the sharpest form. But I will say this about the missing. We have had a large number of wounded come home safely to this country, but I would say about the missing that there may be very many reported missing who will come back home, some day, in one way or another. In the confusion of this fight it is inevitable that many have been left in positions where honour required no further resistance from them.

A COLOSSAL MILITARY DISASTER

Against this loss of over 30,000 men, we can set a far heavier loss certainly inflicted upon the enemy. But our losses in material are enormous. We have perhaps lost one-third of the men we lost in the opening days of the battle of 21st March, 1918, but we have lost nearly

[1] Sir Andrew Duncan.

as many guns—nearly 1,000—and all our transport, all the armoured vehicles that were with the Army in the north. This loss will impose a further delay on the expansion of our military strength. That expansion had not been proceeding as fast as we had hoped. The best of all we had to give had gone to the British Expeditionary Force, and although they had not the numbers of tanks and some articles of equipment which were desirable, they were a very well and finely equipped army. They had the first-fruits of all that our industry had to give, and that is gone. And now here is this further delay. How long it will be, how long it will last, depends upon the exertions which we make in this island. An effort the like of which has never been seen in our records is now being made. Work is proceeding everywhere, night and day, Sundays and weekdays. Capital and labour have cast aside their interests, rights and customs and put them into the common stock. Already the flow of munitions has leapt forward. There is no reason why we should not in a few months overtake the sudden and serious loss that has come upon us, without retarding the development of our general programme.

Nevertheless, our thankfulness at the escape of our Army and so many men, whose loved ones have passed through an agonizing week, must not blind us to the fact that what has happened in France and Belgium is a colossal military disaster. The French Army has been weakened, the Belgian Army has been lost, a large part of those fortified lines upon which so much faith had been reposed is gone, many valuable mining districts and factories have passed into the enemy's possession, the whole of the Channel ports are in his hands, with all the tragic consequences that follow from that, and we must expect another blow to be struck almost immediately at us or at France. We are told that Herr Hitler has a plan for invading the British Isles. This has often been thought of before. When Napoleon lay at Boulogne for a year with his flat-bottomed boats and his Grand Army, he was told by someone, 'There are bitter weeds in England.' There are certainly a great many more of them since the British Expeditionary Force returned.

We Shall Fight...

The whole question of home defence against invasion is, of course, powerfully affected by the fact that we have for the time being in this island incomparably more powerful military forces than we have ever had at any moment in this war or the last. But this will not continue. We shall not be content with a defensive war. We have our duty to our ally. We have to reconstitute and build up the British Expeditionary Force once again, under its gallant Commander-in-Chief, Lord Gort. All this is in train; but in the interval we must put our defences in this island into such a high state of organization that the fewest possible numbers will be required to give effective security and that the largest possible potential of offensive effort may be realized. On this we are now engaged. It will be very convenient, if it be the desire of the House, to enter upon this subject in a Secret Session. Not that the government would necessarily be able to reveal in very great detail military secrets, but we like to have our discussions free, without the restraint imposed by the fact that they will be read the next day by the enemy; and the government would benefit by views freely expressed in all parts of the House by Members with their knowledge of so many different parts of the country. I understand that some request is to be made upon this subject, which will be readily acceded to by His Majesty's Government.

We have found it necessary to take measures of increasing stringency, not only against enemy aliens and suspicious characters of other nationalities, but also against British subjects who may become a danger or a nuisance should the war be transported to the United Kingdom. I know there are a great many people affected by the orders which we have made who are the passionate enemies of Nazi Germany. I am very sorry for them, but we cannot, at the present time and under the present stress, draw all the distinctions which we should like to do. If parachute landings were attempted and fierce fighting attendant upon them followed, these unfortunate people would be far better out of the way, for their own sakes as well as for ours. There is, however, another class, for which I feel not the slightest sympathy. Parliament has given us the powers to put down Fifth Column activities with a strong hand, and we shall use those powers, subject to the supervision and correction of the House, without the slightest hesitation until we are satisfied, and more than satisfied, that this malignancy in our midst has been effectively stamped out.

Turning once again, and this time more generally, to the question of invasion, I would observe that there has never been a period in all these long centuries of which we boast when an absolute guarantee against invasion, still less against serious raids, could have been given to our people. In the days of Napoleon the same wind which would have carried his transports across the Channel might have driven away the blockading fleet. There was always the chance, and it is that chance which has excited and befooled the imaginations of many Continental tyrants. Many are the tales that are told. We are assured that novel methods will be adopted, and when we see the originality of malice, the ingenuity of aggression, which our enemy displays, we may certainly prepare ourselves for every kind of novel stratagem and every kind of brutal and treacherous manœuvre. I think that no idea is so outlandish that it should not be considered and viewed with a searching, but at the same time, I hope, with a steady eye. We must never forget the solid assurances of sea-power and those which belong to air-power if it can be locally exercised.

I have, myself, full confidence that if all do their duty, if nothing is neglected, and if the best arrangements are made, as they are being made, we shall prove ourselves once again able to defend our island home, to ride out the storm of war, and to outlive the menace of tyranny, if necessary for years, if necessary alone. At any rate, that is what we are going to try to do. That is the resolve of His Majesty's Government —every man of them. That is the will of Parliament and the nation. The British Empire and the French Republic, linked together in their cause and in their need, will defend to the death their native soil, aiding each other like good comrades to the utmost of their strength. Even though large tracts of Europe and many old and famous States have fallen or may fall into the grip of the Gestapo and all the odious apparatus of Nazi rule, we shall not flag or fail. We shall go on to the end, we shall fight in France, we shall fight on the seas and oceans, we shall fight with growing confidence and growing strength in the air, we shall defend our island, whatever the cost may be, we shall fight on the beaches, we shall fight on the landing grounds, we shall fight in the fields and in the streets, we shall fight in the hills; we shall never surrender, and even if, which I do not for a moment believe, this island or a large part of it were subjugated and starving, then our Empire beyond the seas, armed and guarded by the British Fleet, would carry on the struggle, until, in God's good time, the new world, with all its power and might, steps forth to the rescue and the liberation of the old.

Their Finest Hour

During the month of June, 1940, disasters fell thick and fast on the Western Front. In the speech which follows Mr Churchill warns the British people that the Battle of Britain is about to begin, and that great trials are imminent. It is worth noting that this speech was delivered first to the House of Commons and then broadcast by Mr Churchill himself on the world-wide services of the British Broadcasting Corporation.

The Second World War was the first war in which leaders of the nations made use of broadcasting. Mr Churchill's oratory was well suited to this new medium. People who listened to him felt that he was speaking as a personal friend and intimate. He had the supreme ability of being elevated but relaxed, lofty but familiar, demanding but sympathetic. The secret of his success lay in the fact that he appealed to all that was best in mankind.

He had also some tricks of expression which endeared him to his audiences. He refused to pronounce any German words according to German pronunciation, so Nazi was 'Nazee' and the German pocket battleship Graf Spee *was pronounced 'Spee' and not 'Spay'. This might seem a small point, but it was singularly effective in conveying his certainty of purpose. The enemy seemed to be less terrifying and to be slightly ridiculous. Only the greatest of orators can adopt this artifice in dealing with a formidable foe.*

DISASTROUS MILITARY EVENTS

I SPOKE the other day of the colossal military disaster which occurred when the French High Command failed to withdraw the northern armies from Belgium at the moment when they knew that the French front was decisively broken at Sedan and on the Meuse. This delay entailed the loss of fifteen or sixteen French divisions and threw out of action for the critical period the whole of the British Expeditionary Force. Our Army and 120,000 French troops were indeed rescued by the British Navy from Dunkirk but only with the loss of their cannon, vehicles and modern equipment. This loss inevitably took some weeks to repair, and in the first two of those weeks the battle in France had been lost. When we consider the heroic resistance made by the French Army against heavy odds in this battle, the enormous losses inflicted upon the enemy and the evident exhaustion of the enemy, it may well be thought that these twenty-five divisions of the best-trained and best-equipped troops might have turned the scale. However, General Weygand had to fight without them. Only three British divisions or their equivalent were able to stand in the line with their French comrades. They have suffered severely, but they have fought well. We sent every man we could to France as fast as we could re-equip and transport their formations.

I am not reciting these facts for the purpose of recrimination. That I judge to be utterly futile and even harmful. We cannot afford it. I recite them in order to explain why it was we did not have, as we could have had, between twelve and fourteen British divisions fighting in the line in this great battle instead of only three. Now I put all this aside. I put it on the shelf, from which the historians, when they have time, will select their documents to tell their stories. We have to think of the future and not of the past. This also applies in a small way to our own affairs at home. There are many who would hold an inquest in the House of Commons on the conduct of the governments—and of Parliaments, for they are in it, too—during the years which led up to this catastrophe. They seek to indict those who were responsible for the guidance of our affairs. This also would be a foolish and pernicious process. There are too many in it. Let each man search his conscience and search his speeches. I frequently search mine.

Of this I am quite sure, that if we open a quarrel between the past and the present, we shall find that we have lost the future. Therefore, I cannot accept the drawing of any distinctions between members of the present government. It was formed at a moment of crisis in order to unite all the parties and all sections of opinion. It has received the almost unanimous support of both Houses of Parliament. Its members are going to stand together, and, subject to the authority of the House of Commons, we are going to govern the country and fight the war. It is absolutely necessary at a time like this that every Minister who tries each day to do his duty shall be respected; and their subordinates must know that their chiefs are not threatened men, men who are here today and gone tomorrow, but that their directions must be punctually and faithfully obeyed. Without this concentrated power we cannot face what lies before us. I should not think it would be very advantageous for the House to prolong this debate this afternoon under conditions of public stress. Many facts are not clear that will be clear in a short time. We are to have a Secret Session on Thursday, and I should think that would be a better opportunity for the many earnest expressions of opinion which members will desire to make and for the House to discuss vital matters without having everything read the next morning by our dangerous foes.

The disastrous military events which have happened during the past fortnight have not come to me with any sense of surprise. Indeed, I indicated a fortnight ago as clearly as I could to the House that the worst possibilities were open; and I made it perfectly clear then that whatever happened in France would make no difference to the resolve of Britain and the British Empire to fight on, 'if necessary for years, if necessary alone'. During the last few days we have successfully brought off the great majority of the troops we had on the lines of communication in France; and seven-eighths of the troops we have sent to France since the beginning of the war—that is to say, about 350,000 out of 400,000 men—are safely back in this country. Others are still fighting with the French, and fighting with considerable success in their local encounters against the enemy. We have also brought back a great mass of stores, rifles and munitions of all kinds which had been accumulated in France during the last nine months.

We have, therefore, in this island today a very large and powerful military force. This force comprises all our best trained and our finest troops, including scores of thousands of those who have already measured their quality against the Germans and found themselves at no disadvantage. We have under arms at the present time in this island over a million and a quarter men. Behind these we have the Local Defence Volunteers, numbering half a million, only a portion of whom, however, are yet armed with rifles or other firearms. We have incorporated into our defence forces every man for whom we have a weapon. We expect very large additions to our weapons in the near future, and in preparation for this we intend forthwith to call up, drill and train further large numbers. Those who are not called up, or else are employed upon the vast business of munitions production in all its branches—and their ramifications are innumerable—will serve their country best by remaining at their ordinary work until they receive their summons. We have also over here Dominions armies. The Canadians had actually landed in France, but have now been safely withdrawn, much disappointed, but in perfect order, with all their artillery and equipment. And these very high-class forces from the Dominions will now take part in the defence of the Mother Country.

Lest the account which I have given of these large forces should raise the question: Why did they not take part in the great battle in France? I must make it clear that, apart from the divisions training and organizing at home, only twelve divisions were equipped to fight upon a scale which justified their being sent abroad. And this was fully up to the number which the French had been led to expect would be available in France at the ninth month of the war. The rest of our forces at home have a fighting value for home defence which will, of course, steadily increase every week that passes. Thus, the invasion of Great Britain would at this time require the transportation across the sea of hostile armies on a very large scale, and after they had been so transported they would have to be continually maintained with all the masses of munitions and supplies which are required for continuous battle—as continuous battle it will surely be.

THE NAVY

Here is where we come to the Navy—and after all, we have a Navy. Some people seem to forget that we have a Navy. We must remind them. For the last thirty years I have been concerned in discussions about the possibilities of oversea invasion, and I took the responsibility on behalf of the Admiralty, at the beginning of the last war, of allowing all regular troops to be sent out of the country. That was a very serious step to take, because our Territorials had only just been called up and were quite untrained. Therefore, this island was for several months practically denuded of fighting troops. The Admiralty had confidence at that time in their ability to prevent a mass invasion even though at that time the Germans had a magnificent battle fleet in the proportion of ten to sixteen, even though they were capable of fighting a general engagement every day and any day, whereas now they have only a couple of heavy ships worth speaking of—the *Scharnhorst* and the

Gneisenau. We are also told that the Italian Navy is to come out and gain sea superiority in these waters. If they seriously intend it, I shall only say that we shall be delighted to offer Signor Mussolini a free and safeguarded passage through the Straits of Gibraltar in order that he may play the part to which he aspires. There is a general curiosity in the British Fleet to find out whether the Italians are up to the level they were at in the last war or whether they have fallen off at all.

Therefore, it seems to me that as far as seaborne invasion on a great scale is concerned, we are far more capable of meeting it today than we were at many periods in the last war and during the early months of this war, before our other troops were trained, and while the B.E.F. had proceeded abroad. Now, the Navy have never pretended to be able to prevent raids by bodies of 5,000 or 10,000 men flung suddenly across and thrown ashore at several points on the coast some dark night or foggy morning. The efficiency of sea-power, especially under modern conditions, depends upon the invading force being of large size. It has to be of large size, in view of our military strength, to be of any use. If it is of large size, then the Navy have something they can find and meet and, as it were, bite on. Now we must remember that even five divisions, however lightly equipped, would require 200 to 250 ships, and with modern air reconnaissance and photography it would not be easy to collect such an armada, marshal it, and conduct it across the sea without any powerful naval forces to escort it; and there would be very great possibilities, to put it mildly, that this armada would be intercepted long before it reached the coast, and all the men drowned in the sea, or, at the worst, blown to pieces with their equipment while they were trying to land. We also have a great system of minefields, recently strongly reinforced, through which we alone know the channels. If the enemy tries to sweep passages through these minefields, it will be the task of the Navy to destroy the mine-sweepers and any other forces employed to protect them. There should be no difficulty in this, owing to our great superiority at sea.

Those are the regular, well-tested, well-proved arguments on which we have relied during many years in peace and war. But the question is whether there are any new methods by which those solid assurances can be circumvented. Odd as it may seem, some attention has been given to this by the Admiralty, whose prime duty and responsibility it is to destroy any large seaborne expedition before it reaches, or at the moment when it reaches these shores. It would not be a good thing for me to go into details of this. It might suggest ideas to other people which they have not thought of, and they would not be likely to give us any of their ideas in exchange. All I will say is that untiring vigilance and mind-searching must be devoted to the subject, because the enemy is crafty and cunning and full of novel treacheries and stratagems. The House may be assured that the utmost ingenuity is being displayed and imagination is being evoked from large numbers of competent officers, well-trained in tactics and thoroughly up to date, to measure and counterwork novel possibilities. Untiring vigilance and untiring searching of the mind is being, and must be, devoted to the subject, because, remember, the enemy is crafty and there is no dirty trick he will not do.

Some people will ask why, then, was it that the British Navy was not able to prevent the movement of a large army from Germany into Norway across the Skagerrak? But the conditions in the Channel and in the North Sea are in no way like those which prevail in the Skagerrak. In the Skagerrak, because of the distance, we could give no air support to our surface ships, and consequently, lying as we did close to the enemy's main air power, we were compelled to use only our submarines. We could not enforce the decisive blockade or interruption which is possible from surface vessels. Our submarines took a heavy toll but could not, by themselves, prevent the invasion of Norway. In the Channel and in the North Sea, on the other hand, our superior naval surface forces, aided by our submarines, will operate with close and effective air assistance.

The Air Force

This brings me, naturally, to the great question of invasion from the air, and of the impending struggle between the British and German Air Forces. It seems quite clear that no invasion on a scale beyond the capacity of our land forces to crush speedily is likely to take place from the air until our Air Force has been definitely overpowered. In the meantime, there may be raids by parachute troops and attempted descents of airborne soldiers. We should be able to give those gentry a warm reception, both in the air and on the ground, if they reach it in any condition to continue the dispute. But the great question is:

Can we break Hitler's air weapon? Now, of course, it is a very great pity that we have not got an Air Force at least equal to that of the most powerful enemy within striking distance of these shores. But we have a very powerful Air Force which has proved itself far superior in quality, both in men and in many types of machine, to what we have met so far in the numerous and fierce air battles which have been fought with the Germans. In France, where we were at a considerable disadvantage and lost many machines on the ground when they were standing around the aerodromes, we were accustomed to inflict in the air losses of as much as two to two-and-a-half to one. In the fighting over Dunkirk, which was a sort of no-man's-land, we undoubtedly beat the German Air Force, and gained the mastery of the local air, inflicting here a loss of three or four to one day after day. Anyone who looks at the photographs which were published a week or so ago of the re-embarkation, showing the masses of troops assembled on the beach and forming an ideal target for hours at a time, must realize that this re-embarkation would not have been possible unless the enemy had resigned all hope of recovering air superiority at that time and at that place.

In the defence of this island the advantages to the defenders will be much greater than they were in the fighting around Dunkirk. We hope to improve on the rate of three or four to one which was realized at Dunkirk; and in addition all our injured machines and their crews which get down safely—and, surprisingly, a very great many injured machines and men do get down safely in modern air fighting—all of these will fall, in an attack upon these islands, on friendly soil and live to fight another day; whereas all the injured enemy machines and their complements will be total losses as far as the war is concerned.

During the great battle in France, we gave very powerful and continuous aid to the French Army, both by fighters and bombers; but in spite of every kind of pressure we never would allow the entire metropolitan fighter strength of the Air Force to be consumed. This decision was painful, but it was also right, because the fortunes of the battle in France could not have been decisively affected even if we had thrown in our entire fighter force. That battle was lost by the unfortunate strategical opening, by the extraordinary and unforeseen power of the armoured columns and by the great preponderance of the German Army in numbers. Our fighter Air Force might easily have been exhausted as a mere accident in that great struggle, and then we should have found ourselves at the present time in a very serious plight. But as it is, I am happy to inform the House that our fighter strength is stronger at the present time relatively to the Germans, who have suffered terrible losses, than it has ever been; and consequently we believe ourselves possessed of the capacity to continue the war in the air under better conditions than we have ever experienced before. I look forward confidently to the exploits of our fighter pilots—these splendid men, this brilliant youth—who will have the glory of saving their native land, their island home, and all they love, from the most deadly of all attacks.

There remains, of course, the danger of bombing attacks, which will certainly be made very soon upon us by the bomber forces of the enemy. It is true that the German bomber force is superior in numbers to ours; but we have a very large bomber force also, which we shall use to strike at military targets in Germany without intermission. I do not at all underrate the severity of the ordeal which lies before us; but I believe our countrymen will show themselves capable of standing up to it like the brave men of Barcelona, and will be able to stand up to it, and carry on in spite of it, at least as well as any other people in the world. Much will depend upon this; every man and every woman will have the chance to show the finest qualities of their race, and render the highest service to their cause. For all of us, at this time, whatever our sphere, our station, our occupation or our duties, it will be a help to remember the famous lines:

> 'He nothing common did or mean,
> Upon that memorable scene.'

I have thought it right upon this occasion to give the House and the country some indication of the solid, practical grounds upon which we base our inflexible resolve to continue the war. There are a good many people who say, 'Never mind. Win or lose, sink or swim, better die than submit to tyranny—and such a tyranny.' And I do not dissociate myself from them. But I can assure them that our professional advisers of the three Services unitedly advise that we carry on the war, and that there are good and reasonable hopes of final victory. We have fully informed and consulted all the self-governing Dominions, these great communities far beyond the oceans who have been built up on our laws and on our civilization, and who are absolutely free to choose their course, but are absolutely devoted to the ancient Motherland, and who feel themselves inspired by the same emotions which lead me to stake our all upon duty and honour. We have fully consulted them, and I have received from their Prime Ministers, Mr Mackenzie King of Canada, Mr Menzies of Australia, Mr Fraser of New Zealand and General Smuts of South Africa—that wonderful man, with his immense profound mind, and his eye watching from a distance the whole panorama of European affairs—I have received from all these eminent men, who all have governments behind them elected on wide franchises, who are all there because they represent the will of their people, messages couched in the most moving terms in which they endorse our decision to fight on, and declare themselves ready to share our fortunes and to persevere to the end. That is what we are going to do.

The Battle of Britain About to Begin

We may now ask ourselves: In what way has our position worsened since the beginning of the war? It has worsened by the fact that the Germans have conquered a large part of the coastline of Western Europe, and many small countries have been overrun by them. This aggravates the possibilities of air attack and adds to our naval pre-occupations. It in no way diminishes, but on the contrary definitely increases, the power of our long-distance blockade. Similarly, the entrance of Italy into the war increases the power of our long-distance blockade. We have stopped the worst leak by that. We do not know whether military resistance will come to an end in France or not, but should it do so, then of course the Germans will be able to concentrate their forces, both military and industrial, upon us. But for the reasons I have given to the House these will not be found so easy to apply. If invasion has become more imminent, as no doubt it has, we, being relieved from the task of maintaining a large army in France, have far larger and more efficient forces to meet it.

If Hitler can bring under his despotic control the industries of the countries he has conquered, this will add greatly to his already vast armament output. On the other hand, this will not happen immediately, and we are now assured of immense, continuous and increasing support in supplies and munitions of all kinds from the United States; and especially of aeroplanes and pilots from the Dominions and across the oceans, coming from regions which are beyond the reach of enemy bombers.

I do not see how any of these factors can operate to our detriment on balance before the winter comes; and the winter will impose a strain upon the Nazi régime, with almost all Europe writhing and starving under its cruel heel, which, for all their ruthlessness, will run them very hard. We must not forget that from the moment when we declared war on 3rd September it was always possible for Germany to turn all her Air Force upon this country, together with any other devices of invasion she might conceive, and that France could have done little or nothing to prevent her doing so. We have, therefore, lived under this danger, in principle and in a slightly modified form, during all these months. In the meanwhile, however, we have enormously improved our methods of defence, and we have learned, what we had no right to assume at the beginning, namely, that the individual aircraft and the individual British pilot have a sure and definite superiority. Therefore, in casting up this dread balance-sheet and contemplating our dangers with a disillusioned eye, I see great reason for intense vigilance and exertion, but none whatever for panic or despair.

During the first four years of the last war the Allies experienced nothing but disaster and disappointment. That was our constant fear: one blow after another, terrible losses, frightful dangers. Everything miscarried. And yet at the end of those four years the morale of the allies was higher than that of the Germans, who had moved from one aggressive triumph to another, and who stood everywhere triumphant invaders of the lands into which they had broken. During that war we repeatedly asked ourselves the question: How are we going to win? and no one was able ever to answer it with much precision, until at the end, quite suddenly, quite unexpectedly, our terrible foe collapsed before us, and we were so glutted with victory that in our folly we threw it away.

We do not yet know what will happen in France or whether the French resistance will be prolonged, both in France and in the French Empire overseas. The French Government will be throwing away great opportunities and casting adrift their future if they do not continue the war in accordance with their treaty obligations, from which we have not felt able to release them. The House will have read the historic declaration in which, at the desire of many Frenchmen—and of our own hearts—we have proclaimed our willingness at the darkest hour in French history to conclude a union of common citizenship in this struggle. However matters may go in France or with the French Government, or other French Governments, we in this island and in the British Empire will never lose our sense of comradeship with the French people. If we are now called upon to endure what they have been suffering, we shall emulate their courage, and if final victory rewards our toils they shall share the gains, aye, and freedom shall be restored to all. We abate nothing of our just demands; not one jot or tittle do we recede. Czechs, Poles, Norwegians, Dutch, Belgians have joined their causes to our own. All these shall be restored.

What General Weygand called the Battle of France is over. I expect that the Battle of Britain is about to begin. Upon this battle depends the survival of Christian civilization. Upon it depends our own British life, and the long continuity of our institutions and our Empire. The whole fury and might of the enemy must very soon be turned on us. Hitler knows that he will have to break us in this island or lose the war. If we can stand up to him, all Europe may be free and the life of the world may move forward into broad, sunlit uplands. But if we fail, then the whole world, including the United States, including all that we have known and cared for, will sink into the abyss of a new dark age made more sinister, and perhaps more protracted, by the lights of perverted science. Let us therefore brace ourselves to our duties, and so bear ourselves that, if the British Empire and its Commonwealth last for a thousand years, men will still say, 'This was their finest hour.'

The Air Raids on London

As Mr Churchill had forecast, the Battle of Britain was fought in the skies above southern England in the summer of 1940. *The Royal Air Force emerged victorious from that struggle, and in a sentence which will be quoted as long as English is spoken, he expressed the gratitude of free people to the young men who made up that force: 'Never in the field of human conflict was so much owed by so many to so few.'*

Thereafter Hitler attempted to bring Britain to her knees by intensive air raids on the great centres of population. In the speech which follows Mr Churchill describes this attack, particularly on London. This speech shows how facts and figures can be woven into the pattern of a great speech without detracting from its majesty and power. Again, one is very conscious of his sympathy and compassion for humble people. He knew that the war pressed heavily upon individuals, and although he was dealing with great events and great ideas and great policies, he never lost sight of the fact that in the long run the war would be won by the patience and the courage of humble people.

It is also worth noticing that he never attempted to encourage by false promises. The last paragraph of this speech is worth studying in this connection.

THE EFFECTS OF THE 'BLITZ'

A MONTH has passed since Herr Hitler turned his rage and malice on to the civil population of our great cities and particularly of London. He declared in his speech of 4th September that he would raze our cities to the ground, and since then he has been trying to carry out his fell purpose. Naturally, the first question we should ask is to what extent the full strength of the German bombing force has been deployed. I will give the House the best opinion I have been able to form on what is necessarily to some extent a matter of speculation. After their very severe mauling on 15th August, the German short-range dive bombers, of which there are several hundred, have been kept carefully out of the air fighting. This may be, of course, because they are being held in reserve so that they may play their part in a general plan of invasion or reappear in some other theatre of war. We have, therefore, had to deal with the long-range German bombers alone.

It would seem that, taking day and night together, nearly 400 of these machines have, on the average, visited our shores every twenty-four hours. We are doubtful whether this rate of sustained attack could be greatly exceeded; no doubt a concentrated effort could be made for a few days at a time, but this would not sensibly affect the monthly average. Certainly there has been a considerable tailing off in the last ten days, and all through the month that has passed since the heavy raids began on 7th September, we have had a steady decline in casualties and damage to so-called vulnerable points. We know, of course, exactly what we are doing in reply, and the size of our own bombing force, and from the many sources which are open to us we believe that the German heavy bomber pilots are being worked at least as hard as, and maybe a great deal harder than, our own. The strain upon them is, therefore, very considerable. The bulk of them do not seem capable of anything beyond blind bombing. I always hesitate to say anything of an optimistic nature, because our people do not mind being told the worst. They resent anything in the nature of soothing statements which are not borne out by later events, and after all, war is full of unpleasant surprises.

On the whole, however, we may, I think, under all reserve reach, provisionally, the conclusion that the German average effort against this country absorbs a very considerable part of their potential strength. I should not like to say that we have the measure of their power, but we feel more confident about it than we have ever done before.

Let us now proceed to examine the effect of this ruthless and indiscriminate attack upon the easiest of all targets, namely, the great built-up areas of this land. The Germans have recently volunteered some statements of a boastful nature about the weight of explosives which they have discharged upon us during the whole war, and also on some particular occasions. These statements are not necessarily untrue, and they do not appear unreasonable to us. We were told on 23rd September that 22,000 tons of explosives had been discharged upon Great Britain since the beginning of the war. No doubt this included the mines on the coast. We were told also, on last Thursday week, that 251 tons were thrown upon London in a single night, that is to say, only a few tons less than the total dropped on the whole country throughout the last war. Now, we know exactly what our casualties have been. On that particular Thursday night 180 persons were killed in London as a result of 251 tons of bombs. That is to say, it took one ton of bombs to kill three-quarters of a person. We know, of course, exactly the ratio of loss in the last war, because all the facts were ascertained after it was over. In that war the small bombs of early patterns which were used killed ten persons for every ton discharged in the built-up areas. Therefore, the deadliness of the attack in this war appears to be only one-thirteenth of that of 1914–18. Let us say, 'less than one-tenth', so as to be on the safe side. That is, the mortality is less than one-tenth of the mortality attaching to the German bombing attacks in the last war. This is a very remarkable fact, deserving of profound consideration. I adduce it, because it is the foundation of some further statements, which I propose to make later on.

What is the explanation? There can only be one, namely, the vastly improved methods of shelter which have been adopted. In the last war there were hardly any air-raid shelters, and very few basements had been strengthened. Now we have this ever-growing system of shelters, among which the Anderson shelter justly deserves its fame, and the mortality has been reduced to one-thirteenth, or, say, at least one-tenth. This appears, as I say, not only to be remarkable, but also reassuring. It has altered, of course, the whole of the estimates we had made of the severity of the attacks to which we should be exposed. Whereas, when we entered the war at the call of duty and honour, we expected to sustain losses which might amount to 3,000 killed in a single night and 12,000 wounded, night after night, and made hospital arrangements on the basis of 250,000 casualties merely as a first pro-vision—whereas that is what we did at the beginning of the war, we have actually had since it began, up to last Saturday, as a result of air bombing, about 8,500 killed and 13,000 wounded. This shows that things do not always turn out as badly as one expects. Also, it shows that one should never hesitate, as a nation or as an individual, to face dangers because they appear to the imagination to be so formidable. Since the heavy raiding began on 7th September, the figures of killed and seriously wounded have declined steadily week by week, from over 6,000 in the first week to just under 5,000 in the second, and from about 4,000 in the third week to under 3,000 in the last of the four weeks.

The destruction of property has, however, been very considerable. Most painful is the number of small houses inhabited by working folk which have been destroyed, but the loss has also fallen heavily upon the West End, and all classes have suffered evenly, as they would desire to do. I do not propose to give exact figures of the houses which have been destroyed or seriously damaged. That is our affair. We will rebuild them, more to our credit than some of them were before. London, Liverpool, Manchester, Birmingham may have much more to suffer, but they will rise from their ruins, more healthy and, I hope, more beautiful. We must not exaggerate the material damage which has been done. The papers are full of pictures of demolished houses, but naturally they do not fill their restricted space with the numbers that are left standing. If you go, I am told, to the top of Primrose Hill or any of the other eminences of London and look around, you would not know that any harm had been done to our city.

Statisticians may amuse themselves by calculating that after making allowance for the working of the law of diminishing returns, through the same house being struck twice or three times over, it would take ten years at the present rate, for half the houses of London to be demolished. After that, of course, progress would be much slower. Quite a lot of things are going to happen to Herr Hitler and the Nazi régime before ten years are up, and even Signor Mussolini has some experiences ahead of him which he had not foreseen at the time when he thought it safe and profitable to stab the stricken and prostrate French Republic in the back. Neither by material damage nor by slaughter will the people of the British Empire be turned from their solemn and inexorable purpose. It is the practice and in some cases the duty of many of my colleagues and many Members of the House to visit the scenes of destruction as promptly as possible, and I go myself from time to time. In all my life, I have never been treated with so much kindness as by the people who have suffered most. One would think one had brought some great benefit to them, instead of the blood and tears, the toil and sweat which is all I have ever promised. On every side, there is the cry, 'We can take it!' but with it, there is also the cry, 'Give it 'em back!'

THE FUTURE

The question of reprisals is being discussed in some quarters as if it were a moral issue. What are reprisals? What we are doing now is to batter continuously, with forces which steadily increase in power, each one of those points in Germany which we believe will do the Germans most injury and will most speedily lessen their power to strike at us. Is that a reprisal? It seems to me very like one. At any rate, it is all we have time for now. We should be foolish to shift off those military targets which the skill of our navigators enables us to find with a very great measure of success, to any other targets at the present stage. Although the bombing force that we are able as yet to employ is, as I have told the House on several occasions, much less numerous than that of which the enemy disposes, I believe it to be true that we have done a great deal more harm to the war-making capacity of Germany than they have done to us. Do not let us get into a sterile controversy as to what are and what are not reprisals. Our object must be to inflict the maximum harm on the enemy's war-making capacity. That is the only object that we shall pursue.

It must not be thought that the mists and storms which enshroud our island in the winter months will by themselves prevent the German bombers from the crude, indiscriminate bombing by night of our built-up areas into which they have relapsed. No one must look forward to any relief merely from the winter weather. We have, however, been thinking about the subject for some time, and it may be that new methods will be devised to make the wholesale bombing of the civilian population by night and in fog more exciting to the enemy than it is at present. The House will not expect me to indicate or foreshadow any of these methods. It would be much better for us to allow our visitors to find them out for themselves in due course by practical experience. I think that is much the best way to handle that particular matter.

As I see it, we must so arrange that, when any district is smitten by bombs which are flung about at utter random, strong, mobile forces will descend on the scene in power and mercy to conquer the flames, as they have done, to rescue sufferers, provide them with food and shelter, to whisk them away to places of rest and refuge, and to place in their hands leaflets which anyone can understand to reassure them that they have not lost all, because all will share their material loss, and in sharing it, sweep it away. These schemes and measures, pursued on the greatest scale and with fierce energy, will require the concentrated attention of the House in the weeks that lie before us. We have to make a job of this business of living and working under fire, and I have not the slightest doubt that when we have settled down to it, we shall establish conditions which will be a credit to our island society and to the whole British family, and will enable us to maintain the production of those weapons in good time upon which our whole safety and future depend. Thus we shall be able to prove to all our friends and sympathizers in every land, bond or free, that Hitler's act of mass terror against the British nation has failed as conspicuously as his magnetic mine and other attempts to strangle our seaborne trade.

Meanwhile, what has happened to the invasion which we have been promised every month and almost every week since the beginning of July? Do not let us be lured into supposing that the danger is past. On the contrary, unwearying vigilance and the swift and steady strengthening of our Forces by land, sea and air which is in progress must be at all costs maintained. Now that we are in October, however, the weather becomes very uncertain, and there are not many lucid intervals of two or three days together in which river barges can cross the narrow seas and land upon our beaches. Still, those intervals may occur. Fogs may aid the foe. Our armies, which are growing continually in numbers, equipment, mobility and training, must be maintained all through the winter, not only along the beaches but in reserve, as the majority are, like leopards crouching to spring at the invader's throat.

The main reason why the invasion has not been attempted up to the present is, of course, the succession of brilliant victories gained by our fighter aircraft, and gained by them over the largely superior numbers which the enemy have launched against us. The three great days of 15th August, 15th September and 27th September have proved to all the world that here at home over our own island we have the mastery of the air. That is a tremendous fact.

Because we feel easier in ourselves and see our way more clearly through our difficulties and dangers than we did some months ago, because foreign countries, friends and foes, recognize the giant, enduring, resilient strength of Britain and the British Empire, do not let us dull for one moment the sense of the awful hazards in which we stand. Do not let us lose the conviction that it is only by supreme and superb exertions, unwearying and indomitable, that we shall save our souls alive. No one can predict, no one can even imagine, how this terrible war against German and Nazi aggression will run its course or how far it will spread or how long it will last. Long, dark months of trials and tribulations lie before us. Not only great dangers, but many more misfortunes, many shortcomings, many mistakes, many disappointments will surely be our lot. Death and sorrow will be the companions of our journey; hardship our garment; constancy and valour our only shield. We must be united, we must be undaunted, we must be inflexible. Our qualities and deeds must burn and glow through the gloom of Europe until they become the veritable beacon of its salvation.

To the French People

The modern miracle of radio presented Mr Churchill with a great opportunity to rally not only the British people but lovers of freedom throughout the world. The spoken word could leap over the barriers and fortifications which the Germans had erected in conquered Europe. The Germans knew this, and stringent penalties were imposed on anyone who listened in to broadcasts from Britain, and particularly to broadcasts made by Mr Churchill.

The following broadcast, made in October, 1940, is typical of the speeches which he made to other countries during the war. One must picture the circumstances in which this speech was heard. Brave French men and French women in a dark October night, would be crouching over their wireless sets, listening eagerly but anxiously to the encouragement which Mr Churchill gave them. Outside there was menace. A footstep in the street, a knock on the door; these threatened danger. Only in the voice was there comfort.

Notice how different his speech is from the more formal speeches which he gave in the House of Commons. Here the tone is friendly and intimate. As always, he appeals to the best in human nature. He recalls the past glories of France. His reference to Napoleon, who, it must be remembered, had been the deadly enemy of Britain, is most apposite.

In his closing remarks he hints at the resistance movement which would one day arise in France and which, in fact, was one of the glorious achievements of the French people in the Second World War. Then there is the closing paragraph: the friendly 'Good night', which, like a benediction, brings a peaceful close to the day and glorious hope for the morning.

FRENCHMEN! For more than thirty years in peace and war I have marched with you, and I am marching still along the same road. Tonight I speak to you at your firesides wherever you may be, or whatever your fortunes are. I repeat the prayer around the louis d'or, '*Dieu protège la France*'. Here at home in England, under the fire of the Boche, we do not forget the ties and links that unite us to France, and we are persevering steadfastly and in good heart in the cause of European freedom and fair dealing for the common people of all countries, for which, with you, we drew the sword. When good people get into trouble because they are attacked and heavily smitten by the vile and wicked, they must be very careful not to get at loggerheads with one another. The common enemy is always trying to bring this about, and, of course, in bad luck a lot of things happen which play into the enemy's hands. We must just make the best of things as they come along.

Here in London, which Herr Hitler says he will reduce to ashes, and which his aeroplanes are now bombarding, our people are bearing up unflinchingly. Our Air Force has more than held its own. We are waiting for the long-promised invasion. So are the fishes. But, of course, this for us is only the beginning. Now in 1940, in spite of occasional losses, we have, as ever, command of the seas. In 1941 we shall have the command of the air. Remember what that means. Herr Hitler with his tanks and other mechanical weapons, and also by Fifth Column intrigue with traitors, has managed to subjugate for the time being most of the finest races in Europe, and his little Italian accomplice is trotting along hopefully and hungrily, but rather wearily and very timidly, at his side. They both wish to carve up France and her Empire as if it were a fowl: to one a leg, to another a wing or perhaps part of the breast. Not only the French Empire will be devoured by these two ugly customers, but Alsace-Lorraine will go once again under the German yoke, and Nice, Savoy and Corsica—Napoleon's Corsica— will be torn from the fair realm of France. But Herr Hitler is not thinking only of stealing other people's territories, or flinging gobbets of them to his little confederate. I tell you truly what you must believe when I say this evil man, this monstrous abortion of hatred and defeat, is resolved on nothing less than the complete wiping out of the French nation, and the disintegration of its whole life and future. By all kinds of sly and savage means, he is plotting and working to quench for ever the fountain of characteristic French culture and of French inspiration to the world. All Europe, if he has his way, will be reduced to one uniform Boche-land, to be exploited, pillaged, and bullied by his Nazi gangsters. You will excuse my speaking frankly because this is not a time to mince words. It is not defeat that France will now be made to suffer at German hands, but the doom of complete obliteration. Army, Navy, Air Force, religion, law, language, culture, institutions, literature, history, tradition, all are to be effaced by the brute strength of a triumphant army and the scientific low-cunning of a ruthless police force.

Frenchmen—re-arm your spirits before it is too late. Remember how Napoleon said before one of his battles: 'These same Prussians who are so boastful today were three to one at Jena, and six to one at Montmirail.' Never will I believe that the soul of France is dead. Never will I believe that her place amongst the greatest nations of the world has been lost for ever! All these schemes and crimes of Herr Hitler's are bringing upon him and upon all who belong to his system a retribution which many of us will live to see. The story is not yet finished, but it will not be so long. We are on his track, and so are our friends across the Atlantic Ocean, and your friends across the Atlantic Ocean. If he cannot destroy us, we will surely destroy him and all his gang, and all their works. Therefore, have hope and faith, for all will come right.

Now what is it we British ask of you in this present hard and bitter time? What we ask at this moment in our struggle to win the victory which we will share with you, is that if you cannot help us, at least you will not hinder us. Presently you will be able to weight the arm that strikes for you, and you ought to do so. But even now we believe that Frenchmen, wherever they may be, feel their hearts warm and a proud blood tingle in their veins when we have some success in the air or on the sea, or presently—for that will come—upon the land.

Remember we shall never stop, never weary, and never give in, and that our whole people and Empire have vowed themselves to the task of cleansing Europe from the Nazi pestilence and saving the world from the new Dark Ages. Do not imagine, as the German-controlled wireless tells you, that we English seek to take your ships and colonies. We seek to beat the life and soul out of Hitler and Hitlerism. That alone, that all the time, that to the end. We do not covet anything from any nation except their respect. Those Frenchmen who are in the French Empire, and those who are in so-called unoccupied France, may see their way from time to time to useful action. I will not go into details. Hostile ears are listening. As for those, to whom English hearts go out in full, because they see them under the sharp discipline, oppression and spying of the Hun—as to those Frenchmen in the occupied regions, to them I say, when they think of the future let them remember the words which Gambetta, that great Frenchman, uttered after 1870 about the future of France and what was to come: 'Think of it always: speak of it never.'

Good night then: sleep to gather strength for the morning. For the morning will come. Brightly will it shine on the brave and true, kindly upon all who suffer for the cause, glorious upon the tombs of heroes. Thus will shine the dawn. *Vive la France!* Long live also the forward march of the common people in all the lands towards their just and true inheritance, and towards the broader and fuller age.

The Iron Curtain

After the end of the war with Germany a General Election took place in Britain on the 26th July, 1945, as a result of which the Conservative Party, led by Mr Churchill, was defeated and the Labour Party, led by Mr Attlee, formed a new government. The war with Japan ended less than a month after the election, and thereafter began the mighty task of reconstruction.

Mr Churchill realized that although the Axis Powers had been defeated a new danger confronted the world. The attitude of Russia was a great disappointment to all who believed that an allied victory would usher in a long period of peace.

In a speech delivered at Fulton, in March, 1946, in the United States of America, he set out his fears. This speech was memorable not only for the lesson which it contained but also because of a phrase which graphically illustrated the new Europe: 'An Iron Curtain has descended across the continent.'

IT is an honour, perhaps almost unique, for a private visitor to be introduced to an academic audience by the President of the United States. Amid his heavy burdens, duties, and responsibilities—unsought but not recoiled from—the President has travelled a thousand miles to dignify and magnify our meeting here today and to give me an opportunity of addressing this kindred nation, as well as my own countrymen across the ocean, and perhaps some other countries too.

The President has told you that it is his wish, as I am sure it is yours, that I should have full liberty to give my true and faithful counsel in these anxious and baffling times. I shall certainly avail myself of this freedom.

Let me, however, make it clear that I have no official mission or status of any kind, and that I speak only for myself. There is nothing here but what you see.

I can therefore allow my mind, with the experience of a lifetime, to play over the problems which beset us on the morrow of our absolute victory in arms, and to try to make sure with what strength I have that what has been gained with so much sacrifice and suffering shall be preserved for the future glory and safety of mankind.

The United States stands at this time at the pinnacle of world power. It is a solemn moment for the American Democracy. For with this primacy in power is also joined an awe-inspiring accountability to the future. If you look around you, you must feel not only the sense of duty done but also you must feel anxiety lest you fall below the level of achievement. Opportunity is here now, clear and shining for both our countries. To reject it or ignore it or fritter it away will bring upon us all the long reproaches of the after-time.

It is necessary that constancy of mind, persistency of purpose, and the grand simplicity of decision shall guide and rule the conduct of the English-speaking peoples in peace as they did in war. We must, and I believe we shall, prove ourselves equal to this severe requirement.

A shadow has fallen upon the scenes so lately lighted by the allied victory. Nobody knows what Soviet Russia and its Communist international organization intends to do in the immediate future, or what are the limits, if any, to their expansive and proselytizing tendencies. I have a strong admiration and regard for the valiant Russian people and for my wartime comrade, Marshal Stalin. There is deep sympathy and good-will in Britain—and I doubt not here also—towards the peoples of all the Russias and a resolve to persevere through many differences and rebuffs in establishing lasting friendships. It is my duty, however, for I am sure you would wish me to state the facts as I see them to you, to place before you certain facts about the present position in Europe.

From Stettin in the Baltic to Trieste in the Adriatic, an iron curtain has descended across the Continent. Behind that line lie all the capitals of the ancient states of central and eastern Europe. Warsaw, Berlin, Prague, Vienna, Budapest, Belgrade, Bucharest and Sofia, all these famous cities and the populations around them lie in what I must call the Soviet sphere, and all are subject, in one form or another, not only to Soviet influence but to a very high and, in many cases, increasing measure of control from Moscow.

Police governments are pervading from Moscow. Athens alone, with its immortal glories, is free to decide its future at an election under British, American, and French observation.

The safety of the world requires a unity in Europe, from which no nation should be permanently outcast. It is from the quarrels of the strong parent races in Europe that the world wars we have witnessed, or which occurred in former times, have sprung.

Twice in our own lifetime we have seen the United States, against their wishes and their traditions, against arguments, the force of which it is impossible not to comprehend, drawn by irresistible forces, into these wars in time to secure the victory of the good cause, but only after frightful slaughter and devastation had occurred. Twice the United States has had to send several millions of its young men across the Atlantic to find the war; but now we all can find any nation, wherever it may dwell, between dusk and dawn. Surely we should work with conscious purpose for a grand pacification of Europe, within the structure of the United Nations and in accordance with its Charter.

However, in a great number of countries, far from the Russian frontiers and throughout the world, Communist fifth columns are established and work in complete unity and absolute obedience to the directions they receive from the Communist centre.

The outlook is also anxious in the Far East and especially in Manchuria. The agreement which was made at Yalta, to which I was a party, was extremely favourable to Soviet Russia, but it was made at a time when no one could say that the German war might not extend all through the summer and autumn of 1945 and when the Japanese war was expected to last for a further eighteen months from the end of the German war.

I have felt bound to portray the shadow which, alike in the West and in the East, falls upon the world. I was a high minister at the time of the Versailles Treaty and a close friend of Mr Lloyd George, who was the head of the British delegation at Versailles. I did not myself agree with many things that were done, but I have a very strong impression in my mind of that situation, and I find it painful to contrast it with that which prevails now. In those days there were high hopes and unbounded confidence that the wars were over, and that the League of Nations would become all-powerful. I do not see or feel that same confidence or even the same hopes in the haggard world at the present time.

On the other hand I repulse the idea that a new war is inevitable; still more that it is imminent. It is because I am sure that our fortunes are still in our own hands and that we hold the power to save the future, that I feel the duty to speak out now that I have the occasion and the opportunity to do so. I do not believe that Soviet Russia desires war. What they desire is the fruits of war and the indefinite expansion of their power and doctrines. But what we have to consider here today while time remains, is the permanent prevention of war and the establishment of conditions of freedom and democracy as rapidly as possible in all countries. Our difficulties and dangers will not be removed by closing our eyes to them. They will not be removed by mere waiting to see what happens; nor will they be removed by a policy of appeasement. What is needed is a settlement, and the longer this is delayed, the more difficult it will be and the greater our dangers will become.

If the population of the English-speaking Commonwealth be added to that of the United States with all that such co-operation implies in the air, on the sea, all over the globe, and in science and in industry, and in moral force, there will be no quivering, precarious balance of power to offer its temptation to ambition or adventure. On the contrary, there will be an overwhelming assurance of security. If we adhere faithfully to the Charter of the United Nations and walk forward in sedate and sober strength, seeking no one's land or treasure, seeking to lay no arbitrary control upon the thoughts of men; if all British moral and material forces and convictions are joined with your own in fraternal association, the high roads of the future will be clear, not only for us but for all, not only for our time, but for a century to come.

WALTER ELLIOT

1888-1958

Anniversary, 3rd September, 1942

Walter Elliot was one of the most famous of the men and women who, during the Second World War, broadcast to the world on the Overseas Service of the B.B.C. In the difficult art of broadcasting nobody excelled the Prime Minister but few excelled Walter Elliot. He was splendidly equipped for this work. He was a scientist but he was also a man of action; he had held high office in government but he was also a man of letters; he was fertile in ideas and resources, but he was thoughtful and balanced.

Of broadcast speeches, Elliot said: 'The speaker must not lecture or harangue. Especially he must not dally. It is a monologue, but a monologue of urgency. It is utterly different from the technique of speechmaking.'

This broadcast shows Elliot at his best. There is first of all his tremendous verve and gusto. We can hear, as it were, the thud of word and sentence. There is the vivid pen picture, the striking word and phrase and the certainty of inward conviction. As always in great speeches, there is the appeal to what is best in human nature. He is friendly and persuasive in approach; he realizes that he is not speaking to an audience in a hall but to individuals seated round a fireside. Remember that this particular speech was addressed to Americans to whom many of the incidents described in the broadcast were but hearsay.

I SUPPOSE we are all thinking and speaking of the same thing today—the Fourth Year, and the three before.

It is difficult to remember exactly what we were doing before the war, and why, so history for this purpose must begin in the autumn of 1939. I well remember when the war came to Great Britain. It came to Parliament here, on the night before the Sunday of the war. Poland had been attacked. Last-minute diplomatic attempts to obtain German withdrawal were still in progress. Parliament met, awaited news, adjourned and met again in an atmosphere of indescribable tension—and then adjourned, till the morrow. There was, I think, only one fear in anyone's heart—that we, or others, should weaken; that the Axis challenge should not be taken up; that the enemy's purpose, now so plainly disclosed, should not be met by a purpose, equal and opposite, from ourselves.

Parliament knew well enough when it dispersed that night into the black streets, with a raging thunderstorm coming up to break like the father and mother of all air raids, what the decision was to be. It was war; we were going to front Germany. We could do no other. And so the decisive step was taken, and the Empire stood up to fight. Poland was the first to take up arms and withstand attack. But Britain and the Empire were the first to declare war, themselves unassailed, on behalf of another. These were great resolves; and worth while recalling when we look back along the road.

What stands out, as we look? I know well enough what stands out first in my own memory. It is—the Evacuation. It was not only a colossal undertaking; it was a great challenge to the nation's spirit. Some three million folk perhaps, to be moved in three days. And we did move a million and three-quarters—ten forces the size of our first Expeditionary Force to France—schools uprooted, homes uprooted, hospitals uprooted, eight thousand women on the verge of child-birth to transport and house from London alone, the lives of countless thousands of households, both town and country, mingled and melted together as the steel is melted for a great gun. But this was to stand by for Rotterdam. The people's resolve took the strain. How much shock and grief was caused will never be known; but there were many shocks, both to hosts and guests, and much grief. And remember, all that movement was being done in the days before the war actually broke out, when we were still nominally at peace; when there was nothing but Danzig, apparently, to explain or justify this vast upheaval. The very casualties to be expected from the air raids had been forecast, forecast repeatedly and in public. They were on a scale sufficient to shake the heart of the most resolute. A quarter of a million in the first ten days was the standard figure. Twenty-five thousand a night, night after night; and then, it was thought, it would slacken, for someone would have lost and won—no guarantee who. Such was the stake Britain placed on the board for the first weeks of three years ago. It was not exacted; but it was laid down. That was the first earnest of victory.

Now, in these war years, all the social service work of the last fifty years, intensified in the last twenty, has been brought to the test.

We have now behind us three years of war. Heavily tested the Home Front has been. Yet the nation is healthy, the nation is strong, the nation's food is competently and adequately distributed. The sick are cared for, the children are at school. There is the audit. It balances; it shows a credit. That strikes very deep. That, far more than a balanced Budget, is a test of resolve—a test of reality.

In May of 1940, the earth moved and the landslides commenced. In six weeks, Europe, as we had known it for centuries, shook and disappeared. Turn, for the experience of these days, from impersonal achievements, such as we have just recalled, to something intensely personal—from acts you could only know by hearsay, to the acts which you shared instantaneously with us here—Churchill's leadership—Churchill's addresses—in which radio almost for the first time came to its full stature. He spoke in English, a universal language; he spoke with a gusto, a zest which made death itself seem but another adventure and made men happy to follow him. He spoke, first, for the Admiralty, and later, for the whole nation, with a swing and a stride which showed that Malbrouk had gone to the wars, and, as in the old ballad, didn't know when he'd return. When swagger was indispensable, swagger was his. There are war passages in the Old Testament which might have been written for him in those days: 'He saith among the trumpets, Ha, ha: he mocketh at fear and is not affrighted, neither turneth he back from the sword.' One might even have gone on to the tremendous phrase 'his neck is clothed with thunder' were it not that Churchill himself laid that one stone dead, in his immortal pun, delivered to the hushed and expectant multitudes of North America, at a flaming crisis of their career, 'Some chicken—some neck'. A people which, in the utmost peril, sought out, and entrusted itself to a leader not merely youthful, but childlike, has a youth movement in its own heart, spontaneous, vigorous, and real; and not a synthetic imitation, in the schoolrooms, of the barrack-square. You heard him; but we saw him; and that was a privilege indeed.

I mentioned his leadership of the Admiralty—but the sea-affair, of which the Admiralty is a part, is greater than any man. The sterling metal, and the professional honour, of her men of the sea has been, for many centuries now, the great achievement of England. It held good. In the earliest days, the murder of the *Athenia* showed what was coming. The assault of the first weeks of the war brought a casualty list amongst the ships comparable with the heaviest figures of 1917. It was subdued, for a time, but the ships sailed as steadily when the slaughter was at its worst as when it fell away. After the submarines, warships in armour came out against the merchant convoys; they were met with a resolution which was manifest in the action of the *Jervis Bay*, only an armed merchant cruiser, yet she closed and fought a ship of the line. And afterwards a thousand times, up to the most recent plod-plod-plod by the Malta convoy through the whole blazing length of the Western Mediterranean. You can't enlarge upon that. You don't need to. Neither need one discuss, nor justify, the Royal Navy. I have in mind pictures of the ports of South Wales, of Bristol with its balloons; of Liverpool, blasted and scarred almost out of recognition, with the ships coming in and going out upon their lawful occasions; and most of all my own furious Clydeside, where the warships and the merchant-men lie down together, head and tail, great and historic ships like hay-cocks in a field, floating light and high after bringing through the booms all the strength of the New World: till one realizes what sea-power means, and some at least of the reasons why this island, in the third year of war, is actually producing more munitions than the United States of America and how we can put twenty-two million people, two-thirds of our adult population, directly on the war effort.

Supported by those strong pillars the nation stood after the avalanche, and began to get its breath. Suddenly another pillar was added—the R.A.F. During all the glorious early summer of 1940 the drone of planes never seemed to stop. Then the Germans launched their air attack, and the smoke of London's burning went up to Heaven—a cloud by day, and a fire by night. These were the days when we listened to the one o'clock news as a man listens to the summing up in a trial for his life; and each day, as the trial closed, and the summing up began to come our way, everyone shook himself, like Kipling's old General, fighting without aid and without expectation on the Roman Wall against the barbarians, who said, 'The Oracle declares that I am not to die today.' And each went to work, or watch, or rare leisure, with the air of folk who had never before seen green leaves or summer weather, high noon, or dawn, and were wrapped in wonder, like men risen from the dead, that earth could be so beautiful, or life so much worth while.

All that was won and held for us by 'so few'. It is a presage of their work when they became 'so many'. But everyone missed something who did not share these days. We have lost it now ourselves; of necessity no doubt, for no man, and certainly no people, can live at such heights for very long. Nor do I say that I rest confidence upon it, as I do upon the steadfastness of the civilians, the sea-honour of the shipmen, or the valour of the R.A.F. It was an end in itself; an exaltation of the spirit, which made it possible to understand certain moments in history. I wish we could gain it again; if we did we should be irresistible.

There is one more highlight to remember, before the Adventure ended and the War began in which we are now engaged, the War which commenced when Hitler marched upon Russia and Japan attacked the United States. That highlight was at the end of 1940; when the Army suddenly began to work miracles too, and stamped about Libya and Central Africa destroying armies, overthrowing empires, and generally making Moab its washpot, and over Edom casting its shoe.

The Army has not been able, so far, to find its steady form. Its fortunes have been most incredibly chequered, and its stock now high, now low. But in these days we all saw—and all the world saw—what a British Army was doing and therefore might do again—and we remember and are not unduly cast down.

These were great days, when we of the British Commonwealth stood by ourselves. 'All alone,' as Churchill said, 'we guarded the treasure of mankind.' Now, we march in the ranks with many others, and are proud to do so; and know well the many mistakes we have made and are still making; and how we shall need all the help we can get from others, just as they in turn may find advantage in help or counsel they may derive from us.

We are going into battle in the fourth year, with many comrades, some of whom have taken the main strain of the war and some of whom are still untried. We have to go forward to the attack, for only so are wars won. In that attack, comradeship of the high heart is not less potent than the comradeship of weight of armour and guns. We believe that we have certain achievements of the spirit, already to our credit, which may be the earnest of more to come; and which in themselves may fittingly be compared with even the shining achievements of many of our comrades, allies of the United Nations.

DYLAN THOMAS

1914–1953

Holiday Memory

The premature death of Dylan Thomas in 1953 deprived modern English literature of one of its greatest writers. As a poet he had a sure eye and a great command of words. In many of his poems he looks at the world through the innocent eyes of a child.

As a story-teller and narrator he found in radio a medium which he made his own. He realized that in order to hold his audience he must be crystal clear. His nouns and his adjectives were carefully chosen to paint a picture and illustrate a scene. He realized that in radio the pictures must be painted by the speaker and that this could only be done by words. His problem was very similar to Shakespeare describing a scene for a bare Elizabethan stage: the words had to create the Forest of Arden, the battlements at Elsinore, and the enchanted island. The visual effect had to be created through the ear.

The following radio broadcast is a good example of the skill of Dylan Thomas. Note how the short, sharp phrases in the first paragraph build up the scene. The dialogue, too, is interesting. Thomas had a most flexible voice and he used it as a musician uses an instrument.

AUGUST BANK HOLIDAY. A tune on an ice-cream cornet. A slap of sea and a tickle of sand. A fanfare of sunshades opening. A wince and whinny of bathers dancing into deceptive water. A tack of dresses. A rolling of trousers. A compromise of paddlers. A sunburn of girls and a lark of boys. A silent hullabaloo of balloons.

I remember the sea telling lies in a shell held to my ear for a whole harmonious, hollow minute by a small, wet girl in an enormous bathing-suit marked 'Corporation Property'.

I remember sharing the last of my moist buns with a boy and a lion. Tawny and savage, with cruel nails and capacious mouth, the little boy tore and devoured. Wild as seed-cake, ferocious as a hearth-rug, the depressed and verminous lion nibbled like a mouse at his half a bun, and hiccupped in the sad dusk of his cage.

I remember a man like an alderman or a bailiff, bowlered and collarless, with a bag of monkey-nuts in his hand, crying 'Ride 'em, cowboy!' time and again as he whirled in his chairoplane giddily above the upturned laughing faces of the town girls bold as brass and the boys with padded shoulders and shoes sharp as knives; and the monkey-nuts flew through the air like salty hail.

Children all day capered or squealed by the glazed or bashing sea, and the steam-organ wheezed its waltzes in the threadbare playground and the waste lot, where the dodgems dodged, behind the pickle factory.

And mothers loudly warned their proud pink daughters or sons to put that jellyfish down; and fathers spread newspapers over their faces; and sand-fleas hopped on the picnic lettuce; and someone had forgotten the salt.

In those always radiant, rainless, lazily rowdy and sky-blue summers departed, I remember August Monday from the rising of the sun over the stained and royal town to the husky hushing of the roundabout music and the dowsing of the naphtha jets in the seaside fair; from bubble-and-squeak to the last of the sandy sandwiches.

There was no need, that holiday morning, for the sluggardly boys to be shouted down to breakfast; out of their jumbled beds they tumbled, scrambled into their rumpled clothes; quickly at the bathroom basin they catlicked their hands and faces but never forgot to run the water loud and long as though they washed like colliers; in front of the cracked looking-glass bordered with cigarette-cards, in their treasure-trove bedrooms, they whisked a gap-tooth comb through their surly hair; and with shining cheeks and noses and tide-marked necks, they took the stairs three at a time.

But for all their scramble and scamper, clamour on the landing, catlick and toothbrush flick, hair-whisk and stair-jump, their sisters were always there before them. Up with the lady lark, they had prinked and frizzed and hot-ironed; and smug in their blossoming dresses, ribboned for the sun, in gym-shoes white as the blanco'd snow, neat and silly with doilies and tomatoes they helped in the higgledy kitchen. They were calm; they were virtuous; they had washed their necks; they did not romp, or fidget; and only the smallest sister put out her tongue at the noisy boys.

And the woman who lived next door came into the kitchen and said that her mother, an ancient uncertain body who wore a hat with cherries, was having 'one of her days' and had insisted, that very holiday morning, in carrying all the way to the tram-stop a photograph album and the cut-glass fruit-bowl from the front room.

This was the morning when father, mending one hole in the thermos-flask, made three; when the sun declared war on the butter, and the butter ran; when dogs, with all the sweet-binned backyards to wag and sniff and bicker in, chased their tails in the jostling kitchen, worried sandshoes, snapped at flies, writhed between legs, scratched among towels, sat smiling on hampers.

And if you could have listened at some of the open doors of some of the houses in the street you might have heard:

'Uncle Owen says he can't find the bottle opener. . . .'

'Has he looked under the hallstand?'

'Willy's cut his finger. . . .'

'Got your spade?'

'If somebody doesn't kill that dog . . .'

'Uncle Owen says why should the bottle-opener be under the hall-stand?'

'Never again, never again. . . .'

'I know I put the pepper somewhere. . . .'

'Willy's bleeding. . . .'

'Look, there's a bootlace in my bucket. . . .'

'Oh come *on*, come on. . . .'

'Let's have a look at the bootlace in your bucket. . . .'

'If I lay my hands on that dog . . .'

'Uncle Owen's found the bottle-opener. . . .'

'Willy's bleeding over the cheese. . . .'

And the trams that hissed like ganders took us all to the beautiful beach.

There was cricket on the sand, and sand in the sponge cake, sand-flies in the watercress, and foolish, mulish, religious donkeys on the unwilling trot. Girls undressed in slipping tents of propriety; under invisible umbrellas, stout ladies dressed for the male and immoral sea.

Little naked navvies dug canals; children with spades and no ambition built fleeting castles; whispy young men, outside the bathing-huts, whistled at substantial young women and dogs who desired thrown stones, more than the bones of elephants. Recalcitrant uncles huddled over luke ale in the tiger-striped marquees. Mothers in black, like wobbling mountains, gasped under the discarded dresses of daughters who shrilly braved the goblin waves. And fathers, in the once-a-year sun, took fifty winks. Oh, think of all the fifty winks along the paper-bagged sand.

Liquorice Allsorts, and Welsh Hearts, were melting, and the sticks of rock, that we all sucked, were like barbers' poles made of rhubarb.

In the distance, surrounded by disappointed theoreticians and an ironmonger with a drum, a cross man on an orange-box shouted that holidays were wrong.

And the waves rolled in, with rubber ducks and clerks upon them.

I remember the patient, laborious, and enamouring hobby, or profession, of burying relatives in sand.

I remember the princely pastime of pouring sand, from cupped hands, or buckets, down collars and tops of dresses; the shriek, the shake, the slap.

I can remember the boy by himself, the beachcombing lone-wolf, hungrily waiting at the edge of family cricket; the friendless fielder, the boy uninvited to bat or to tea.

I remember the smell of sea and seaweed, wet flesh, wet hair, wet bathing-dresses, the warm smell as of a rabbity field after rain, the smell of pop and splashed sunshades and toffee, the stable-and-straw smell of hot, tossed, tumbled, dug, and trodden sand, the swill-and-gas lamp smell of Saturday night, though the sun shone strong, from the bellying beer-tents, the smell of the vinegar on shelled cockles, winkle-smell, shrimp-smell, the dripping-oily backstreet winter-smell of chips in newspapers, the smell of ships from the sun-dazed docks round the corner of the sand-hills, the smell of the known and paddled-in sea moving, full of the drowned and herrings, out and away and beyond and further still towards the Antipodes that hung their koala-bears and Maoris, kangaroos and boomerangs, upside down over the backs of the stars.

And the noise of pummelling Punch, and Judy falling, and a clock tolling or telling no time in the tenantless town; now and again a bell from a lost tower or a train on the lines behind us clearing its throat, and always the hopeless, ravenous swearing and pleading of the gulls, donkey-bray and hawker-cry, harmonicas and toy trumpets, shouting and laughing and singing, hooting of tugs and tramps, the clip of the chair-attendant's puncher, the motor-boat coughing in the bay, and the same hymn and washing of the sea that was heard in the Bible.

'If it could only just, if it could only just?' your lips said again and again as you scooped, in the hob-hot sand, dungeons, garages, torture-chambers, train tunnels, arsenals, hangars for zeppelins, witches' kitchens, vampires' parlours, smugglers' cellars, trolls' grog-shops, sewers, under a ponderous and cracking castle, 'If it could only just be like this for ever and ever amen.' August Monday all over the earth, from Mumbles where the aunties grew like ladies on a seaside tree to brown bear-hugging Henty-land and the turtled Ballantyne Islands.

'Could donkeys go on the ice?'

'Only if they got snowshoes.'

We snowshoed a meek, complaining donkey and galloped him off in the wake of the ten-foot-tall and Atlas-muscled Mounties, rifled and pemmicanned, who always, in the white Gold Rush wastes, got their black-oathed-and-bearded Man.

'Are there donkeys on desert islands?'

'Only sort-of-donkeys.'

'What d'you mean, sort-of-donkeys?'

'Native donkeys. They hunt things on them!'

'Sort-of walruses and seals and things?'

'Donkeys can't swim!'

'These donkeys can. They swim like whales, they swim like anything, they swim like——'

'Liar.'

'Liar yourself.'

And two small boys fought fiercely and silently in the sand, rolling together in a ball of legs and bottoms.

Then they went and saw the pierrots, or bought vanilla ices.

Lolling or larrikin that unsoiled, boiling beauty of a common day, great gods with their braces over their vests sang, spat pips, puffed smoke at wasps, gulped and ogled, forgot the rent, embraced, posed for the dicky-bird, were coarse, had rainbow-coloured armpits, winked, belched, blamed the radishes, looked at Ilfracombe, played hymns on paper-and-comb, peeled bananas, scratched, found seaweed in their panamas, blew up paper-bags and banged them, wished for nothing.

But over all the beautiful beach I remember most the children playing, boys and girls tumbling, moving jewels, who might never be happy again. And 'happy as a sandboy' is true as the heat of the sun.

Dusk came down; or grew up out of the sands and the sea; or curled around us from the calling docks and the bloodily smoking sun. The day was done, the sands brushed and ruffled suddenly with a sea-broom of cold wind.

And we gathered together all the spades and buckets and towels, empty hampers and bottles, umbrellas and fish-frails, bats and balls and knitting, and went—oh, listen, Dad!—to the fair in the dusk on the bald seaside field.

Fairs were no good in the day; then they were shoddy and tired; the voices of hoop-la girls were crimped as elocutionists; no cannon-ball could shake the roosting coco-nuts; the gondolas mechanically repeating their sober lurch; the Wall of Death was safe as a governess cart; the wooden animals were waiting for the night.

But in the night, the hoop-la girls, like operatic crows, croaked at the coming moon; whizz, whirl, and ten for a tanner, the coco-nuts rained from their sawdust like grouse from the Highland sky; tipsy the griffin-prowed gondolas weaved on dizzy rails and the Wall of Death was a spinning rim of ruin, and the neighing wooden horses took, to a haunting hunting tune, a thousand Becher's Brooks as easily and breezily as hooved swallows.

Approaching, at dusk, the fair-field from the beach, we scorched and gritty boys heard above the belabouring of the batherless sea the siren voices of the raucous, horsy barkers.

'Roll up, roll up!'

In her tent and her rolls of flesh the Fattest Woman in the World sat sewing her winter frock, another tent, and fixed her little eyes, blackcurrants in blancmange, on the skeletons who filed and sniggered by.

'Roll up, roll up, roll up to see the Largest Rat on Earth, the Rover or Bonzo of vermin.'

Here scampered the smallest pony, like a Shetland shrew. And here 'The Most Intelligent Fleas', trained, reined, bridled, and bitted, minutely cavorted in their glass corral.

Round galleries and shies and stalls, pennies were burning holes in a hundred pockets.

Pale young men with larded hair and Valentino-black side-whiskers, fags stuck to their lower lips, squinted along their swivel-sighted rifles and aimed at ping-pong balls dancing on fountains.

In knife-creased, silver-grey, skirt-like Oxford bags, and a sleeveless, scarlet zip-fastened shirt with yellow horizontal stripes, a collier at the strength machine spat on his hands, raised the hammer, and brought it Thor-ing down. The bell rang for Blaina.

Outside his booth stood a bitten-eared and barndoor-chested pug with a nose like a twisted swede and hair that started from his eyebrows and three teeth yellow as a camel's inviting any sportsman to a sudden and sickening basting in the sandy ring or a quid if he lasted a round; and wiry, cocky, bow-legged, coal-scarred, boozed, sportsmen by the dozen strutted in and reeled out; and still those three teeth remained, chipped and camel-yellow in the bored, teak face.

Draggled and stout-wanting mothers, with haphazard hats, hostile hatpins, buns awry, bursting bags, and children at their skirts like pop-filled and jam-smeared limpets, screamed before distorting mirrors, at their suddenly tapering or tubular bodies and huge ballconing heads, and the children gaily bellowing at their own reflected bodies withering and bulging in the glass.

Old men, smelling of Milford Haven in the rain, shuffled, badgering and cadging, round the edges of the swaggering crowd, their only wares a handful of damp confetti.

A daring dash of schoolboys, safely, shoulder to shoulder, with their father's trilbies cocked at a desperate angle over one eye, winked at and whistled after the procession past the swings of two girls arm-in-arm: always one pert and pretty, and always one with glasses.

Girls in skulled and cross-boned tunnels shrieked, and were comforted.

Young men, heroic after pints, stood up on the flying chairoplanes, tousled, crimson, and against the rules.

Jaunty girls gave sailors sauce.

All the fun of the fair in the hot, bubbling night. The man in the sand-yellow moon over the hurdy of gurdies. The swing-boats swimming to and fro like slices of the moon. Dragons and hippogriffs at the prows of the gondolas breathing fire and Sousa. Midnight roundabout riders tantivying under the fairy-lights, huntsmen on billygoats and zebras hallooing under a circle of glow-worms.

And as we climbed home, up the gas-lit hill, to the still homes over the mumbling bay, we heard the music die and the voices drift like sand. And we saw the lights of the fair fade. And, at the far end of the seaside field, they lit their lamps, one by one, in the caravans.

LORD BIRKETT
1883–

Advocacy

Lord Birkett is one of the outstanding legal minds of the present generation. As a barrister practising in the courts he won renown for his powers in advocacy; as a judge he was famous for the wisdom of his judgments; as a speaker on formal and informal occasions alike he is rightly regarded as one of the best in the country.

His mind is richly stored. It has been nourished in all that is best in English literature. His speeches are compounded of thought and reflection, delivered in a most pleasing voice and revealing a personality wise and amiable.

This address on Advocacy which in itself is a masterpiece was delivered in 1954 to the Holdsworth Club of Birmingham University. The extracts from this address show Lord Birkett's skill and charm as a speaker. They are also valuable in that they reveal his considered views regarding some of the qualities which are required by the successful public speaker. This address is memorable for the student of public speaking both for its manner and its matter.

No address on Advocacy by me could give me any satisfaction if I did not pay tribute to the men whose methods I was privileged to observe in daily practice, whose example was a perpetual fount of inspiration, and whose kindness to me can never be forgotten. The city of Birmingham nourished and nurtured these men, and for seven years allowed me to learn their great language and catch their clear accents.

Since that time I have seen, I suppose, almost every type of advocate in almost every type of Court. I have seen the great occasions, naturally rare, when as Lord Campbell said of the first speech of Thomas Erskine 'every eye was fixed on the great advocate, every syllable he uttered was quickly caught up, breathing was almost suspended, and such was the silence, that if a flake of snow had fallen, it would have been heard to fall'. But at all times and in all Courts, I have remembered the men that I first saw in action in this city practising the art of advocacy, and to them, and to the city itself, I bring today this grateful acknowledgment of my debt.

Truth, it is said, hath a quiet breast: but truth can sometimes be disturbing. And the disturbing truth must be faced at once that it is extremely doubtful whether anything can now be said on the subject of advocacy that has not already been said with complete authority some eighteen centuries ago, when Quintilian spoke with such discernment and insight. Many writers in all succeeding ages have embroidered and embellished the theme; but the essential things have long since been said. My modest purpose, therefore, is merely to set down some of the thoughts I have entertained on the subject of advocacy during the forty years I have followed the profession of the law. I do not aspire to teach or to instruct or to exhort: I am content to express the pleasure to be derived from the exercise of the art, to discuss some of its elements, and to assert, in the face of all detractors, that the career of the advocate is a high and honourable calling, essential to the good government of any civilized state, and one to which men and women might well devote their greatest gifts and powers.

How then shall we define the art of advocacy about which so many words have been spoken? It is not easy to give a short answer that will be entirely satisfactory, for advocacy is composed of so many diverse elements; but in its essence, advocacy may still be called the art of persuasion if that term is used in its widest sense. It is not confined wholly to persuasive speech, though persuasive speech is infinitely important, and may with truth be said to dominate everything else. Quintilian quotes with approval the saying of the Greek grammarian that forensic oratory has one main task—'to persuade the judge and lead his mind to the conclusions desired by the speaker'. But whilst I am referring to persuasive speech, may I go a little out of my way to touch upon a wider theme than advocacy in the courts of law? The uses of persuasive speech are too often considered as belonging exclusively to counsel and solicitors. The truth is that wherever men seek to win others to their own opinion, the art of advocacy is being displayed, and men everywhere would do well to remember the immense power that lies in persuasive speech, and would do well also to make the necessary effort to acquire it.

We are living in what is sometimes called the Welfare State, and it is plain that one of the features of that state is that the duty of public speaking is now cast upon a larger number of people than ever before. It would be unreasonable to expect the same excessive care to be given to the art of persuasive speech as was bestowed upon it when the world was very much different. Men have ceased to 'smooth the locks, to adjust the tresses, and to vary the braids of their comely creations' as did the Greeks and the Romans. But the Chairman of the Board of Directors, the Leader of the Trade Union, the parliamentarian, the preacher, equally with the advocate in the law courts, would do well to remember that the rewards of persuasive speech are not only exceeding great, but that they are not to be won without much labour. The notion that attractive and persuasive speech comes unbidden to the lips as a gift from Heaven's treasury dies hard, and the speech that delights you with its ease and spontaneity is not uncommonly the result of prolonged labour in the silent watches of the night. Men can be stirred and moved, thrilled and delighted, calmed and assured, stimulated to high endeavour or encouraged to follow the path of duty by the simple and skilful use of the English tongue. The primary rules are not many and they are easily mastered. They are to seek simplicity, to avoid verbiage, to use familiar words of plain meaning and to be natural. It is lucidity that makes speech enjoyable to the hearer; it is grace of speech that makes the spoken word memorable; and grace and lucidity come only from the observance of the primary rules and the willingness to take pains. Lincoln's ten sentences spoken at Gettysburg will live so long as the language endures, and the speeches of John Bright, many of them made in this city, to use the phrase of Lord Morley, 'will live to be a lamp for many a generation of Englishmen in times to come'.

They stand as great examples of the unrivalled efficacy of simple speech, from which all lesser mortals in courts of law or wherever men are called upon to address their fellows, may find guidance and inspiration.

But it is of the advocate in the courts of law that I have undertaken to speak, and I must therefore say a word or two about the serious misconception in the public mind concerning him. Respect for the law is widespread, but the lawyer himself is not a very popular figure. The strongest condemnation has always been, and is, reserved for the lawyer who is also an advocate. Curiously enough (or do I live behind an iron curtain in this matter?), judges appear to be exempt from the universal disparagement. It would seem that when an advocate is made a judge he ceases to be a lawyer, a belief that is widely held in circles other than those of the general public. But the advocate is said to be a man utterly devoid of moral scruple, who will willingly espouse any cause whether he believes in it or not, and will defend the right or the wrong without hesitation, so long as he is paid. It is most unfortunate that one of the greatest of the English stylists and satirists gave currency to this view in *Gulliver's Travels*. There it was that Swift permitted himself to say that lawyers were 'a society of men bred up from their youth in the art of proving by words multiplied for the purpose that white is black and black is white according as they are paid'. Swift was in fact a disappointed litigant, and was venting his spleen in that capacity; but the power of his writing was such that his words are likely to endure. It is scarcely necessary for me to say that the disfavour in which the advocate is sometimes held arises almost wholly from the grave misconception of the advocate's true function. He does not profess to present his own point of view or his own beliefs to the Court. He is there as the mouthpiece of the client to say for him what he would wish to say for himself, were he able to do so with knowledge and understanding. When Thomas Erskine, perhaps the greatest advocate this country has ever produced, defended Tom Paine for a seditious libel contained in *The Rights of Man*, he was subjected to severe criticism and much abuse for undertaking the defence, and in the course of his address to the jury he took the opportunity to vindicate himself, and the vocation of the advocate in general, in language that is still remembered and quoted. He said:

> If the advocate refuses to defend from what he may think of the charge or the defence, he assumes the character of the judge; nay, he assumes it before the hour of judgment, and in proportion to his rank and reputation, puts the heavy influence of a perhaps mistaken opinion into the scale against the accused, in whose favour the benevolent principles of the English law makes all allowance and which command the very judge to be his counsel.

Boswell records Dr Johnson as saying pretty much the same thing in his conversation with Sir William Forbes, who had suggested that a lawyer should never undertake a cause which he was satisfied was not a just one.

> Sir [said Dr. Johnson], a lawyer has no business with the justice or the injustice of the cause which he undertakes, unless the client asks his opinion, and then he is bound to give it honestly. The justice or the injustice of the cause is to be decided by the Judge. Consider, Sir, what is the purpose of the courts of justice. It is that every man shall have his cause fairly tried by men appointed to try causes. A lawyer . . . is not to usurp the functions of the jury or judge, and determine what shall be the effect of evidence, what shall be the result of legal argument. . . . A lawyer is to do for his client all that his client might fairly do for himself, if he could.

It must be conceded, of course, that the art of advocacy is therefore beset with perils of a very special kind, and for that reason the first quality beyond all others in the advocate, whatever his particular type of advocacy may be, is that he must be a man of character. The Court must be able to rely on the advocate's word; his word must indeed be his bond; and when he asserts to the Court those matters which are within his personal knowledge, the Court must know for a surety that those things are as represented. The advocate has a duty to his client, a duty to the Court, and a duty to the State; but he has above all a duty to himself that he shall be, as far as lies in his power, a man of integrity. No profession calls for higher standards of honour and uprightness, and no profession, perhaps, offers greater temptations to forsake them; but whatever gifts an advocate may possess, be they never so dazzling, without the supreme qualification of an inner integrity he will fall short of the highest. 'I, for one,' said Quintilian, 'restrict the name of orator and the art itself to those who are good.' Lord Rosebery, himself a great master of the spoken and the written word, said of the oratory of Chatham—

> Assiduous study of words, constant exercise in choice language, so that it was habitual to him even in conversation, and could not be other than elegant in pre-meditated speech—this combined with

poetical imagination, passion, a mordant wit and great dramatic skill, would probably seem to be the secrets of Chatham's oratorical supremacy . . . And yet it is safe to predict that a clever fellow who had mastered all this would produce but a pale reflection of the original. It is not merely the thing that is said, but the man who says it that counts, the character which breathes through the sentences.

If the argument of the advocate is presented in clear and choice language, and language which seems to come naturally and easily from the speaker, and if in addition the advocate can make use of what appears to be quite natural gesture, the very argument itself seems the more persuasive.

But in the main task of advocacy, the exposition, the narrative, the summing-up, the persuasion, the advocate may use, and as I think ought to use, the full range of our wonderfully flexible English speech. For there is no speech to equal it in its amazing richness of expression, being as it is described in the Preface to *The Oxford Book of English Prose* 'as malleable and pliant as Attic, dignified as Latin, masculine, yet free from Teutonic guttural, capable of being as precise as French, dulcet as Italian, sonorous as Spanish', and the advocate may captain all these excellencies to his service. The advocate must therefore be a student of words; he must know something at least of their history; their sound, their meaning, their associations, and, above all, the use that has been made of them by the great masters of the tongue. It is well if he knows his Bible in the Authorized Version, and has drunk in the glories of the Book of Common Prayer. It is well, too, if he knows something of the great triumvirate—Chaucer, Dryden and Shakespeare—who did so much to mould and fashion the language, and of men like Swift and Sterne and Defoe and the great stylists.

For I am one of those who believe that in the ordinary everyday affairs of life, even in casual conversation, the use of natural and graceful English is an accomplishment greatly to be desired. And how much more is it to be desired when the whole purpose of the advocate is to gain the ends he seeks by the impression he creates upon the particular tribunal before which he appears.

H.R.H. THE PRINCE PHILIP, DUKE OF EDINBURGH

1921–

Presidential address to the British Association for the Advancement of Science

Edinburgh, 8th August, 1951

Speeches must always be considered in relation to the circumstances in which they are delivered. A speech appropriate to the House of Commons on a great occasion would be different from that appropriate to a village-hall discussion on arrangements for a summer fête; a speech appealing to the emotions would be different from one appealing to reason; a speech which would be of significance to a body of learned men and women would be beyond the comprehension of young children.

The following speech, delivered by H.R.H. Prince Philip, Duke of Edinburgh, is a good example of the speech which is appropriate to an important but select audience. It was given at Edinburgh in 1951 to the British Association for the Advancement of Science. H.R.H. Prince Philip was President of the Association.

It is worthy of study because of the skilful presentation of facts taken from a wide range of scientific achievement. Yet it is no mere catalogue. The facts are marshalled with understanding and with pride in order that they might create in his distinguished but critical audience a sense of past achievement and a hope for the future.

In this scientific age it is important that reviews of this kind should be given. Science has become so specialized that very few people are able to survey the whole field. Speeches similar to that given by H.R.H. Prince Philip must be given in the future to show how science is pushing back the frontiers of knowledge and affecting the lives of everyone. This speech will be regarded as a model of its kind and will be studied not only for the facts which it contains but for the manner of their presentation.

THE STARTING-POINT

IN a review of British science and technology 1851 is a convenient starting-point for two reasons. Firstly, the Exhibition of that year can be regarded as a gigantic stocktaking of the national resources and technical skill. Secondly, because it marked the end of the Industrial Revolution and the conversion of Victorian England to the policy of industrial expansion on which our future still depends. The period as a whole saw the climax of our industrial supremacy and its inevitable decline when countries with greater resources and population learned from us the lessons of the mechanization of industry. It also covers the birth and growth of the new concepts of modern science.

Social conditions of a hundred years ago were, generally speaking, the outcome of the Industrial Revolution, but with all the traditions of the England of agriculture, cottage industry, and small market towns. The population of twenty millions was growing fast but still small compared to our fifty millions of today. Education was limited to a minority and was almost entirely classical, so the new profession of engineering had to draw its recruits from a different sphere, that of self-educated men. A new wealthy class was growing up in the commercial world to rival the old aristocracy. There was unbounded optimism about the future and ample scope in commerce and industry to attract all intelligent and enterprising men. The number of poor was on the increase and their conditions were deteriorating because, as yet, no social conscience had grown up to replace the patriarchal responsibility of the landowners and master craftsmen.

In the domestic field, lighting was by candle and oil lamps, cooking and heating by coal or wood in ranges or open fires with the consequent enormous waste of energy. Food had to be fresh or crudely preserved, and thus needed to be produced locally. In health and hygiene the figures speak for themselves. In 1851 the infant death-rate was 150 per 1,000 living births compared with 25 per 1,000 today. Anæsthetics, antiseptic surgery, biochemistry, tropical medicine were all virtually unknown or in their infancy. Psychology had not yet achieved independence from philosophy on the one hand and physiology on the other.

This was the age of the practical engineer and of processes arrived at by intuition born of experience and by trial and error. Technology was concerned with the application of steam power, with metallurgy and the working of metals for various purposes, and with the production of machine tools and precision machinery. Men were already turning their minds to other types of engines and the internal-combustion engine was in the process of development.

Scientists, while continuing their search for the secrets of nature, were beginning to turn their attention to exploring the empirical developments of industry. Their numbers as yet were small, the endowments for research were negligible and much of their work was carried out in the watertight compartments of the different sciences. But the seed had been sown and it was not long before scientists and engineers were preparing the way for the great technological harvest of the twentieth century.

THE CONDITIONS

The changes brought about in the lives of men and women in the last hundred years have been greater and more rapid than during any other period in history, and these changes have been almost entirely due to the work of scientists and technologists all over the world. They have not only affected the way of living of all civilized peoples but have also vastly increased our knowledge about ourselves, the earth we live on, and the universe around us. I cannot emphasize too much that the sum total of scientific knowledge and technological progress is an international achievement to which every civilized country has made some contribution.

And now before considering the contribution of the British Commonwealth, I should like to sketch what appear to a layman like myself to have been the main influences on the course of scientific and technical achievement since 1851 and their relation to one another.

The great stimulus of the 1851 Exhibition created a growing interest in technical education and research, followed by a widening of the scientific horizon which was soon to find expression in borderline subjects. For the next fifty years science advanced rapidly, but in most fields there was a wide gap between science and industry. Electricity was an exception and the groundwork was already being laid for the electrical revolution of the Victorian age. Medicine was on the verge of breaking away from medieval practice and taking the first steps towards its modern pattern, while British colonial development stimulated the study of tropical disease.

Between 1851 and 1870 practice, in many industries, was ahead of science, and in that period the large number of inventions of the Industrial Revolution were progressively improved and widely applied. These inventions, which added so much to our industrial production, were mainly the work of British genius. They were of great economic advantage to this country and were quickly exploited commercially. New factories and plants were built to include the very latest ideas, and with the expansion of industry came the demand for more and more new ideas and greater efficiency. This demand was a direct stimulus to technological invention as well as an indirect stimulus to science. We are still struggling with the social results of this vast expansion.

From 1870 to 1890 the high-water mark of British industrial expansion, as compared with other countries, had been reached and the competition of the United States and Europe was just beginning to be felt. But the lack of serious competition hitherto had bred a feeling of over-confidence and satisfaction in the methods and processes employed. The result was a conservative attitude towards technical change, and, particularly in the older industries, neglect of scientific research. Accumulation of wealth and the income from foreign investments in any case made the country as a whole less dependent on the efficiency of her industries. Concurrently a subtle change occurred in the type of British exports. So far the products of our machinery, such as rails and rolling-stock, had been shipped abroad for immediate use, but now machines themselves were exported to do their work in the factories of Europe and America instead of in Britain. The result of this was to intensify foreign industrial competition between 1890 and 1914, but with the increasing demands from the Colonies the volume of British exports was not greatly affected.

Then came the critical years of the First World War, bringing a realization of the part science must play in the industrial and military strength of the nation. For the first time in history a real attempt was made to enlist the services of science in the war effort and the Department of Scientific and Industrial Research was founded to further the application of science in industry through government laboratories and research associations.

The effects of these measures appeared clearly in the inter-war years when there was a marked swing of education from classics towards science. Coupled with this the war had directed the attention of many research scientists to practical objectives so that after the war there was a rapid expansion of industrial research. Scientific progress was no longer confined to the work of a few brilliant individuals, but came also from teams of research scientists each working on different parts of the same problem. It was during this period that many new commercial research laboratories grew up, employing scientists to discover new processes and materials connected with their industry as a direct weapon of competition.

The war had also shown a great weakness in our dependence on foreign production for many vital articles, such as dyestuffs, scientific instruments, and optical glass, in the manufacture of which scientific research played an essential part. This weakness was remedied with the help of the Key Industry Import Duties which gave the necessary support and encouragement to the establishment of these industries at home.

It is true that manufacturers in some of the older industries still clung to traditional methods in spite of the pressure of competition from America and other countries. And in this connexion it is significant that the history of production engineering after 1890 is almost entirely confined to the United States.

It was, however, a period of rapid development in Britain. The invention of the internal-combustion engine and the pneumatic tyre had opened new branches of industrial engineering, and the demand for fuel for motor-cars and aircraft gave birth to the new technology of oil. In the electrical, chemical, and aircraft industries, science was fully enlisted in the fields of electronics, synthetic fibres, plastics, aerodynamics, and light alloys. Consequently the outbreak of war in 1939 found us in a much stronger position to meet the immense demands it made on all branches of technology for new gadgets, machines, and weapons. From the outset science in all its forms and branches was harnessed and completely co-ordinated with the war effort. It was only the intimate partnership of science and engineering with the staffs of the Fighting Services that enabled us to meet swiftly and effectively the ever-changing menace of total war.

The tremendous demands on our industries had some good after-effects. Once again these demands revealed weaknesses where our industrial capacity was out of date. The realization of this has initiated comprehensive reconstruction on most modern lines. The almost complete absence of income from our foreign investments has forced us to rely once more on our capacity to make the goods the world requires. Our industry and productivity have shown a wonderful improvement, but there is still a lot more that can be done. The rate at which scientific knowledge is being applied in many industries is too small and too slow. Our physical resources have dwindled, but the intellectual capacity of our scientists and engineers is as great as ever and it is upon their ingenuity that our future prosperity largely depends.

THE CONTRIBUTION

I would now like to make a brief survey of the British contribution to natural knowledge and technology and pay a tribute to some of the great men of science of the last hundred years.

In some branches almost the whole story can be told since one problem after another has been solved by British scientists. In others there are many blanks and gaps where the vital links in the chain were forged abroad. But looking at the whole vast field of abstract and practical science there can be no doubt that during this period the contribution of the British Commonwealth has been of outstanding importance.

Our knowledge of the stars, the heavens, and our place in the universe has increased steadily through the centuries, but since 1851 some of the most important links were supplied by such men as Eddington, Jeans, and Milne in their work on mass, luminosity, and stellar evolution. Huggins made a great contribution with his application of spectrum analysis to astronomy, and Lockyer's discovery of helium in the sun had a significance far beyond the realms of astrophysics.

Coming nearer to the earth, the work of Abercromby and Shaw on the behaviour of the earth's atmosphere in the troposphere started the scientific study of weather and weather prediction, and Appleton's research into the ionosphere extended this to the upper air.

Chemistry has fascinated man from the earliest times, and vast progress has been made in the last hundred years both in knowledge and theory. Much fresh ground was broken by Crookes by his work on spectra, his discovery of thallium and of 'radiant matter', known later as cathode rays. Long after everyone was quite sure of the composition of the air, Rayleigh found another ingredient which he called argon and so started the hunt for other inert gases. In organic chemistry both Perkin and Robinson have added enormously to our knowledge of the structure of carbon compounds, and to our power to copy natural products synthetically. The development of X-ray analysis by the two Braggs, father and son, has given us a means of finding the actual arrangement of the atoms in the molecule and has revealed the accuracy of the chemists' conclusions about the architecture of molecules based on their reactions with one another. This is a most striking example of the power of the theoretical and practical scientist to penetrate nature's secrets.

Going beyond the chemist and his molecules we come to the physicist and the study of even smaller particles. Thomson's discovery of the nature of the electron was the first attack upon the integrity of the atom. Next, thanks to Rutherford's brilliant research and keen intuition, came the nuclear theory which revolutionized our ideas of matter. To prove it, he was the first man to succeed in the transmutation of an element. It is appropriate to mention Moseley's work on the X-ray spectra of the elements, as it already showed such great promise, before he was killed at Gallipoli.

Parallel with this activity in the physical sciences there occurred a technological revolution of even greater scope and variety. The Darbys of Coalbrookdale were the lineal ancestors of Bessemer, Thomas, and Siemens, and the whole technology of metals. First cheap cast iron followed by cheap steel, then steel from phosphatic ores, completely changed the materials available to engineers, shipbuilders, and architects. Scientific metallurgy can be said to have started when Sorby first applied a microscope to the surface of metals. The way was opened for the investigation of the metallic alloys which came in quick succession from developments in which Hadfield and Rosenhain made outstanding contributions.

It was not long before the possibilities of these new materials were recognized, and the great majority of the mechanical developments of the period were due to new alloys which could withstand higher stresses. But before these materials could be fully used, Maudsley and Whitworth had to lay the foundations of production engineering, and Mushet had to do pioneer work in developing tungsten steel as the first high-speed cutting tool.

The reciprocating steam engine of the Industrial Revolution was the main source of power until Parsons invented the steam turbine, which revolutionized large-scale power production on land and sea. But that was not the only source of power to rival the push-and-pull engine. The internal-combustion engine, in which Dugald Clerk and Ackroyd-Stuart were among the early pioneers, has proved to be a formidable challenger in many fields. In marine engineering, Froude's work on hull forms and propellers enabled the full benefit of the new prime movers to be reaped at sea.

Here I wish I could mention early British pioneers of motor vehicles but, as is well known, restrictive legislation drove the development of the motor-car abroad, until the repeal of the speed limit in 1903 gave scope to the genius of Royce, Lanchester, and Ricardo. In place of the motor-car, however, we have Lawson to thank for the invention of the safety bicycle; and all wheeled vehicles, except those running on rails, owe their rapid development to Dunlop's invention of the pneumatic tyre. The material required for this started the vast natural and synthetic rubber industry, and has made famous the name of Wickham for a brilliant feat of smuggling, when he brought the rubber seeds from Brazil to Kew, from which sprang the rubber plantation industry of the east.

In flying, the names of the pioneers and their feats are legion, and more than in any other mechanical science the development of aerodynamics has been shared by many nations, but Lanchester's vortex theory was one of the stepping-stones to powered flight, and the achievement of Alcock and Brown in making the first Atlantic flight in 1919 speaks highly for the tremendous scientific and technological background of flying in this country. Of outstanding importance and consequence was the genius which Mitchell brought to aircraft design, and, more recently, Whittle's pioneer work has given us the lead in jet-engine production both in civil and military use.

Following on the immense progress in metallurgy and mechanical engineering the most far-reaching development of the period has been that of electricity and electronics. Although the key discovery belongs to Faraday in an earlier period, the second founder of the science is undoubtedly Clerk Maxwell, with his classic treatise on electromagnetism. The use of electricity for domestic and industrial purposes was helped by Wilde's development of the dynamo and then by Swan's incandescent lamps. Wheatstone and Kelvin pioneered the use of electricity for communication by their work on line and cable telegraphy. Wireless telegraphy soon followed and the work on tuned circuits by Lodge, and Marconi's many brilliant developments, made in this country with the General Post Office and the Navy, soon made radio a practical proposition. Heaviside and Appleton made further contributions on the propagation of radio waves. It is interesting to see that the technique used by Appleton in his pulse-ranging on the ionosphere and upper layers was later developed by Watson-Watt into radar which is now almost indispensable to airmen and seamen all over the world. And here Randall's development of the magnetron for high-frequency radar was one of the major contributions to the allies' equipment for war.

Television has a wide parentage, but Baird's name will always be linked with the first successful pictures.

Another great innovation of this hundred years was the discovery and development of plastic and synthetic materials. The story starts with Parke's discovery of celluloid and Cross and Bevan's manufacture of viscose, which gave birth to the rayon industry and the many later types of synthetic fibre. Perkin's mauve, first of the aniline dyes, and Kipping's new silicon compounds were, however, disregarded by industry in this country. But we see today a change of heart in the development in our industrial laboratories of two new plastics, perspex and polythene, with an almost unlimited range of applications in the air, on the ground, and at sea.

The effect all this has had upon the citizen varies naturally with where and how he lives, but basically it has given him reliable light and heat in his home, push-button communication with almost any part of the world, and home entertainment of a high quality. His transport on land, at sea, and in the air is quick, comfortable, and clean. In addition he has a vast range of materials with which to clothe himself and to furnish and embellish his home. Almost more important, these developments have brought about a complete change in his conditions of work.

But if the citizen has benefited, so too has science from the great array of new techniques that have been invented, and the new tools with which the scientist and technologist can burrow, hack, and worry at the growing mountain of problems to be solved.

So far I have dealt with the physical sciences. Now I would like to turn briefly to the biological and psychological sides, which after a slow beginning in this country have made increasingly rapid progress.

The whole field of biological science in this period is overshadowed by the words of Darwin presented in his *Origin of Species* and *The Descent of Man*. Nothing has done so much to widen man's thoughts as his conception of evolution as the great law controlling living things, 'that progress comes from unceasing competition, through increasing selection and rejection'.

In the basic study of living things some of the most important contributions from this country were the pioneer work of Francis Galton and William Bateson in the field of heredity, Sherrington's work on the integrative action of the nervous system, and Dale's and Adrian's contributions to our knowledge of the transmission of nervous impulses.

The science of biochemistry is relatively new and Gowland Hopkins was its founder in this country. His discovery of the significance of accessory food factors, leading up to the recognition of vitamins, started the modern science of nutrition. Other landmarks were Bayliss's and Starling's recognition of the part played by hormones in the bloodstream, followed by Banting's and Best's isolation of insulin, and Harington's synthesis of thyroxin here in Edinburgh.

Fleming working on mould cultures discovered the antibacterial properties of penicillin, and later Florey and Chain, at Oxford, found that penicillin could be extracted in a highly purified form, and used it to treat human disease.

Modern surgery can be said to have been born in Scotland with Simpson's discovery of the use of chloroform as an anæsthetic and Lister's antiseptic technique based on Pasteur's bacteriological discoveries. A further advance of the greatest value to surgery as a science was Macewen's aseptic technique which made surgery clean and safe, followed by his classic work on the brain and spinal cord.

If Lister was the father of modern surgery, then Manson was the father of tropical medicine, and it is particularly in this field that the British contribution has led the world. The discovery by Ross that malaria is carried by the anopheles mosquito and, much later, the work of Fairley in Australia on its prevention and cure have been of the greatest benefit to mankind. Bruce will always be remembered for his discovery of the part played by the deadly tsetse-fly in the transmission of sleeping-sickness and his work on Malta fever. Finlay, Adrian Stokes, and Hindle stand high among the names linked with the study and prevention of yellow fever.

These were all vital efforts towards the prevention of sickness, but there is another aspect of medical practice in which the Commonwealth has taken a leading part—the promotion of health. It was Sir John Simon, the first Medical Officer appointed to a central authority, who made a careful statistical study of the causes of sickness, with a view to taking effective measure for the health of the community at large. Through his leadership health services have been provided in regular stages throughout the country. At first these were largely aimed at providing pure water, effective sanitation, and the abolition of slums; but since the beginning of the present century the personal health services, especially in the case of mothers, babies, and school children, have become national in scope and lead the world.

There are two other fields in which the biological sciences play a major part. The first is in the preservation of food and in nutrition which has had the most profound economic, and social, effects. The ability through freezing, drying, and canning to import large quantities of food has enabled a rapidly inceasing population to maintain and increase its standards of living, which would have been impossible had it been dependent on British agriculture alone. The scientific study of nutrition has made it possible to improve the health of the population and in war to feed the people with the minimum of waste.

Mort had the first freezing works in the world at Sydney, and was a pioneer in refrigeration, but success in transporting meat to Britain had to wait for the development of more reliable refrigerating plant. Since 1918 the Food Investigation Laboratories of the Department of Scientific and Industrial Research, of which Sir William Hardy was the first director, have established the basic biological knowledge on which the storage and transport of meat, fish, and fruit are now largely based.

The second field is in agriculture, where in order to compete with cheap foreign foods the most successful farmer is one who enlists the full assistance of science. Lawes, who discovered how to make and use superphosphate, and started the great fertilizer industry, was quick to realize this. He founded Rothamsted, now the oldest agricultural research station in the world, and there he and Gilbert carried out the first scientifically controlled field experiments which laid the foundation of agricultural science. Later, Biffen's pioneer work in plant breeding at Cambridge became one of the greatest contributions to the problem of feeding the world's growing population. He showed how it was possible to breed strains of wheat combining resistance to disease with high yields and good milling properties. In the field of animal breeding, the foundation of the most important aspect of British agriculture today, I will mention amongst the many investigators only Cossar Ewart and Crew who did so much to advance its scientific study here in Edinburgh. The mechanization which was to revolutionize farming in all parts of the world was also under way and Britain was playing a leading part. The reaping machine, for instance, was invented by Patrick Bell in 1826 although it was not manufactured until 1853.

There is no need to point out the effect which all these improvements, discoveries, and inventions have had on society. It is this group of biological sciences which have had the most far-reaching social results, and it is particularly during and since the last war that it has been possible to exploit them.

There is one science which I have not yet mentioned. It is both the youngest science and the oldest problem. The study of man's mind was the province of the philosopher until the middle of the nineteenth century, when it separated from him and began its independent existence as the science of psychology. The foundations were not laid in this country, but important contributions were made, both from the biological and the philosophical sides, by men like Ferrier, Bain, and Ward. Sully's work on child psychology was the first of its kind. But probably the most outstanding figure in this country was Galton, whose teaching is widely respected in all psychological laboratories, and who was the first to develop an interest in the mental differences between individuals—a field in which British psychology has made some of its greatest contributions. Again it is only recently that full practical advantage is being taken of the progress made in this branch of science, but the results of that application may be as important as the many more easily understood developments in the purely physical world.

PRESIDENTIAL ADDRESS TO THE BRITISH ASSOCIATION

THE IMPLICATIONS

The story of the British contribution to science in the past century is indeed impressive and I am very pleased to have this opportunity to pay tribute to the men whose achievements I have been discussing. But this story would not be complete without studying the wider implications of their work and examining some of the lessons to be learnt from it.

The concrete measurement and indirect effect of all scientific effort is the general improvement in the conditions in which people live and work, it is in the improvement in health, in the expectation of life and standards of living, the latter including not only food and clothing, but housing, home comforts, medical care, education, books and newspapers, recreations, and travel facilities. In every one of these directions the progress that has been made has amounted to a revolution.

Not all this springs directly from science and invention. Much has been due to the politicians and administrators, and behind them to religion, morals, education, art, and the complex influences which we call culture. But even there science has stood beside the authors of progress to advise, to help, and sometimes to guide.

Now as science and technology are so vital to the future strength and prosperity of the British Commonwealth, the great problem is to discover the conditions under which they are most likely to flourish. The records show that both depend very much on co-operation and upon the linking up of a long chain of discoveries, one with another; so that it is quite exceptional for the credit of a great advance to belong to one man or even to one country, although it will always require the flash of inspiration to weld the links into the chain. Today the development of teamwork in laboratories has made this truer than ever. For many reasons, but principally because of the increasing complexity of research and its cost, such teamwork is becoming more and more the rule. We need not repine at this but it would be a disaster if the individual inquirer working in his own laboratory were discouraged out of existence.

While the quality of scientific work is determined by the quality of the scientist, the quantity of scientific output is determined by the money available. The rapid progress of science in Britain has owed much to the growing support and sympathy of government and individual benefactors and to the endowment of research by industrial corporations. However, the basic discoveries that mark the great advances depend on the accident of individual genius and are not at our command.

The scope and intensity of the progress of applied science and technology, on the other hand, bear a close relationship to the circumstances of the time. Technology, as the combination of scientific knowledge with the practical ability of the inventor to apply that knowledge to the solution of particular problems, comes into play with any new discovery of scientific fact. The latest particle of truth is then developed, according to the circumstances of the time, for military, commercial, or medico-social purposes. It is a sad reflection that the urgent demands of modern war can produce advances that might otherwise take many years to develop, especially in the costly and uncertain experimental stages.

The rivalry between large commercial undertakings, using science to improve their products or processes as a direct means of competition, has produced a steady flow of improvements and developments. However, the fruits of this form of scientific work are sometimes open to considerable misuse. The discoveries of these commercial laboratories may be kept secret and in some cases a number of teams may be working on the same problem, which may have already been solved elsewhere. The buying up and suppression of patents and discoveries to protect equipment from becoming obsolete has also been known to happen. I am glad to see, however, a change of outlook in the growing quantity of publication of the results of industrial research.

It would seem that science has become so well established that nothing can stand in the way of its natural growth. This is far from the truth. Since the earliest times the natural conservatism of laymen has acted as a powerful brake to the adoption of new ideas which do not rigidly conform to this notion of the correct order of things. In its most violent form it will produce unreasoning anger, utter disbelief in face of the clearest evidence, or provoke plain ordinary laughter. The storm raised by Darwin's *Origin of Species* is an excellent example where even scientists failed to keep an open mind.

The position seems better today, and I am sure that Sir Harold Hartley, our immediate past President, spoke for all scientists when he said: 'Today, with our greater understanding, there is humility in the minds of all scientists. The further we penetrate into Nature's secrets the more closely we see the ever-receding frontiers of knowledge.'

The resistance towards anything new or unexpected is balanced on the other hand by bursts of enthusiasm that some particular discovery or invention will see the end of all our troubles. The belief in the philosopher's stone seems to be just as great as ever.

As the front of pure science has advanced so its lines of communication to practical exploitation have got longer and longer. The time was when the whole process of discovery, application, and exploitation could be achieved by one man. In our time a great army of scientists, technicians, inventors, designers, and production engineers are required to keep the lines of communication open. Quite how important some of the members of this follow-up team become is not always appreciated. In his presidential address in 1948 Sir Henry Tizard emphasized this point when he said: 'All depends on good design and production. Our weakness in the war was not to be found in what was best to do, nor in the scientific work of how to do it. It was when the stage of design and production was reached that we fell short of the best standards.'

This was true already when Whitworth invented the screw micrometer, which was subsequently put into production in Germany and the United States and up to the 1914 war all micrometers had to be imported into this country.

To Professor Kipping of Nottingham goes the credit for the basic work which led to the development of silicones in Russia and the United States and yet until this year we have been dependent on imports from America of marketable silicone products.

There are many cases in the Navy where a piece of apparatus has been used operationally exactly as the inventor put it together, with all the resulting disadvantages in maintenance and efficient operation. The limitation in performance, except in some cases, is practical as opposed to scientific. Where the basic scientific principles are known by all nations the advantage lies in the good design of equipment for practical use.

A more general and far-reaching matter for concern and possibly the most vital factor affecting the industrial application of scientific research is the lack of a co-ordinated system of scientific and technological education in this country. Excellent as they are, the existing institutions, which have grown up to meet particular circumstances, do not produce anything like enough trained technologists to meet the urgent needs of scientific development in industry and to provide leaders for the future.

It is to be hoped that the new and rather uncertain science of education will develop sufficiently quickly to point the way to a speedy solution of this problem.

The shortage in Britain of 'personnel trained and eager to apply scientific knowledge and scientific methods to practical ends'—as Sir Ewart Smith said last year—is only one of the many shortages which the world is now facing. Among them are food, non-ferrous metals, steel alloy metals, and sulphur. These very shortages are due to the scientific complexity of present-day life and it is only by science that they can be overcome. Naturally there are many ways of tackling this problem; but the most obvious are firstly by improved design to secure economy in production and the minimum use of scarce materials. Secondly by the development of substitutes made from raw materials which are still abundant. Thirdly by the reclamation of scrap and improved methods of using low-grade ores. Finally the development of renewable raw materials such as timber to satisfy the world demand for cellulose. Some of these shortages are partly due to the huge inevitable waste of war and its consequences, and partly to the lack of any comprehensive survey of the world's resources and requirements. It is only by an accurate knowledge of the world's resources that we can foresee the scope and magnitude of the future problems that science and technology have to meet and that only they can solve.

It is, therefore, good news that the Economic and Social Council of the United Nations has resolved 'to promote the systematic survey and inventory' of those resources which are not already covered by the Food and Agriculture Organization.

We have evolved a civilization based on the material benefits which science and technology can provide. The present shortages are a timely reminder of the slender material foundation on which our civilization rests and of our dependence upon science and technology.

The Conclusion

The pursuit of truth in itself cannot produce anything evil. It is in the later stage when the facts dug up enter the process of application that the choice between the beneficent and destructive development has to be made. It is quite certain that it is an exception if any particular discovery cannot be used equally well for good and evil purposes.

Happily the beneficent exploitation of scientific knowledge has kept pace with its destructive application.

In a mid-century article *The Times* put it this way:

> ... It has been an age of great achievement. The lines of progress in which the Victorians trusted have been pursued farther and faster than they foresaw. Scientific discovery, from which above all their doctrines of progress derived, has swept forward on an enormous front. The conquest of the air has made possible an intercourse and understanding between distant peoples such as our ancestors could not imagine—and it has been diverted to the vast destruction of men and cities. The invention of wireless telephony has opened a channel through which liberating truths might be proclaimed to all the listening earth—and every would-be despot has used it to suborn the blind masses into the worship of false gods. The medical art has performed miracles; the cures of immemorial pestilences have been found, infancy has been safeguarded and old age tended, so that the normal expectation of life has been extended by years—aside from the new and universal apprehension of sudden death.

To my mind it is vital that the two sides of scientific development are fully and clearly understood, not only by the research scientist, inventor, designer, and the whole scientific team, but also by all laymen. The instrument of scientific knowledge in our hands is growing more powerful every day, indeed it has reached a point when we can either set the world free from drudgery, fear, hunger, and pestilence or obliterate life itself.

Progress in almost every form of human activity depends upon the continued efforts of scientists. The nation's wealth and prosperity are governed by the rapid application of science to its industries and commerce. The nation's workers depend upon science for the maintenance and improvement in their standard of health, housing, and food. Finally, superiority or even our ability to survive in war is a direct measure of the excellence and capacity of the scientific team.

This team of research workers and engineers has a dual responsibility, one for its work and the other as informed citizens, and it can only fulfil its proper functions if its members have a sound general education as well as a thorough training in science. It is no less important that the people who control the scientific machine, both laymen and scientists, should have a proper understanding of what science has grown into and its place among the great forces of the world.

Ladies and gentlemen, it is clearly our duty as citizens to see that science is used for the benefit of mankind. For, of what use is science if man does not survive?